Applied Theology
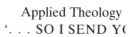

'. . . SO I SEND Y(

CW00446523

The SPCK International Study Guides incorporate the much loved and respected TEF series, and follow the tradition of: clarity and simplicity; a worldwide, ecumenical perspective; and an emphasis on application of the material studied, drawing out its relevance for Christians today. The Guides are ideal for first year students and Bible study groups, as well as for multi-cultural classes, and students for whom English is a second language.

SPCK International Study Guide 34

Applied Theology 4
'. . . SO I SEND YOU'
A Study Guide to Mission

Roger Bowen

First published in Great Britain 1996

Society for Promoting Christian Knowledge
Holy Trinity Church
Marylebone Road
London NW1 4DU

Fourth impression 2002

© Roger Bowen 1996

All rights reserved. No part of this book
may be reproduced or transmitted in any
form or by any means, electronic or mechanical,
including photocopying, recording, or by any
information storage or retrieval system,
without permission in writing from the publishers.

Unless otherwise stated the Scripture quotations
in this book are from the Revised Standard Version
of the Bible (Ecumenical Edition), copyrighted
1973 by the Division of Christian Education of the
National Council of the Churches of Christ
in the USA.

ACKNOWLEDGEMENTS
The photographs in this book are reproduced by courtesy
of Andes Press Agency (pp. 119, 215, 231),
Borneo Mission Association/Rhodes House Library (p. 98),
CAFOD/George Arnison (p. 70), CAFOD/David Mtidieri (p. 39),
CAFOD/Paul Smith (p. 138), CAFOD/Sean Sprague (p. 45),
Christian Aid/Chris Steele-Perkins (p. 23),
Christian Aid/Stuart Franklin (pp. 67, 155),
Easton Family Centre (p. 193), the Leprosy Mission (p. 20),
the Malaysia Tourist Promotion Board (p. 86),
the Mansell Collection, London (pp. 33, 104),
Methodist Church Overseas Division (p. 135),
USPG (pp. 51, 53, 162 (top), 167, 173, 176, 223),
USPG Archives/Rhodes House Library (p. 10).

British Library Cataloguing-in-Publication Data
A catalogue record for this book is available from the
British Library

ISBN 0 281 04939 4

Printed in Great Britain by
The University Press, Cambridge

Contents

Preface

The appearance of this book is due largely to the help and encouragement I have received from a considerable number of people. The Rev. Nick Beddow urged me to start on the project, and St. John's College, Nottingham, allowed me a term's study leave to do the writing. Kate Hughes put in many hours of editorial work and made unfailingly helpful suggestions.

I confess that I have drawn freely from the work of many authors, not with the aim of claiming credit for the wisdom of others, but rather to make their wisdom accessible—as it deserves to be—to a large number of people throughout the world who are engaged on the frontiers of the Church's mission. Mission, of all theological tasks, can only be done by collaborating with other people, and I hope that this Guide not only says this but also provides a model for it. The whole of the bibliography on pp. 235–6 shows my debt to other writers, particularly those books which are marked with an asterisk(*). The writings of Bishop Lesslie Newbigin have always been a special source of inspiration to me, as to many others.

My own firsthand experience of mission in Africa has needed to be supplemented with examples from other parts of the world, and I am indebted to the Rev. George Kovoor (India) for his help in providing some of these. Individual chapters owe much to specialist insights from John Padwick (Kenya) and Philip West. Elizabeth Jordan read through the whole manuscript and helped me to clarify much of it. Malcolm Riches and Malcolm Rogers gave freely of their computer expertise to help with the graphics.

But my chief debt is to successive generations of students who called me their 'Teacher' in Tanzania, Kenya, England, South Africa and Singapore. In reality they taught me more than I taught them—the evidence for this appears in the pages of this Guide, especially in the stories of their experiences of God's grace which they were generous enough to share with me. It is *their* obedient response to the missionary call of Jesus which is chiefly celebrated here.

St John's College, Nottingham   ROGER BOWEN

Editor's Note: About This Book

The first volume of the Applied Theology course in the International Study Guide series deals with Christian ministry to communities—both outreach to the unevangelized and nurture of Christian congregations. The second volume focuses on the pastoral care of individuals. The first volume relates primarily to rural settings in the Third World, the second to a variety of situations worldwide. A further volume on Church Administration is also planned.

This present volume concentrates on the theme of mission, i.e. how God sends and uses His people to do His work in the world. This theme is specially important at present for three reasons:

(1) Most Churches in the world have recently committed themselves to a 'Decade of Evangelization (or Evangelism)', because they realize how dangerous it is to concentrate their energies on the maintenance and organization of the Church, i.e. in caring for the sheep in the fold, instead of going to do God's work out on the frontiers of the Church. In fact history shows that the Church always declines in numbers and vitality when it becomes preoccupied with itself.

(2) A second reason why this topic is important today is that the centre of mission has shifted from the North (Europe and North America) to the South (Africa, South-East Asia, Latin America), where Churches are growing fast.

(3) In the 'Global Village' of the twentieth century we have all become aware of the miseries and disasters that overwhelm the human race. These are not new and are probably no worse than in previous generations, but the difference is that *now we know* about these things. People see pictures on TV or hear stories about human misery on the radio, and they ask, 'Where is God?' and 'Where are God's people?' in these terrible events. This is also part of mission.

This volume begins by looking at history, theology and the Bible in order to find a definition of mission. We shall then turn to the problem of how we can relate the Good News of Jesus to the wide variety of cultures in the world today, and look at examples of attempts to do this during the last sixty years. We shall try to learn from these examples and also to evaluate them. The third section of this Guide is about urban mission, which seems necessary because in the past the Church has been less successful in cities than in the countryside. But this was not true of St Paul's mission strategy, and should not be true today, for it is the world's cities which present the biggest challenge to the Churches. Finally, we shall reflect on how the Christian faith relates to the other world faiths with which it lives.

There are some Special Notes throughout the book which either discuss missiological issues (questions about mission), or offer longer examples of mission practice. One main purpose of this book is to help the reader to know more about how God is at work in the different parts of His world, so that our own missionary task can be inspired by His mission worldwide. The topic is much wider than 'missionary work overseas' or 'holding a Gospel crusade', because it involves all that the Church is and does.

A list of Further Reading suggests the books that will be most helpful to those who wish to study more about any of these issues. Mission is, however, a very wide topic on which many hundreds of good books and articles have been written. You will probably get most help from those books which come out of your own culture and are even written in your own language—so you should seek local advice about local resources.

STUDY SUGGESTIONS

Suggestions for further study and revision appear at the end of each chapter. They are intended to help you to study more thoroughly, and to relate what you have read to your own experience and circumstances, and the ideas held by the people amongst whom you live. There are a large number of Study Suggestions in this Guide; you are therefore advised to *select* those questions which are most appropriate for your own situation.

The *Key to Study Suggestions* is given on pp. 237–8. Usually, the Key does not give a complete answer. Instead, it shows where in the Guide the answer can be found. Some of the questions for discussion and debate depend on local circumstances. No exact answer to this type of question can be given in the Key.

BIBLE VERSION

The English translation of the Bible used and quoted in this Study Guide is the Common Bible Edition of the Revised Standard Version (RSV). The abbreviations used in this Guide for the titles of the books of the Bible are the same as those listed at the front of the Common Bible, except for the following: Exodus (Exod.), Isaiah (Isa.) and Matthew (Matt.).

INDEX

The Index (pp. 243–8) includes all the proper names of important people mentioned, and the main subjects dealt with in the Guide.

Introduction

The word 'mission' expresses the idea of movement, because it is all about sending and being sent. 'As the Father sent me, so I send you,' said Jesus. It is therefore strange that in many parts of the world Christians have set up 'Mission Stations'—for the word 'station' expresses the idea of standing still. But the Church cannot really be itself unless it is on the move and reaching out beyond itself. It has only to look at the example of Jesus to see how it should do this. The Church is missionary by its nature.

Recently most Churches in the world have begun to recognize this. The 1990s have been named 'A Decade of Evangelization (or Evangelism)'. We shall discuss later in this Guide the relationship between mission and evangelism, but think for a few moments, either alone or in group discussion, about what ideas come at once into your mind when you hear the word 'mission' or 'missionary'. For some people, a mission may refer to the special effort made occasionally by a local Church, to bring new people to Jesus. Or 'mission' may refer to the activity of sending people overseas, usually from the 'North' to the 'South', in order to bring the blessings of Christianity to others. In the past, people sometimes thought that 'mission' was aimed at people who were *not yet* Christians, but 'evangelism' was aimed at those who were *no longer* Christians.

We shall think about the proper definition of mission in chapter 6, but now you need to know how three important words will be used in this book:

Evangelism describes the activity of making people disciples of Jesus Christ, often (but not only) by the proclamation of the Gospel. This word is very commonly used by Protestants and those connected with the World Council of Churches. In the Three Circle diagram on p. 63 of chapter 6, evangelism is represented by one circle.

Mission is the way in which the Church is sent out into the world, i.e. the ways in which it moves out beyond itself. Mission does not include activities like teaching, worship, brotherly love, renewal. It is represented by two circles in the diagram.

Evangelization describes *everything* the Church does, considered in relation to its impact on society. Therefore evangelization relates to all three circles in the diagram. The word is used with this meaning especially by Roman Catholics, but now other Churches increasingly use it as well. Some Protestants, however, use it to mean exactly the same as evangelism—indeed, there are people who use all three of these words to mean exactly the same as each other. In this Guide we shall use these words as we have defined them here.

In the past, many good reasons were given for mission activity aimed at those who were not yet Christians. Some of these reasons are listed on p. 8. This type of mission flourished in the nineteenth and twentieth centuries, but today many Christians are impatient with these 'old' ideas. There are fewer of the old forms of missionary activity for the following reasons:

1. Because of *independence movements* both within nations and within Churches, people have stopped feeling that they must depend on colonial leaders or even foreign ways of thinking and acting.

2. People have discovered their *local cultural and religious roots* and learnt to value them in new ways. They now see that customs and ideas which were once thrown away as 'backward' actually enshrine values needed by the whole world.

3. *Two world wars* have shown everybody that the so-called 'civilized' countries of the North can be as barbaric and cruel as anyone else. The way in which the northern countries now use 80 per cent of the world's resources for the benefit of 20 per cent of the world's people represents an abuse of the earth. This abuse means that these nations have no right to lead the rest of the world.

4. *The decline of the Churches of the North* makes us wonder whether in fact there is anything that the Churches of the South can learn from them. In England, for example, Church attendance has dropped from 40 per cent of the population in 1865 to less than 10 per cent in 1990. It is said that an average of 53,000 people leave the Churches in the North every week (though this figure may be misleading).

5. *Church growth in the Third World*, on the other hand, has been and continues to be dramatic, as the following chart of numbers of Christians in the South shows ('m' represents 'millions'):

	1900	*1985*	*2000 (estimated)*
Africa	10m	236m	400m
Latin America	62m	392m	571m
South-East Asia	19m	148m	225m

An average of 115,000 people become Christians in Africa every week. Brazil is estimated to have 35 million evangelical Christians—more than in the whole of Europe. Therefore it is no surprise to learn that in 1994 more missionaries were recruited and sent out in the South than in the North. Indian Churches and indigenous missions are supporting 8000 missionaries, and Nigerians support over 2000. Every year Korea sends more than a thousand new missionaries.

6. *Religions should not compete but co-operate*, say world political leaders. Even though religion is used in some countries to support domination by one race or tribe, people see (a) that they are united by God's gift of the humanity that they share, and (b) that light and truth are not found only in one faith but throughout humankind.

7. *The big problems are not solved by faith*, say many world leaders, but by social and economic action which applies modern technology to them.

Some of the above observations are clear matters of fact; others are more open to dispute. What is clear as we approach the end of the twentieth century is that there has been a shift in the 'centre of gravity' of the Christian faith, away from Europe and North America to the Third World. This is not just a matter of numbers, it is also changing the way the faith is practised and preached. We shall see many examples of this on the following pages.

For the moment, however, we can be encouraged by the fact that shifts of this kind are not a new experience for Christian believers. On the contrary, there have been three distinct theological phases or periods of the Church:

1. *Jewish Christianity* This was the first phase of the Church, which was culturally Jewish and centred on Jerusalem. This phase lasted perhaps until St Paul's mission to the Gentiles, or until the destruction of the Jerusalem Temple in AD 70, or until the Jews were finally expelled from Jerusalem by the Romans in AD 130.

2. *Hellenistic (or Greek) Christianity* This phase began as a result of the conversion of large numbers of Gentiles, who spoke Greek, and Rome rapidly became the centre of the faith (see the last two verses of Acts). Apart from small groups of Christians in Syria, India, Ethiopia (and perhaps Arabia), the culture of Christianity remained Greek (or European) until the present day, the twentieth century. Missions which brought the Gospel inevitably brought it in European wrappings (see chapter 8).

3. *Universal Christianity*. Today, as we have already seen, the Christian faith does not have one single cultural or geographical centre, and the Gospel is presented to people in a variety of different ways. The Church has begun to see the true meaning of universality and pluralism. This understanding almost certainly fulfils the intention of Jesus, for it was reflected in His own ministry (see chapter 7, p. 77), and He sent His followers 'to all nations'. We should therefore rejoice in this view of Christianity, even though it

creates problems for us all, problems which lie at the heart of mission.

The word 'universal' recognizes the social fact that all human beings relate to one another and must respect each other. The word 'Christianity' recognizes the theological fact that we are committed to witness to the claims of Jesus Christ as Lord without any apology. Christians have always been involved in the process of discovering what this commitment to witness means in every situation in which they find themselves. They discovered this as they moved from phase one to phase two, and they are doing the same now as they move to phase three. It means adjusting to new geographical centres, cultures, languages, moralities, forms of worship and ways of knowing. This adjustment was one of the most difficult problems which Christians had to face in the time of Paul (see Acts 15), and it is even more difficult for us today, because the cultural and technological changes which affect the world are bigger and more rapid than they have ever been before. Although there are a few rural peoples who are not much affected by them, there is no nation, no city dweller, no educated person who can avoid their impact. In some places 'Western' values seem to have triumphed without question. In other places they are being sharply questioned. The local Church is called by God to be courageous and to discern what is good in every culture, and also what is suitable for the culture of its own people.

This need for cultural adjustment has not always been recognized in mission, and many people feel alarmed by the bewildering speed of the changes which face them. But change has happened before, and the Holy Spirit uses such changes to bring new life to new parts of His Church. We should not be discouraged; instead, we should be excited to see the new possibilities which God sets before us. In the next section we shall trace some of the ways in which this has happened in Church history.

STUDY SUGGESTIONS

WORD STUDY

1. Note the meaning of the three words listed on p. 1 (evangelism, mission, and evangelization). If you use a language other than English, which words would you use to express these ideas?

BIBLE STUDY

2. What major changes faced people in the following pas-

sages of the New Testament? Why did they fear these changes, and what was the effect of them?

    Luke 12.50   Acts 13.45   Acts 15.14   Phil. 1.13 2   Tim. 4.6

CONTEXTUAL APPLICATION

3. What thoughts, words and ideas come into your mind *first* when you hear the word 'mission'? What comes into your mind after you have had time to reflect about this word?

4. In what ways is Jesus an example of mission?

5. What reasons are given to explain why it is important to study mission? What other good reasons can you think of?

6. What evidence is there to show that the Church is growing in numbers—or declining—in your own country? What evidence is there for other sorts of growth? Are there aspects of Church life which cannot be measured in terms of growth?

7. Do you agree that the Church declines when it becomes preoccupied with itself? Give any examples known to you which support or question this statement.

8. List in order of importance the seven reasons given for the change of attitude to traditional forms of mission. Give any other reasons you may have noticed.

9. What are the biggest changes and adjustments facing Christians in your country today? Do you welcome these changes or do you dislike them? How could they encourage you?

PART 1
THE FOUNDATIONS OF THE CHRISTIAN MISSION

1. Historical and Theological Foundations

THE HISTORICAL FOUNDATION: SERIAL EXPANSION

The Christian faith has only survived because it has been able to develop through different phases, as described in the Introduction (p. 3). This has not been true of any other faith. Islam, the other great missionary faith, has embraced many cultures but it has expanded in a *progressive* way. It grew by moving on to new areas while retaining its hold on the lands where it had already taken root: first Arabia, then the Middle East, then North Africa, then the coasts of Africa, India and the Far East. Spain is the only region which Islam lost and has never regained. But Christianity has expanded in a *serial* way, i.e. when it lost ground in those regions where it was most strong and secure, it won new followers from those people who seemed to threaten its existence. The survival of Christianity has depended upon its ability to adapt to new and hostile cultures.

JEWS AND GENTILES

The first Christians were Jews who had experienced in Jesus the fulfilment of their nation's hope. The Gospel was the good news of the Messiah for God's people, the Jews. But in Acts 10 Peter found himself welcoming as equals Gentiles such as Cornelius and his family. Although some Gentiles worshipped God and supported the Jewish faith, Jews were not allowed to accept hospitality in Gentile homes (see Acts 10.2,15). God had to send Peter a special message before he was ready to accept Cornelius as an equal in Christ.

Then at Antioch some rather uneducated Jewish Christians from the country areas started to tell Greeks, complete outsiders, about the good news of Jesus (Acts 11.20). It is difficult for us today to realize what a revolutionary step this was, but Jews had never thought that Gentiles could become God's people unless they were circumcised like Jews, i.e. by first becoming a Jew. The new

7

movement (Christianity) would have to be stopped, they thought, but that was not really possible because it had been amazingly successful—so successful, in fact, that within a generation the majority of Christians in the world were not Jews but Greeks. If the situation had not been like this, it is hard to see how Christianity could ever have survived the Roman invasion of Judaea in AD 70. The original (Jewish) Church vanished; yet the Church was stronger and bigger than ever. This was not because humans had planned it but through what looked like an accident. The story of how the Church came to terms with the new situation is told in Acts 15.

GREEKS AND BARBARIANS

In the seventh century AD the Greek- and Latin-speaking Church in North Africa and the eastern Mediterranean seemed to be strong and secure. The only people they feared were the savage barbarians who threatened them from Northern Europe. Yet it was not those barbarians who destroyed the Church. The Church was destroyed by the brotherhood of Islam, which swept all before it and took over all the areas which had been proud of being Christian. The Church remained, stronger and bigger than ever, but it was not in the places where it had been. Now its central area was among those despised barbarians of the North. If we colour the Muslim expansion on a map, the area of colour grows progressively bigger. If we colour the Christian expansion on a map, we have to move the area of colour constantly out of old regions into new ones—and new regions were often those areas which seemed least likely to respond to Jesus.

NORTH AND SOUTH

After the changes caused by the advance of Islam, the Church did not expand very much for several centuries. But movement began again in the eighteenth century. The European Church gradually became aware of its obligation to share the faith and it had enough self-confidence to do it. European Christians thought they had everything to offer to a needy world—education for the ignorant, wealth for the poor, ethics for the amoral, peace for the warlike, civilization and skills for the savages, religion for the godless—and even English to replace 'barbaric' languages. The traffic was strictly one-way, and for a time the expansion of Christianity seemed to be progressive and triumphant. There were local reasons for this movement in the Churches of Europe. *Politically*, the nineteenth century was an age of individual enthusiasms, without control by a central government. It was a time when individual people formed voluntary societies together in order to promote their special interests. *Economically*, there was a surplus of cash which could be freely moved around the world. *Religiously*, Christians were self-confident and needed outlets for their energies—they needed the mission field just as much as the mission field needed them. They needed to be needed and they needed to be missionary heroes. We must also not overlook a fourth reason for the missionary movement of the nineteenth century. This was the humanitarian reason of repentance for the harm which European nations had done to Africa by the slave trade. Before 1800 Europeans knew very little about Africans except as slaves, but the revivals led by John Wesley and others awakened the consciences of many Christians, and so the first missionaries sent out by the Church Missionary Society in 1804 were told:

> Africa has not only . . . received from us our diseases and our vices, but it has ever been the chief theatre of the inhuman Slave Trade; and tens of thousands of its children have been annually torn from their dearest connexions to minister to the luxuries of men bearing the Christian name, and who had no more right to exercise this violence than the Africans had to depopulate our coasts with a similar view. The wickedness and wretchedness consequent upon this trade of blood have deeply and extensively infected these shores; and . . . the British nation is now, and has long been, most deeply criminal. We desire therefore, while we pray and labour for the removal of this evil, to make Western Africa the best remuneration in our power for its manifold wrongs.

But big changes took place during the twentieth century. Signs of these changes appeared as early as 1897. Apolo Kivebulaya of Uganda spent his life as a missionary to the Congo. He was a far more effective missionary than a white person could ever have been, and he was only one of many Africans engaged in such ministries. Another sign of change was Bishop Tucker's constitution for the Church of Uganda, which put all missionaries under the control of the local church. African Independent Churches began to emerge, such as the Kimbanguist Church (1921), and Ugandan Anglican delegates at the International Missionary Council at Jerusalem in 1928 declared that they were in control of their own affairs and had not been dominated by foreign missions.

By 1975 the change was unmistakable. Uganda was more than eighty per cent Christian, and South Korea and Singapore were rapidly becoming Christian lands. In the West, however, Christen-

Nineteenth-century missionaries like this one, photographed pulling out a rotten tooth, have been greatly criticized for treating their converts like children and destroying local culture. Did they really do everything wrong, or was some of their work of great help to the countries to which they went?

dom was in decline. The serial expansion of Christianity has begun again; the era of Constantine, the emperor who made the Roman Empire Christian, has ended and we can no longer think in simple terms of lands which have been mission fields, and those which have not. The Gospel is no longer given by the rich to the poor or by rulers to their subjects. On the contrary, like evangelists in the New Testament, those who are bearers of the Gospel today will bring no gifts with them except the Gospel itself. The Church's new centre of gravity can be found in Latin America, Africa and the Far East, and perhaps we stand at the beginning of a new era of cross-cultural mission. Many lands which until recently were Communist are now open to the Gospel, and it may be that the Islamic world will also open up, just as Muslims have flooded into the lands of Europe which were once Christian. The new missionaries from the Third World may be more acceptable to their hearers than the affluent Westerner could ever have been. This is beginning to happen even in Britain, where only the poorer, black-led Churches are growing rapidly.

As a result of observations like these, some Western Christians have begun to lament the sins of their missionary ancestors. It is right to do this, but they should also recognize the power of the Holy Spirit in the younger Churches and praise God for it. He has brought new peoples to birth from the seed of the Gospel planted by missionaries, in spite of the fact that those who preached the Gospel often did not understand it properly. They were ready to die for the Gospel, but they had often wrapped it up in their own culture, like a baby in swaddling-clothes. The miracle was that very often those who received the Gospel understood it better than the missionaries. But that has been the normal experience of the Church ever since the events described in Acts 10.

THE THEOLOGICAL FOUNDATION:
THE MISSION OF GOD

If you ask most Christians to say what they understand by the word 'mission', they will answer in terms of the tasks committed to the Church. But Roman Catholics have used the term *Missio Dei* (= the Mission of God) to describe how the Father, the Son and the Holy Spirit relate to one another. It is a relationship of movement. The idea of relationship must be in the front of our minds if we are to understand about God, His Kingdom and His mission (see p. 61). The Father sends the Son and the Spirit: this is what the God who is One in Three is like in Himself. This movement of sending out is revealed both in the creation of the world and in the coming

11

of the Son to live a human life on earth. The word 'mission' therefore describes what God is like and also what the Church is like, in which His life is reproduced. The Church is in its nature missionary, 'It exists by mission, as fire by burning'. Moreover, mission creates the Church, so it comes before the Church's doctrine and theology. Theology only exists to serve the Church in the mission of God. Mission bridges the gap between the Church and the Kingdom of God. The goal of the Church is not its own good but the Rule of God; the Church was founded for a future in the Kingdom of God and so it is for all humankind (see chapter 6).

KARL BARTH'S VIEW OF MISSION

It is not only Roman Catholics who teach that mission belongs to the very nature of the Church. The Swiss Protestant theologian Karl Barth also pointed out that the Church does not exist for itself; it cannot consider its own security and dignity. 'As Jesus' community,' he wrote in *Church Dogmatics* (vol. IV, pp. 724ff.),

> it is always free from itself . . . It is not churchly but worldly—the Church with open doors and great windows, behind which it does better not to close itself in upon itself again by putting in pious stained-glass windows . . . Its mission is not additional to its being. It exists as it is sent and active in its mission.

This is because the Church's model is Jesus Christ, who was born in the world, died for it and rose in it. Therefore the Church has no choice in the matter. In Christ,

> God has chosen His community to be for the sake of those outside, to be visible, worldly and like the people . . . To set aside this likeness with the world . . . would mean separating itself from the God who came, lived, suffered, died and rose in the flesh. How else can the Church be a witness of Jesus Christ? It is amazing and wonderful that just as the Son of God came, so the Church is called to be a people like others which precisely as such is His people and may exist in His service.

The life of God himself is therefore reflected in what the Church is and does when it is sent out to belong to the world. It is therefore not surprising that when people begin to study the Bible from the standpoint of mission, they find themselves led to the very heart of its message.

ATTITUDE AND ACTIVITY

We shall find it helpful to distinguish between the missionary attitude and missionary activity (which some missiologists call

The Swiss Protestant theologian Karl Barth said that the Church must have 'open doors and great windows' (p. 12), so that Christians could go out in mission to other people. Do the members of your own congregation go out to the people around them, to share the good news of Jesus, or do you close the doors and shut yourselves away from non-Christians?

'missionary dimension' and 'missionary intention'). The missionary attitude sees 'being sent' or (to invent a word which sums it up) 'sentness' as belonging to the nature of the Church. Only a Church which has this dimension can truly be the Church which confesses Jesus, the one whom God sent, as Lord. This missionary attitude affects every part of the Church's nature and work, because the Church is the society in which the life of Jesus lives on and His mission continues in the form of death and resurrection. (For signs of 'sentness', see p. 117.)

However, at times the Church engages in activities which are deliberately missionary. These may involve conversion, church-planting, social work, political action, etc. By doing this, the Church's intention is to bring about change in areas outside itself. But sometimes a church engages in missionary activity (perhaps by holding a mission or recruiting new members) when it does not have the missionary attitude. This is one reason why missions of this sort often fail. People can see when a church is concerned first with itself and not with the people to whom it has been sent. In these cases the church becomes an institution and loses touch with the Kingdom of God. It may engage in missionary activities, but people see that it lacks the love which is at the heart of the mission of Jesus.

Perhaps we ought to ask questions about the missionary activities of our churches, and measure them against the presence of the missionary attitude. For example, if the whole Church was truly missionary, would it need to create missionary societies? If the parish church was outward-looking, would it need to organize a parish mission? If the Christians in a city were witnesses to Jesus in their daily lives, would they need to invite Billy Graham to hold a 'crusade'? Is it only seminaries which focus chiefly on academic and pastoral studies which need to teach the missionary attitude by offering courses in missiology?

There is, of course, an opposite danger (a danger into which the Eastern Orthodox Churches have fallen at some times in their history). This danger is that Christians will see the Church itself as the centre of mission, and think that if you renew the Church you are engaging in missionary activity. Christians who think in this way may fall into the trap of being satisfied that they have got a missionary attitude—but never actually *doing* any kind of missionary activity at all!

Mission is an attitude of mind which should be at the heart of the Church's life and work, just as it is at the heart of God, both as He is in Himself and in all He does.

14

STUDY SUGGESTIONS

WORD STUDY

1. Explain what is meant by
   (a) progressive expansion
   (b) serial expansion.
2. What is the difference between the missionary *attitude* and missionary *activity*?

CONTEXTUAL APPLICATION

3. Have you ever heard of the Gospel message coming to a person or group of people because other people have rejected it? If you know of an example of this, what happened?
4. Mission may take place for a variety of reasons, both good and bad. List some good motives which people have for doing mission; and then list some of the bad motives. How have you seen God do good even when human motives are wrong?
5. Give examples of local churches being ruled, or dominated, by outsiders. Is this ever right? If so, why? If not, what steps could be taken to change the situation?
6. Has the Church you belong to found new opportunities for mission in the past six months? If so, what are they?
7. What new lessons about God or the faith have you learned from people (perhaps people of a different culture) who have only recently become Christians?
8. What is the theological significance of the term *Missio Dei*?
9. Describe any missionary *activity* your Church has engaged in. Do these intentions arise out of the mission *attitude*? How would you describe the difference between the two in your local church? How should a local church express the mission attitude in practice?

2. The Mission of God in the Old Testament

The New Testament contains many commands to take the Good News to all peoples. It also contains many examples of people doing this, beginning with Jesus Himself. But many people find it harder to see the idea of mission in the Old Testament. Israel's scriptures seem to require the nation to belong to Yahweh alone, and to be separate from all other peoples. If God had any message for the heathen nations, this message seemed to be one of judgement, not of salvation. In other words, God's love for Israel seemed to be *particular* (focused on them specially) and *exclusive* (not for anyone else).

THE CALL OF ABRAHAM

This exclusivism can be seen most clearly in Genesis 12, where God told Abram to leave his family and all that was sacred to him and to go to a new land. But in fact the context of this text is a situation which is *inclusive* and *universal* and this context can guide us to the true meaning of the text. For before Abram's call we find the list of the seventy nations (Genesis 10), and Israel was not fundamentally different from them in origin (see Amos 9.7 and 1.3–2.16). Most people tell mythical stories about how their nation came into being, but Israel's beginnings were in real world history. God intended the nations to receive His blessing but they obstinately refused to co-operate wih His purposes (Gen. 9.17; 11.9). Patiently God made a new beginning and from the nations chose Abram by grace (Gen. 12.1–13)—not just to receive His blessing but to carry it to others, not just to have privileges but to have responsibilities—'In you shall all the nations of the world be blessed'.

And yet God's choice continued to become more and more narrow: Isaac was chosen, but not Ishmael; Jacob, not Esau; Judah, not Israel; and so on. This exclusivism (which seems to us to be contrary to the spirit of the New Testament) is always, in the end, for the sake of including everyone in God's purposes of mercy, and the biblical revelation never ceases to remind Israel and the Church about this purpose. 'You only have I known of all the families of the earth,' said the Lord to Israel, and 'Therefore I will punish you for all your iniquities' (Amos 3.2). It is true that Israel enjoys a privileged position—but it also carries the heaviest responsibility.

THE BOOK OF THE COVENANT

Deuteronomy is called 'The Book of the Covenant', the covenant which Yahweh made with Israel. The book contains the most important statement of God's love in action, i.e. *Grace* (Deut. 5.6), and His requirements for their life, i.e. the *Law* (Deut. 5.7–21). When the people of Israel were wandering in the desert they had experienced God's love and heard His voice—God and His people were together. Humbly they knew they had not yet arrived where they were going, so they were open to receive the clearest revelation of His grace:

> The Lord, the Lord, a God compassionate and gracious, long-suffering, ever faithful and true, remaining faithful to thousands, forgiving iniquity, rebellion and sin but without acquitting the guilty, one who punishes children and grandchildren to the third and fourth generation. (Exod. 34.6,7)

But now, in the book of Deuteronomy, they were at the end of their desert wandering and stood on the brink of a new and frightening experience. They were about to enter the land of Canaan, where they would find themselves mixing with people who worshipped idols, followed pagan rituals, had sexual activity with children, prostitutes and people of the same sex, and even killed children in sacrifice. The land of Canaan therefore presented the people of Israel with both danger and opportunity.

1. Canaan was *dangerous* because it would be easy for the Israelites to *imitate* the life of their Canaanite neighbours. When everybody is living in a certain way—and boasting about it—it is difficult not to do the same. See Deut. 7.1–6.

2. Canaan was a great *opportunity* to *challenge* the godless ideas and practices of their neighbours in the name of Yahweh.

Therefore Deuteronomy contains the call to *love* God (Deut. 6.4–9). He is the one and only God, unique and different from all the false gods of Canaan, especially because He had taken action in loving His people and rescuing them from Egypt (6.20–23). Deut. 6.4–9 is called the 'Shem'a'. Today the Shem'a is still the most solemn creed of all Jews. Jesus quoted it as 'The Great Commandment' (Matt. 22.37; Mark 12.29–30). Here in the Jewish scriptures this text formed the basis of God's special 'Great Commission' to Israel. This was God's call to Israel to belong to Him for ever and to be separate from their neighbours who denied the one true God.

Deuteronomy also contains the call to loyalty (7.6). Faced with the threat of idolatry and immorality, Israel understood the call to loyalty as a call to fight against their pagan neighbours—precisely so that the Israelites would not join them and become like them (7.4,16). The basis of this call to loyalty was Yahweh's special love for them (7.6–15). The heart of this love is seen in v. 9, which echoes Yahweh's great revelation to Moses in Exod. 34.6,7. But in spite of the warnings, idolatry was the chief fault of Israel and is mentioned in the Bible more frequently than any other sin. Deuteronomy's call to loyalty did not simply mean believing that there is only one God. It was a call to the people actually to enthrone Yahweh as the one King in their lives. This meant refusing and denouncing the many false and evil gods which were freely offered to the people of Israel in Canaan, in the same way that idols like materialism, sex and superstition are, literally, sold to people in the market-places of modern society. Deuteronomy warned the Israelites against these things not only for their own benefit but also for the sake of the nations of the world (Deut. 4.5–8). Would the people of Israel remain true to God or not, when so many other 'gods' called for their attention? Over and over again Yahweh brought His people back to Himself in a renewed loyalty (see Jer. 9.12–14). Christians are called to the same loyalty to the one God and to a spiritual warfare against the powers of evil that draw them away from Him. Like Israel, we are witnesses to the whole world.

Both *love* and *loyalty* demand that God's people should be like Him in character and behaviour. In the Law of Moses this meant caring for the poor, the stranger and the oppressed, just as God had cared for the Israelites when they were strangers in the land of Egypt. Even though the people of Israel were told to destroy idols and idolaters, at the same time they were obliged to love, welcome, shelter and feed oppressed people. This was their mission because it was the nature of their God (Deut. 10.18–21). If the people were like God in this way, then God would take care of the nation (Deut. 15.6). Many governments today say they do not have enough resources to aid the poor—but Deuteronomy teaches that the nation cannot prosper if it neglects its poor people.

Like God's people in the past, Christians today must ask what great events, like the Exodus, show God's care for those in need. These events can become signs or stories which give us vivid pictures of God's love for all. Many preachers in Africa have used the story of their own nation's struggle for independence from colonial powers to illustrate how God sets us free. In Latin America small groups of poor people meet to tell of injustices suffered at the hands of the rich—and God is with them, showing them how together they can begin to put things right (see chapter 13). The

Lord's Supper is a powerful story of God acting with ordinary things and ordinary people to mend His world (see chapter 4).

THE BOOK OF JONAH

The dramatic tale of the prophet Jonah is more about a gracious God than about a reluctant missionary. In order to avoid God's call, Jonah journeyed in the opposite direction until the storm stopped him completely. Then Jonah slept while the pagan sailors prayed. Finally, Jonah, like 'the sleeping Church', was awakened to reality, and he told them his story. Hearing about the Lord, the pagans prayed and turned to God—but Jonah, apparently, did not.

After a series of adventures, Jonah found himself proclaiming divine judgement upon the city of Nineveh—an act which was rather like a Jew daring to denounce the Nazis in Berlin in 1935. And this was the moment when Jonah's worst fears were realized. The King of Nineveh covered himself in sackcloth and ashes and the whole city prayed and fasted. God changed his mind and forgave them, and Jonah said, 'How typical! I knew it! I told you so! No wonder I ran away. What justice can there be in a world where God is so absurdly generous? What is the point of missions if judgement is going to be abolished? What does He mean by putting them in the same category as me, His prophet? And it's worse than that—He's even made me a laughing-stock because He made me tell them He would destroy them. Who will believe me now? I look such a fool!' While God was saving people, Jonah sat outside in the mission compound sulking. And he quoted—in frank disapproval—that supreme revelation given to Moses in Exod. 34.6:

> 'I knew that you are a gracious and compassionate God, long-suffering, ever constant, always ready to relent and not inflict punishment. Now take away my life . . . ' (Jonah 4.2,3)

The scriptures return to this revelation over and over again (see, for example, Ps. 89.1,3,24; Jer. 22.13–17; Lam. 3.22,31; Luke 4.22ff.). And the writers of the Bible quote this revelation over and over again to correct the constant desire of God's people to be exclusively His. The fact is that the real missionary is God, who wants everyone to receive His mercy. The question is whether His people (who often wish to be a small, exclusive group) can keep up with Him and catch His vision.

The story of the Book of Jonah seems to be told as a warning to the Jewish people not to be self-satisfied in their enjoyment of God's favour. They were a tiny nation threatened on all sides by enemies, just as Jonah's little ship was threatened by the storm.

These sufferers from leprosy in Burma (now Myanmar) in 1920 had to live together in a special hospital, completely separated from their families and other people. The Jews in the Old Testament saw themselves as God's special people and tried to keep themselves separate from everyone else and not mix with other nations who were not God's people. What did the Book of Jonah try to teach the Jewish people? What can Christians learn from Jonah?

They were thrown out of their land into exile just as Jonah was thrown out of the ship. Yahweh saved His people who cried to Him, just as He saved Jonah when he prayed from inside the fish (Jonah 2.10)—but, like Jonah, they needed to learn that God's love was not only for them. As Isaiah saw in his first vision (Isa. 5.3), Yahweh is Lord of the whole earth. This means that even the King of Assyria did not act on his own, but was the rod of Yahweh's anger (Isa. 10.5); Nebuchadnezzar of Babylon was 'My servant' (Jer. 27.6); and Cyrus King of Persia was 'the Lord's anointed' (Isa. 45.1). So it is not surprising that in the end God's saving power is able to reach out to all nations (Isa. 49.6).

The pagan people of the world thought that each territory had its own god to whom you had to pray when you were in that territory. Even the Israelites in exile were tempted to ask 'How can we sing Yahweh's song in a strange land?' (Ps. 137.4). But the prophets told them to pray for their land of exile and to settle there as witnesses to Yahweh, for He was there also— indeed it was Yahweh rather than Nebuchadnezzar who had deported the Israelites there (see Jer. 29.1, 4–7).

This is missionary thinking, and it is difficult to put into action when everyone around you assumes that each nation or tribe has its own god. Even today many Christians think that the Good News of Jesus is only for pagans who have no religious faith, Christians, and those who were once Christians—not for Muslims, Hindus, Sikhs and Jews. This is what Jonah really thought, even though he 'knew' (in his head) the text which said that God's mercy is boundless. He could only learn what this text *really* meant by experience. The writer told Jonah's story to help other Jews learn the following lessons:

1. God is more of a missionary than we are.
2. We are often afraid of mission and do not want to evangelize.
3. We often misunderstand and misrepresent our God.
4. True love for God can often be found outside the Church.
5. It is often hard for us to see what is happening when God works in new ways.
6. Mission does not make us successful, it makes us amazed and humble.

A CHRISTIAN REFLECTION

Christians can be just as exclusive as God's people in the Old Testament, especially perhaps when they think what the Sacraments of the Church mean to them. People often think, for example, that Baptism is an occasion when people come to receive

God's blessings for themselves. Baptism is, however, the 'ordination' or setting apart of everyone who responds to God's call—and ordination, like Abraham's call, is for responsibility and service. In volume IV of his *Church Dogmatics*, Karl Barth asked the question, 'What is it that makes Christians Christian? What is the controlling principle, the primary thing which makes them how they are?' He suggested several possible answers to this question.

1. The most common answer is the fact that Christians possess the salvation which God gives through Jesus Christ. Evangelists offer people salvation, and Christians rejoice in finding Jesus as their Saviour because nothing is more relevant to people than the salvation of their souls. Yet Barth thinks that this answer is unacceptable for four reasons:

(a) In New Testament times people confessed Christ as Lord, not as Saviour and Benefactor.

(b) Many non-Christians seem to live good lives and experience peace, patience, trust and freedom, i.e. they show many of the signs of salvation that Christians claim to have.

(c) All this seems to depend on the Christian believer's personal awareness or assurance of salvation. In normal experience this assurance is sometimes weak and sometimes strong, and it cannot be relied upon always to scatter the doubts and difficulties which attack us.

(d) Finally, Barth asked this question: 'Can it really be the purpose and meaning of my Christian life . . . that I should be blessed, that my soul should be saved . . . that I should finally attain to eternal bliss, that I should go not to hell but to heaven?' Is not an attitude like this thoroughly selfish and self-centred—even worse than the sinfulness which Christ offers to save us from? If we see the main characteristic of being a Christian as my personal enjoyment of 'this indescribably magnificent private good fortune', then this is completely opposite to the selflessness and self-giving of God in Jesus Christ. It is more like the sin of Adam in Gen. 3.5, 6. This answer is the opposite of mission.

2. The only satisfactory—and biblical—answer to the question 'What makes a Christian a Christian?', according to Barth, is this: the controlling principle of the Christian life is not found in our personal well-being; it is found in the task which we are called to do. The blessings received by Paul at his conversion were less important than his call to ministry and to witness. The call of God means living in order to fulfil His will, and everything else comes second to this. God's will is that we should be His disciples and use the variety of gifts which He has given (for an example of this, see p. 68). Christians do, of course, at the same time receive salvation,

We are not Christians simply because salvation makes us feel good. Like the Jews, we have to behave like the God we follow. This means caring for the poor and the oppressed, and looking after the environment in which we live. This man in Bangladesh is planting trees to provide shelter and hold the soil, a practical way of improving living conditions for everyone in the area.

peace, joy, grace and hundreds of other personal blessings, but these are secondary benefits which come to those who respond to God's call 'Follow me'.

There are two reasons why this is the best answer to the question 'What is the primary characteristic of a Christian?'.

First, if the controlling principle of the Christian life is God's call to be His disciple, this means that we are restored to the relationship with God and the life with purpose and meaning which were lost at the Fall, i.e. we are restored to the task of being God's stewards or representatives.

Secondly, in this way the life and character of Jesus Christ, especially his self-giving and obedient love, are reproduced in the Christian.

STUDY SUGGESTIONS

WORD STUDY

1. What do we mean when we say that God's love for Israel seemed to be
   (a) particular, and
   (b) exclusive?
2. What do we mean when we say that God's love for human beings is
   (a) inclusive, and
   (b) universal?
3. Which book in the Bible is called 'The Book of the Covenant'?

CONTEXTUAL APPLICATION

4. How were God's loving purposes for the whole world channelled through Israel in (a) the ministry of Jesus and (b) the teaching of Paul in Romans 11?
5. The Church often needs to face danger if it is to discover new opportunities for witness. What risks were taken by (a) Abraham, (b) the Israelites who entered Canaan, (c) Jonah, (d) Jesus, and (e) Paul? What good resulted from taking these risks? What risks might you—or your Church—need to take, and what might be the result?
6. How was Jesus' Great Commission to His followers (a) unlike and (b) similar to the task given to Israel in Deuteronomy?
7. What idols are God's people tempted to worship today?
8. What ministry does your Church exercise to the poor and oppressed?

9. How did the pagan sailors challenge Jonah? In what way do unbelievers challenge Christians today?
10. What is God like, according to Exod. 34.6–9? Why do you think Christians today might find this revelation uncomfortable? What are the implications of it for our lives?
11. Comment on Psalm 47, in the light of Isa. 10.5; 45.1; Jer. 34.1–6.
12. Read the list on p. 21. Which of these lessons have you and your own Church learnt by experience?
13. If the chief calling of a Christian is the task God has given us (p. 22), what difference could this make to the way in which we proclaim the Gospel?

3. The Mission of the Son in Mark's Gospel

We could take any book of the Bible and examine the writer's theology of mission. In this Guide we shall look only at the Gospels of St Mark and St Luke. Although these writers emphasized different aspects of the mission of Jesus, our mission should be based on the models that Jesus left for us, which Mark and Luke record. This is as important for us as it was for the first Christians. Before turning to Mark we shall consider briefly the tradition about Jesus which is reflected in all the Gospels.

THE MISSION OF JESUS

Jesus Himself did not have a universal mission programme, because He limited His ministry to Jews (Matt. 10.5; 15.24). He did not clearly prepare the disciples for such a universal programme, either; we can see this from their great reluctance to go to non-Jews (Acts 10.14; 11.3, 19; 15.1). Many of the disciples believed that the final age of salvation had dawned in the coming of Jesus and that as a result the nations would *come to* Zion (Mic. 4.1, 2). This belief did not make them *go out* in mission to the nations.

However, the one feature of Jesus' ministry which made a great impression on the early Church was His readiness to welcome outcasts and sinners. The religious leaders of His time condemned or excluded these people; Jesus affirmed and included them. He crossed all the customary barriers and went out to people, i.e. his ministry was 'centrifugal' (see p. 40). He crossed the widest barrier of all when He left His glory with the Father and became incarnate as a human being belonging to a particular place and time. His disciples did not learn very quickly, but eventually they followed His example by crossing what was for them the widest barrier of all, i.e. the barrier between Jews and Gentiles.

The main theme of Jesus' teaching in the first three Gospels was the coming of the Kingdom (i.e. the reign or rule of God). God's reign was revealed in many different ways:

(a) God's action in history, which began to fulfil His promises now in anticipation of the final triumph of His rule, promised in Matt. 13.8.

(b) The presence of Jesus the King, here and now, which brought people into a new relationship with God who loves them even though they do not deserve it (Matt. 20:1–16; Luke 15.11–32).

(c) Setting people free from sin, demons, disease, ignorance, poverty, oppression, wrong relationships and death, and making them whole—this is what the Bible means by 'salvation', not just new ideas but new freedoms and new happenings (Luke 11.20).

(d) Love for all the outcasts. Religious leaders called them 'sinners' but Jesus could see in them the goodness of God: women, children, lepers, the poor, tax-collectors, prostitutes, Gentiles, Nineveh (Matt. 9.10–13).

(e) Unlimited forgiveness and reconciliation both between people and between them and God—the two were related (Matt. 18.21–35).

(f) Reinterpreting the Law of Moses, as the Northern prophets (e.g. Amos and Hosea) had done. This made love more important than keeping rules (Mark 1.23–3.5; 7.1–13).

(g) The gathering of the Twelve, a symbolic number which showed that God is not concerned with a small remnant in Zion (as many Jewish leaders thought), but is restoring the whole people of God (Mark 3.14).

Jesus' claim that he was the King who was bringing in the rule of God, with the help of a band of simple fishermen, was incredible to the religious leaders of His time. In everything He did, he truly represented God who cared for the poor and outcast; at the same time, He was Himself one of those poor and powerless people, a fact which was finally shown by His death as a common criminal. But after He had risen from death His followers were set free to continue His ministry of weakness—and even failure—knowing that God was with them and building His Kingdom. See also chapter 6, 'Mission and the Kingdom of God'.

THE STORY THAT MARK TOLD

It is important to realize that Mark was not writing history as scholars do today. Rather, he was telling a story which was very important to his readers because it gave them guidance for their life and witness as Christians, not because it gave them information. Mark's readers may have lived in Rome at about the time of the Jewish revolt against Roman rule in AD 70, although we do not know this for certain. What we can be sure about is that his readers were confused and bewildered Christians who were facing (a) the collapse of the familiar religious structures of Judaism, (b) the rapid expansion of the Church, which now included people from a wide variety of different cultures, and (c) various problems about how to live (see Mark 12.17), what to believe (Mark 12.25–27) and how to witness (Mark 6.7–12). Many Christians today who live in a world of rapid change are like Mark's readers, and have the same sort of problems.

In order to help his readers, Mark wrote his story in short episodes which move on in quick succession. Almost every episode throws new light on some matter and calls the reader to respond. It is in fact a mission document for people sent out as witnesses in the world. The story is built round three confessions:

1. *God's* confession of Jesus in Mark 1.11. He confesses Jesus as both King ('You are my beloved Son', quoting from Ps. 2.7) and Servant ('in you I take delight', quoting from Isa. 42.1). This confession leads into Mark's account of Jesus' kingly ministry of power (1.14–8.26).

2. *Peter's* confession of Jesus as Messianic King (Mark 8.29). This confession leads into Jesus' teaching about His suffering in Jerusalem (8.31–15.38).

3. *The centurion's* confession of Jesus as son of God (Mark 15.39). For Mark, this confession is the climax of the story and it is followed by a very small hint about the coming world mission which would begin in Galilee.

This structure of Mark's Gospel can be set out in the form of a diagram as shown in Figure 1 below.

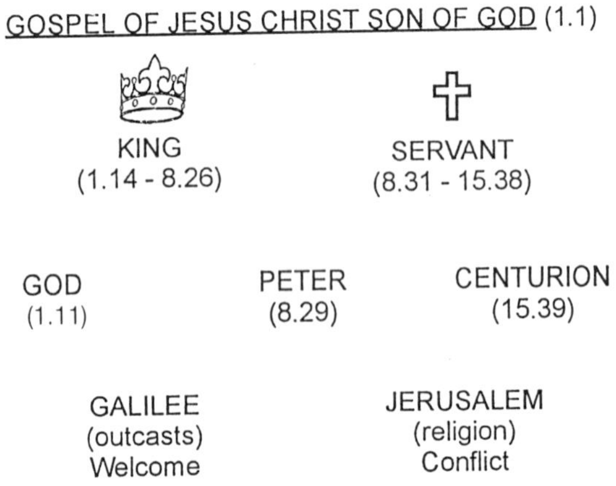

GOSPEL OF JESUS CHRIST SON OF GOD (1.1)

| KING | SERVANT |
| (1.14 - 8.26) | (8.31 - 15.38) |

| GOD | PETER | CENTURION |
| (1.11) | (8.29) | (15.39) |

GALILEE	JERUSALEM
(outcasts)	(religion)
Welcome	Conflict

Figure 1 The structure of Mark's Gospel.

THE WAY OF JESUS

Mark took the theme of 'The Way' to describe Jesus' ministry. John the Baptist had prepared the Way (1.2) for Jesus' coming (1.14). Jesus continued on the Way through Galilee, and His Way became the Way of the Twelve (6.8). On their Way together Peter showed that he had learnt the lesson of Jesus the Messiah—or King—(8.27–29), and so Jesus started on the Way of the Servant, to Jerusalem and His suffering (9.33; 10.17, 32, 46, 52; 12.14) and finally to Galilee (14.28; 16.7). Perhaps Mark's own readers thought of themselves not as 'Christians' but as 'Followers of the Way' (Acts 9.2). Mark wanted his story to help them to understand more about the Way of Jesus which they were following, a Way of power and suffering and mission.

The journeys of Jesus through Galilee were the beginning of his mission. For Mark, Galilee was not just a geographical area. It was also a region with a mixed population of Jews and Gentiles. They welcomed Jesus and He preached freely among them. People in Judaea rather despised the Gentile population and regarded the Jews in Galilee as uneducated northerners. But key people in the witness and mission of the early Church such as the faithful women at the cross and Peter were Galileans (14.70; 15.41). From 4.35 to 8.10 Mark shows Jesus going backwards and forwards across the Sea of Galilee. Some people saw the lake as a barrier to keep outsiders away; Jesus saw it as a bridge to reach them. He was welcomed on both sides of the lake, by both Jews and Gentiles, but the chief opposition to him came from the Jews (6.1–6; 6.27; 7.1–13). From this we can see that Mark's story of Jesus reflects the life of the ordinary Christian community to which Mark himself belonged thirty years later:

1. The mission is for Galileans and everyone;
2. Jews and Gentiles can enjoy Jesus' presence together;
3. Jews are still opposing the mission of the Church.

In Mark, going to 'Jews first' (7.27) gives way to going to 'all nations' (13.10).

This is why Jesus' promise to lead the disciples into Galilee after his resurrection (14.28; 16.8) is so significant. His promise was not just travel instructions; it was a commission to go to all peoples, and an assurance that they would have the same success which they had experienced in Galilee.

The first Christians were called 'Followers of the Way'. What is the Way of Jesus like? What do we have to do to follow him on the road?

CHARACTERISTICS OF JESUS' MINISTRY

St Paul did not say much about the life of Jesus, because he was so interested in the way that the death and resurrection of Jesus are reproduced in the lives of Christians. Mark, on the other hand, clearly believed that what Jesus did is the key to what we should do in our ministry, even though our situation may be different (see Special Note A, p. 44). Mark's stories provide many theological clues to the Church's mission (e.g. 3.31–35; 7.29). His Gospel shows us the following features of Jesus' ministry:

1. *Jesus used the ordinary language of the world in His teaching* and related his teaching to the needs which people really felt in daily life.

2. *He was open to outsiders*, unlike the religious leaders of His time; therefore He came into conflict with those leaders.

3. *He delivered people from oppression of all kinds*—physical, social, religious and political. Therefore He came into conflict with the demonic powers of evil.

4. *He commissioned the Twelve to continue His work*, although they failed to understand it; therefore He came into conflict with His disciples.

5. *He suffered and died in weakness at the hands of His opponents*; this brought Him into an internal conflict within Himself.

This list of the features of Jesus' ministry helps us to understand why He experienced conflicts in His life. We may call them His spiritual warfare, which went on from the time of His temptation by the devil in the desert. On the one hand, His ministry was in the power of the Spirit and the new age promised by the prophets (e.g. Isa. 61.1–3; Joel 2.28–31); on the other hand, He lived and died as the radically powerless one, always at the mercy of those who opposed Him. This was His choice. It was the opposite of the choice made by the prophet Muhammad when he faced opposition at Mecca. He escaped to Medina to preserve the message of Allah and accepted political and military power. The choice which Jesus made, to be powerless, commits His followers to a similar choice (see below).

One special feature of Mark's Gospel is that the kingship of Jesus is hidden. This has been called Mark's 'messianic secret'. We can see this 'secret' when Jesus commands those He has healed 'not to tell anybody' (Mark 1.44, 45); we can see it in His use of parables so that he does not reveal everything about God's rule all at once (4.10, 11, 33, 34); and we can see it especially in His use of the mysterious name 'Son of Man' to describe Himself. This title was almost never used by His followers after His resurrection, so when it is used in the first three Gospels it must reflect the fact that it was Jesus' own idea. Scholars do not all agree about the origin or significance of the name 'Son of Man', but Jesus probably used it because (a) it was not a clear claim to be the Messiah; (b) it spoke about Jesus' humanity; (c) it reminded his hearers of the name 'Son of Man' in Dan. 7.13, 14, which describes a 'Son of Man' who belongs to heaven and has a special destiny from God to receive kingly power over all the world. And in Dan. 7.27 the same kingly power was also given 'to the holy people of the Most High'. Mark's Gospel may reflect this shared power when it shows Jesus calling the Twelve 'to be with Him' and to exercise the same power that He did (3.14, 15; 6.7).

THE DISCIPLES OF JESUS

Although Jesus' followers shared His power, Mark described clearly their weakness and foolishness.

(i) They were blind to the true significance of Jesus and what He was doing (6.52; 8.17–21). They could not recognize His mission or their own mission (8.32; 10.41–45) and ultimately they betrayed, denied and forsook Him.

(ii) The followers of Jesus have to experience crucifixion in their lives. This teaching is particularly clear in Paul, but Jesus referred to it in Mark 8.34, 35. Jesus' followers have to say 'No' to their own way of life and self-interest in order to live the new life He offers them. Therefore their mission cannot be carried out by means of worldly power and authority.

(iii) When the followers of Jesus fail through weakness or persecution (e.g. 14.17–21; 27–31), they need not be dismayed. This was the experience of their Lord and they should expect it. Strangely, it is the key to the success of the Christian mission. The Church does not grow because it is strong but because it is weak. This weakness, this hidden power of God, is not only a theme of Mark the evangelist but it also belongs to the life of the Church. It can set missionaries free for mission, for they do not have to wait for strength in order to 'succeed', nor do they need to worry too much when they fail (as they will)—the mission is God's, and He works through human weakness. 'Power Evangelism' and weakness evangelism are closely connected!

Mark ended his Gospel abruptly and unexpectedly, with the words 'They said nothing to anyone, for they were afraid' (16.8). (Verses 9–20 are printed in many Bibles, but did not form part of the original manuscript of Mark.) Yet of course the readers know

Mark emphasizes the weakness of Jesus and His disciples. Yet weakness is the hidden power of God. Mahatma Gandhi was a weak and powerless man who refused to use violence, but his peaceful protest helped to make India independent. What other examples do you know of power in weakness?

that the women *did* eventually speak—otherwise this Gospel which we read today could not have come into being. But Mark has left his readers deliberately in suspense, with an implied question which they had to answer for themselves (and which we have to answer when we read the Gospel today): 'Are you afraid? Are you silent? Can you find the courage to be a witness to what you have seen and know, like those women did? Jesus is now calling you to go into "Galilee" and all the world with His mission. The matter rests now with you.' We can say that this verse is Mark's version of the Great Commission, better known to us in the words of Matt. 28.18–20 and Luke 24.47–49.

Perhaps at this point, at the very end of his Gospel, Mark was using a teaching method which he had learnt from Jesus. Jesus often left people with a question which He wanted them to go away and think about. This was part of the hiddenness of His teaching (see p. 31). One way in which missionaries and other preachers can provoke people to think and respond in ways which are appropriate for them is to ask questions, instead of giving answers.

STUDY SUGGESTIONS

REVIEW OF CONTENT

1. What aspects of Jesus' ministry prepared the early Church for its mission to be universal?
2. Why was the story of Jesus important for the early Church's mission?
3. Why did Mark consider Galilee important?

BIBLE STUDY

4. Find words in Mark 1 which express the idea of movement; then note other such words when you read the rest of Mark.
5. Give two examples of crossing the barrier between Jews and Gentiles from (a) Jesus's ministry and (b) the Acts of the Apostles.
6. Name two Old Testament prophecies which spoke about the Day of the Lord and said that it would be a new way of living and God's Spirit would be present.
7. Find two episodes from the first part of Mark's Gospel which show Jesus as King, and two from the second half which show Him as Suffering Servant.
8. Mark might have recorded the following sayings in order to help his readers who were facing problems. What do you think those problems were?
   3.33–35; 7.14–19; 7.29; 12.17.

9. Find texts in Mark which reflect Jesus' conflict with each of the following: (a) religious leaders; (b) demons; (c) His disciples.

CONTEXTUAL APPLICATION

10. Note the seven signs of the Kingdom of God (p. 26): which of these signs can you see in the Church in your country, through what it is or does?
11. What was the situation of the people for whom Mark was writing? How is your situation today (a) similar, and (b) different from that situation?
12. 'Some people saw the lake as a barrier to keep outsiders away; Jesus saw it as a bridge to reach them' (p. 29). What sort of people does the Church try to keep away from? How could the Church change its attitude so that it can reach out to these people in love?
13. What features of Jesus' spiritual warfare do you encounter in your discipleship?
14. What sorts of (a) power and (b) weakness on the part of Jesus and His disciples are revealed in the following passages:
    Mark 2.10, 11; 6.5; 6.13; 8.33; 9.34; 10.45; 14.37; 14.62; 15.40, 41; 16.8; 1 Cor. 2.1–5.
    What sort of power and weakness does your own Church experience? What sort of weakness is good for mission and what sort is bad?

4. The Mission of the Spirit in Luke's Gospel and Acts

St Luke was the author of two New Testament books, his Gospel and Acts, which he was careful to relate closely to one another. More than any other New Testament writer, Luke related the life and mission of the early Church to the life of Jesus of Nazareth. For example, Acts 1.1 suggests that Luke's Gospel told the story of the beginning of Jesus' ministry but that Acts tells the story of the continuation of His ministry through the Spirit whom He sent, not through Jesus personally. We could rename Luke's second volume 'The Acts of the Holy Spirit'. When he wrote at the beginning of his Gospel that he was writing 'an *orderly* narrative', he probably did not mean that he recorded events in the order in which they happened, but rather that he was setting them out in a *logical* order which Theophilus, his non-Jewish reader, would find easy to follow.

There is a good example of this in Luke 4.16–30. This passage tells the story of Jesus' visit to his home town of Nazareth and the opposition which He met there. Mark (6.1–6) and Matthew (13.53–58) say that this event took place later in His ministry, but Luke probably placed it right at the beginning because he wanted to show especially clearly the pattern and principles of the whole of Jesus' ministry. We shall therefore pay special attention to this passage.

JESUS' MESSAGE AT NAZARETH

The key verse is Luke 4.21, in which Jesus claimed that He was now fulfilling the prophecy of God's coming new age. He used Isa. 61.1–2 to support His claim, but he does not quote it word for word in 4.18. Luke was clearly relying on the Greek version of the book of Isaiah, with which he was familiar, not on the Hebrew version. He altered Isa. 61.1–2 in four ways:

(a) He left out the phrase in 61.1 '. . . to bind up the broken-hearted'.

(b) He inserted the phrase 'to send out the oppressed' which comes from Isa. 58.6. This use of other texts was allowed in Jewish teaching, provided that the text which was inserted did not come from too far away from the original text.

(c) He wrote 'proclaim' instead of Isaiah's word 'call' in v. 19.

(d) Finally, Jesus did not go on with the words of Isaiah which speak of God's vengeance and Israel's domination over the Gentiles.

Isaiah / Luke

Isaiah 61.1 & 2 (Greek)	Luke 4.18 & 19
The Spirit of the Lord is upon me	The Spirit of the Lord is upon me
because he has anointed me to preach good news to the poor	Because he has anointed me to preach good news to the poor
He has sent me to bind up the broken-hearted	(omitted)
to proclaim freedom for the captives	to proclaim freedom for the captives
and recovery of sight for the blind	and recovery of sight for the blind
(inserted from Isa. 58.6)	to send out the oppressed in freedom
to call the Year of the Lord's favour	to proclaim the Year of the Lord's favour
and the day of vengeance	(omitted)

Figure 2 The Isaiah and Luke passages.

These alterations (which could easily have come from Jesus Himself) can be seen by setting out the Isaiah and Luke passages side by side, as in Figure 2.

If we look at the structure of a literal translation of Luke 4.18, 19, it seems as if Jesus (or Luke when he reported His words) intentionally made the lines balance in such a way that they emphasised certain key points. A literal translation also shows that most of our English translations are rather inaccurate. Figure 3 over the page shows how the passage reads literally. Key ideas are printed in bold type; these ideas balance one another as follows:

Line 1 speaks of the Spirit who is at work in Jesus (4.14) and whom Jesus will send in power upon His followers at the Day of Pentecost, as a sign that the promised day of the Lord has now arrived (4.21). *Line 7* balances line 1 by repeating the idea of the promised time of the Lord with a reference to the Year of Jubilee

37

1-   The **Spirit of the Lord** is upon me
2-   for he has anointed me to **preach** to the poor
3-   for he has **sent me** to proclaim to the captives
      freedom
4-   and recovering of **sight to the blind**
5-   to **send out** the oppressed in **freedom**
6-   and to **proclaim**
7-   the **Year of the Lord** which is welcome

Figure 3 The structure of a literal translation of Luke 4.18,19.

(see Lev. 25.10–55) when, every fifty years, all debts were can-
celled, land was returned to its original owners and all slaves were
freed. In other words, it was a time of good news for the poor
—though the rich were probably not so pleased about it! (Even
though this law was probably not observed in practice, everyone
would have understood the reference to it.)

Lines 2 and 6 use the two Greek words (*euangelizomai* and *kerusso*)
which the New Testament uses regularly for preaching the Gospel.
This shows the readers that the evangelism of the churches to which
they (and Luke) belonged was the same as the evangelism of Jesus.

Line 3 has the Greek word *apostello* which is used regularly for God
sending out His messengers (or *apostles*). Exactly the same word is
found in *line 5* (though this is not clear in most English translations). Jesus was saying that God had sent Him on a special
mission to the world, especially to the poor, and that the poor and
oppressed share this same mission with Him. Both lines also have
the word 'freedom' which means both forgiveness and release from
all that spoils people's lives (Luke 13.16).

Line 4 stands alone and is important because Luke had already
announced that Jesus would bring light to the Gentiles (2.32). This
line therefore suggests that spiritual as well as physical blindness
will be healed.

OPPOSITION TO THE MESSAGE OF JESUS

After Jesus had spoken these words from Isaiah, he was immediately criticized for his claim. Again, the English versions are not

38

According to Luke, Jesus came to bring good news to the poor, like this street child in Bombay. Who are the poor in your community? What is good news for them? What would be good news for this child?

accurate in Luke 4.22, which means literally: 'And they all bore witness about him, and wondered at the words of grace . . . "Is not this Joseph's son?" ' This suggests that the people in the synagogue criticized Him from the start, and that is how Jesus understood it (vv. 23–24). They criticized Him because they did not believe that this person they had known since childhood could be a special messenger from God. They also criticized Him because He had declared that God was specially concerned for the poor and despised, not for the rich and comfortable. God was apparently even concerned for the Gentiles, because the people in the synagogue probably noticed that Jesus did *not* quote what Isaiah had said about God's judgement on the nations (Isa. 61.2, 5).

Jesus went on to emphasize this point again when He referred to the history of Elijah and Elisha (Luke 4.25–27). He seems to have made two main points in these verses:

1. God's love and grace have always been available to anyone, especially the outcasts, as Israel's two greatest prophets bear witness.

2. Mission is both *centrifugal*, i.e., it sends the message *out* to outsiders, as Elijah *went to* the widow at Sidon, and *centripetal*, i.e., it attracts outsiders *into* the Church, as Naaman *came into* Israel to be cured by Elisha and was then 'sent out in freedom' to be a witness to the God of Israel. In the same way God's mission was to send Jesus into the world so that people might *come to* Him to be set free and then be *sent out* on His mission. So the centrifugal and centripetal mission of Jesus is also the model for His Church to follow. (See Figure 4 opposite.)

This message of God's grace to outsiders was one of the chief causes of the hostility towards Jesus (4.28; 15.2; see point 3 opposite), because most Jews of the time thought that only those whom God had chosen and made prosperous could be blessed and saved.

THE MAIN THEMES OF JESUS' MESSAGE

1. Jesus fulfilled the Jewish scriptures (4.21) in His ministry and especially in His birth and death (3.22–38; 13.33; 18.31). The story of Jesus is not simply religious history; it is part of the ordinary history of the whole human race. Just as Abraham was called in the midst of the nations under God (see p. 16), so Jesus was 'son of Adam' (3.38) and part of human history (3.1, 2). In the same way, at the end of Luke's second volume (Acts) he showed Paul, the great missionary, in Rome, the centre of the secular world of his time (Acts 28.31). The Church follows this pattern of being part of

Luke 4.25-27

Centrifugal	Centripetal
Sent to someone to proclaim freedom	**Sends out** someone else in freedom (someone must come in first)
Elijah **goes out** of Israel and helps the woman of Zarephath	Elisha ministers to Naaman who is attracted **in** and comes to him in Israel

Go out and proclaim freedom	Attract in, then send out in freedom

Figure 4 The centrifugal and centripetal mission of Jesus.

ordinary human life. The Church quotes the scriptures in its mission (as it did especially when preaching to Jews) but it also relates its mission to the life and thought of all those to whom it is sent.

2. Jesus came in the power of the Spirit (4.18). The new age promised by the prophets and fulfilled in Acts was the age of the Spirit of God (Acts 2.16–18). Here Luke showed how all the activity of the Spirit was really focused on Jesus Himself. If His followers were filled with the Spirit, it was only because He was, before them (see also 3.16, 22; 4.1, 14). See p. 37.

3. Jesus had a special concern for the poor (4.18). In the Gospels 'the poor' refers not only to those with little money but to all the people who had been edged out of respectable society, e.g. women, Samaritans, lepers, sinners, tax-collectors. These were the disreputable people whose religious ignorance and immorality meant that they could not be saved through the Temple or the synagogue. They were, however, welcomed at Jesus' table (5.30; 7.39; 19.7) and at God's heavenly banquet (14.21, 23). There are no laws of religion or class or tribe which can set limits on the people God will

accept. This example has not always been followed by leaders in the Church—or by the Jewish religious leaders, as Jesus showed in His vivid story of the elder son who refused to join His father in welcoming his younger brother back home (the Parable of the Two Lost Sons, Luke 15.28). This is clearly a picture of the Jewish leaders in the time of Jesus.

4. Jesus was concerned for all parts of human life (Luke 4.18). The Greek word translated as 'freedom' means release from sin (5.20; 7.47) but also release from captivity and handicap (13.16). And, we could also add, freedom from sickness, hunger, poverty, ignorance and oppression. Freedom of all these kinds is good news, and Luke 4.18, 19 has a clear message of good news both in word and in deed. The ordinary people at that time were under foreign rule and in debt to tax collectors. Because of their religious impurity they were often excluded from the worship in the synagogue and the Temple, which was only for the 'righteous'. Jesus' message was relevant to what they felt they needed and they welcomed it. But others opposed His message. Rich people today often read the message of Jesus as if it is only a matter of words and spiritual ideas, but in fact it brings a definite and material challenge to their lives (i.e. it is 'holistic', concerned with every aspect of life). See also chapter 6.

5. Jesus gave people a role in life (4.18). He did not just bestow blessings, but he commissioned His people as God's stewards with authority over the created order, and also as His witnesses in all the world. Elijah did not go to the widow in Sidon primarily so that he might save her, but so that *she* might feed and save him! See 1 Kings 17.9. She was given a task and a sense of worth (see p. 22). The gospel does not make people dependent or independent, but interdependent.

THE ENDING OF LUKE'S GOSPEL

The same themes described above appear consistently all through Luke's Gospel to the very end, when they appear again in 24.44–49. This passage also relates to the central message of the gospel as it was preached in Acts (compare Acts 10.36–43). But these words, which were spoken just before Jesus departed from the disciples, emphasize new things which the disciples would need to remember through all their ministry. These new emphases are:

1. Their ministry began in Jerusalem (24.47). For Luke, unlike Mark, Jerusalem was the focus of the mission. Jesus had set His face to go there (9.51–19.40). Jerusalem was the place of suffering both for Him and His followers. The result of this suffering was

resurrection for Jesus and renewed spiritual power for His missionaries (Acts 5.40–42; 8:1–4; 11:19, 20). Jerusalem was the place
where the missionaries had to give an account of their work, and
where every new missionary advance had to be approved as
authentic (8.7; 9.27; 11.2; 15.2).

2. The ministry of the disciples was for all nations (24.47), but it
took them a long time to see this. It was not the outward command
of Jesus but the inward work of the Spirit which led them to
understand it, when the Spirit sent them first into Samaria through
persecution, secondly to Cornelius (a God-fearer) through a series
of visions, and thirdly to Gentiles, also through persecution.

3. The ministry of the disciples was in the power of the Spirit
(24.49) who alone could enable them to fulfil it. The Holy Spirit is
the subject of Acts, for He continues the work of Jesus both then
and up to the present time (Acts 1.1–5). The mission does not go
forward because of the apostles' plans but because of the way in
which the Spirit leads (16.7). All these three emphases are found
together again in Acts 1.8. There is however one other emphasis at
the end of Luke's Gospel:

4. Suffering was a characteristic of the ministry of the disciples
(24.46). If their Master suffered, so will they, and this suffering will
mark the greatest advances of the mission of Jesus (see 1 and 2,
above). For the disciples, for St Paul and for the Church in all ages,
it is power, wealth and prestige which are the greatest dangers to
the Church—and it is weakness, poverty, suffering and humility
which make the Church an effective instrument in the hand of God,
for then it is like Jesus its Lord. Perhaps the greatest example of this
was Stephen, the first martyr. It was to him, just as he was about to
die, that the Holy Spirit gave the first really clear vision of the fact
that the Kingdom of God belonged not only to Israel but to the
whole world (Acts 7).

Special Note A

USING THE BIBLE IN MISSION

One of the problems faced by all Christians is to decide how the
Bible can help them solve the problems of living and mission which
they meet today. It is tempting to look in the Bible for ready-made
answers to our questions. Just before the Second World War, at a
big Christian gathering in England, two leaders noticed that many
women were not wearing hats. So they published a pamphlet which

declared that the judgement of God was about to fall on the country because of this sin against the teaching of the Bible in 1 Cor. 11.5, 6. When war broke out, these leaders felt that they had been proved right, but the culture of twentieth-century England was so different from that of first-century Corinth that it was not possible to make such a direct connection.

Today, no one would tell the *same* stories as Jesus did in order to catch people's attention, but you might tell (different) stories . . . You would not do the same things as the apostles did, but you might follow the same principles. In the example given on p. 36, Jesus used the Jewish scriptures in His ministry to Jews because they knew them and accepted their authority. The apostles did the same—but only when they were speaking to Jews. When they preached to pagans they followed the same principle, but instead of quoting from the Bible (which pagans would not have read) they quoted from the secular literature which their hearers knew and revered. This is what Paul did in Athens (Acts 17.28). Like the apostles we need to ask two questions:

1. If Jesus and His followers made that particular response in the situation of their culture in those days, how would they act if they faced this situation which confronts me today?

2. How can we continue the principles of Jesus' ministry in an imaginative and creative way in our very different culture and place and time?

Only thirty years after the resurrection of Jesus, the writers of the Gospels realized that they were not writing for Jews in Galilee and Jerusalem but for Christians in different parts of the Roman Empire who spoke Greek. Some of their questions were the same as those the hearers of Jesus asked, but some of their questions were very different. So the Gospel writers edited their material so that their readers could see the relevance of Jesus for them. Luke did this in 4.25b, to help his Gentile readers understand a story which was familiar to all Jesus' Jewish hearers.

Bible translators today follow the same principle, which is called 'dynamic equivalence'. They do not translate the actual words of the Bible but what the words *mean*. See p. 79 for two examples of this.

One of the principles we must follow is the incarnation of Jesus. Of course, we cannot become incarnate as He did, because all human beings are already 'in the flesh'. But we can and should identify ourselves as He did with the particular cultures to which we are sent as God's witnesses. Even if it is our own culture which we know well, it unfortunately often happens that Christians lose touch with their own culture when they join the Church. Or

Bible translators today follow a principle of 'dynamic equivalence' to translate what the words of the Bible *mean*. These men washing in a Calcutta street, for example, may find it difficult to understand Jesus as a good shepherd. They need to have the idea of God's tender care translated into words which mean the same thing for them. What words, ideas or pictures of God might be meaningful for these men?

perhaps, because they were born into a Church culture, they never make contact with the secular culture which surrounds them. Jesus never made this mistake (although the religious leaders of His day had done so), and we should be like Him in this respect.

Because of differences in culture and circumstances, people perceive the gospel differently. A London student may see the good news as bringing peace in his heart and a purpose in life. An Indian Dalit (untouchable) will probably see the good news more as justice and equality for him and his family. A villager went to a successful church in Singapore and noticed that it used an overhead projector in its services. 'Our church at home needs one of these,' he said, 'to achieve similar success.' What he should have asked was, 'In my village, how can I communicate visually, by showing people, as well as verbally, by speaking to them?'

A United States visitor to Tanzania noticed that the church there used wind-up cassette players in evangelism. He could see that these would not be effective in the streets of his city parish back home, so he decided that Tanzanians had little to teach him about evangelism. Instead of deciding this, he should have tried to discover what the equivalent of wind-up cassette players would be in terms of American culture and technology.

See also chapter 7 and Special Note C.

STUDY SUGGESTIONS

WORD STUDY
1. What is the meaning of the following words:
   (a) centrifugal
   (b) centripetal
   (c) holistic
   (d) dynamic equivalence?

CONTEXTUAL APPLICATION
2. Why do you think Jesus left out the words about judgement when He quoted Isaiah 61? What can we learn from this example?
3. Note which words and phrases occur twice in Luke 4.18, 19. Why are these words significant for the mission of the Church?
4. Which of these seven lines (p. 38) is most relevant for your Church's ministry today?
5. How does the story of the early Church in Acts show that God entrusted His mission to the poor, the weak and the oppressed?

6. Why might rich or powerful people find the message of Jesus unattractive?

7. Which of the following passages refer to centripetal mission, and which to centrifugal mission?
   Jonah 3.1–10; Micah 4.1,2; John 1.4,5; John 1.38; Acts 2.5–12; Acts 8.4–8.

8. What aspects of the life of your Church (a) are outgoing (centrifugal) and (b) draw people in (centripetal)? Which of these two movements is most effective as mission?

9. To what extent is your Church involved in the secular life of the country and its citizens, as Jesus was?

10. If Jesus used the Jewish Scriptures to support His message among Jews, what methods should we use today to convince different sorts of people of the truth of His message?

11. What was the role of the Holy Spirit in the ministry of (a) Jesus, and (b) the early Church in Acts?

12. What sort of people might be excluded from worship today by religious leaders? Are there any people like this near you, who feel excluded? Should you welcome them? What good news has the Church got which might meet their needs?

13. If God intends Christians to be interdependent and need each other, how far is this also true of our relationship with God? Is there any way in which God needs us?

14. How was Luke's theology of mission (a) like and (b) unlike the mission theology of Mark?

5. Eucharist and Mission

The word 'eucharist' means thanksgiving and is the name given in many Churches to the meal instituted by Jesus on the evening before His crucifixion. Other Churches call it 'Holy Communion', 'The Lord's Supper', 'The Breaking of Bread' or 'The Mass'. Many writers about mission do not mention the Eucharist, either because their theology does not give a prominent place to the sacraments or because many people assume that mission means being sent out, but Holy Communion seems to mean staying inside with the Church fellowship. However, this is a misunderstanding of the Eucharist; in fact the word 'Mass' is a short form of the last sentence of the Eucharist in Latin: 'Ite, missa est', which means 'Go, the Church is sent out'.

It is easy to see how the sacrament of Baptism relates to mission because at a Baptism the Church celebrates the new birth of those who turn to Christ in faith and confess Him as Lord. Baptism also commits people to serve Him in the fellowship of His Church—in fact, it has been called 'the ordination service of every believer'. But the Eucharist is the continuation of our Baptism, and it is at least as much about mission as Baptism is. In this chapter we shall look first at the three different aspects of the Eucharist which we find in the New Testament. Then we shall consider ways in which the Eucharist can serve the Church's mission today. Before reading further, please read 1 Cor. 11.17–34.

TABLE FELLOWSHIP WITH JESUS

As we saw in chapter 4, Jesus often enjoyed meals with His disciples and with 'sinners'. He provided food for the hungry. He went to parties and enjoyed eating and drinking in good (and often in bad!) company. So did His disciples. However, there came a sad day when the disciples realized that they were eating with Jesus for the last time. Then, three days later, when they were in misery and despair, He came to eat with them again (Luke 24.30, 43; John 21.13; Acts 10.41) and they were overjoyed at His presence.

But then He left them again—but this time He promised that He would send them His Spirit and so would be with them for ever. This time—after the Holy Spirit came upon them—nothing could rob them of their joy, and the meals when they broke bread together were transformed into parties of celebration (Acts 2.46, 47). Eucharist is a suitable name for such an occasion, because joyful celebration of Jesus' presence and the spiritual gifts He gives to His people should be an essential part of our worship together. Unbelievers should notice this joy, and so it is an important part of witness. However, Paul had to criticize the Christians at Corinth for overdoing the celebration. They did wrong because

(a) they brought their own food and drink to church, which meant luxury meals for the rich and bread and water for the poor;

(b) they brought the social and class divisions (which were one of the chief problems of the church at Corinth) right into the heart of the fellowship and so destroyed it (1 Cor. 11.17–22; compare 1.11);

(c) they forgot the significance of the solemn event which they recalled in the bread and wine.

Paul solved this problem when he warned the Corinthian Christians to take their meals at home (11.33, 34), and when they were in church simply to eat the bread and drink the wine as a ritual, or memorial, action. It seems likely that Paul's solution prepared the way for a major shift in how the Eucharist was celebrated. To this we now turn.

THE MEMORIAL OF JESUS' DEATH

When Jesus told his disciples to 'do this', he was not merely telling them to have parties together. They were to eat the bread and drink the wine primarily in order to remember Him, and especially to remember His death on the cross for them. The Eucharist has been called a 'visible word' from God to us, because we not only hear it, but we also see, touch and taste it. God is therefore the subject of the Eucharist. He brings His grace to His people who respond by (a) eating and drinking as individuals and (b) thanking Him corporately with one another. In this way they really do receive Christ, and the Eucharist is much more than just remembering a past event in your mind. The Greek word for remembering (*anamnesis*) suggests that the past event becomes present as a reality among us here and now, and this is what happens when God's people eat and drink this bread and wine together (1 Cor. 11.26).

In this way the Eucharist is like the Jewish Passover meal. According to the first three Gospels, Jesus was eating the Passover meal when he instituted the Eucharist. The Eucharist and the Passover resemble one another in five ways:

1. They both recall in word and symbol a past, historical event when God acted in mercy and love to set His people free.

2. They both give thanks in word and action for the covenant fellowship with God which His people now enjoy (Mark 14.24).

49

3. They represent both an individual, personal relationship with God and also a corporate, family relationship with Him.

4. They both refer to sacrifice. In the Passover the sacrifice is the lamb now offered and eaten. In the Eucharist the sacrifice is the one, final sacrifice offered once by Jesus on the cross.

5. They both look forward to a future hope (Mark 14.25; and see below).

Therefore in the Eucharist Christians receive the benefits of Christ's death which sets them right with God. This is a movement of grace *from God to human beings, and we are passive receivers.* This is why, when we understand it in this way, the Eucharist 'proclaims' the good news from God to us (see 1 Cor. 11.26), i.e. it is evangelism.

But we can also understand the Eucharist in another way. Because Christ's death is also our death (Rom. 6.4,5), and we are united to Him by His Spirit, therefore when Christ consecrates and offers Himself to the Father, we who belong to Him share in that action. Thus the whole Church takes part in the self-offering of Christ to the Father. The movement is *from human beings to God and we are active participants.* Both views have support in Scripture and in the liturgies of the early Church. But the risk with the second view of the Eucharist is that it does not distinguish clearly between what Christ did for us by grace and how we respond to that in faith. God moves towards us first, before we respond by turning to Him— and 1 Cor. 11.29 may be a warning to the Corinthians not to lose sight of how important and central is what Christ did for us.

The liturgies of the Church during the first two centuries presented the Eucharist in these two ways: some liturgies showed it as a celebration of Christ's presence, others showed it as a memorial of His death. But there is a third way of looking at the Eucharist, which the Churches of the North have usually neglected but which has been rediscovered by the Churches in the South.

THE PROMISE OF RENEWED CREATION

As I mentioned in point 5 above, at the Last Supper Jesus looked forward to the fulfilment of all God's promises (Luke 22.16, 18) in His coming kingdom. This kingdom was often described as a big banquet—and the Eucharist is like a small banquet which looks forward to the big one. In the same way that the Holy Spirit makes the absent Lord Jesus present, so the Eucharist is the 'not-yet' heavenly banquet 'already' here. As Christians must celebrate the Eucharist here and now, so they must here and now work for the

This Eucharist is taking place in Zimbabwe. The bearded priest to the left of the celebrant, Fr Michael Lapsley, lost both his hands and the sight of one eye when a parcel bomb exploded, the result of his work for liberation in South Africa – a reminder that the Eucharist is a sharing in Christ's suffering as well as a celebration of the Resurrection.

renewal of creation which Jesus Himself promised. Taking part in the Eucharist means accepting that commitment.

It was in this area that the Corinthians were failing. The disciples' common life in Acts 2.42–47 came out of their breaking bread together. But the Eucharist at Corinth did not point to the Corinthians' common life, it pointed to their divisions and squabbles. They failed to see that their fellowship was the body of Christ (1 Cor 11.29). If they did not care for their brothers and sisters, then they received the Eucharist unworthily and so experienced the judgement of God in their lives (11.27–32). The Eucharist must therefore make us want to tell everyone about Christ's 'blood shed for many', to love all those who are sisters and brothers in Christ, and to bring God's healing to a broken world. This is why Zacchaeus, having shared a meal with Jesus, immediately gave half his goods to the poor and gave back four times as much as all the sums of money he had stolen (Luke 19.8). At the Eucharist we learn to belong to everyone that Jesus invites to His supper—and that means especially the poor and outcast. 'What is the bread and wine?' asks Bishop Anthony Bloom, and he answers his own question: 'What all creation is destined to become: renewed by Christ.'

The Eucharist, therefore, is only the beginning, because it sends God's people out. It sends them out first into Christ's new society where there is no room for doing things on your own (individualism), being competitive, or for divisions of race or class (1 Cor. 12.25, 26). Secondly, the Eucharist sends God's people out into the streets and trouble spots of the world. Eucharistic people are called to *praxis* (a Greek word which means 'action'), in order to change the world they live in. Sometimes this may look like a hopeless task, but God's promise encourages us that our efforts are not useless (1 Cor. 15.58).

HOLDING IT ALL TOGETHER

The mission of the Church can therefore be seen in three ways in the Eucharist: present, past and future. All these were mentioned by Paul when he wrote the very earliest record we have of Jesus' words of institution in 1 Cor. 11.26:

Present: As often as you eat this bread and drink this cup,
Past: you proclaim the Lord's death
Future: until he comes.

'The Eucharist . . . is only a beginning, because it sends God's people out' (p. 52). What does God send you out to do for your neighbours?

The Roman Catholic theologian, Thomas Aquinas, also described these three aspects of the Eucharist: 'The sacrament is a sign which recalls a past event, the passion of Christ, indicates the effect of Christ's passion in us, i.e. grace, and foretells the glory that is to come.'

The main points can be shown in the form of a chart:

PRESENT	PAST	FUTURE
The presence of Jesus	The death of Jesus	The coming of Jesus
gifts of grace	God's love	God's promise
fellowship	good news	service
share	remember	work
love & thanks	believe	hope

For a fuller version of this chart, see p. 57.

Readers of this book who belong to the Anglican Church may like to note that these three different aspects of the Eucharist are reflected in different Anglican liturgies. The *Alternative Service Book* in England (1980), like modern liturgies in India and elsewhere, mentions all God's saving acts in Christ and we rejoice in His presence with us now in fellowship together. The *Book of Common Prayer* (1662), which has been translated into many languages, focuses on the past event of Jesus' death so that we can solemnly and quietly recall it and receive its benefits by faith. There are not many liturgies yet which focus on the future—but the ecumenical liturgy of Lima calls worshippers to oneness in Christ, and the Kenyan liturgy speaks strongly of social and political justice and care of the environment.

However, all Christians need to ask themselves whether the worship in their local church reflects these three aspects of the Eucharist in equal balance. Almost every congregation has a bias towards one or two aspects and may ignore one or two aspects. Our aim should be to commit ourselves to reflect each of these aspects equally: (a) to show such love and care that people are attracted to the Church, (b) to go out to proclaim the death of Christ for all humanity, and (c) to work energetically to transform the world according to God's will for it, which He has promised will happen one day. The logo of the Church Mission Society portrays these three commitments (see Figure 5 opposite).

No one group of Christians can do this alone, for we need the help, wisdom and inspiration of other Christians (who may have a

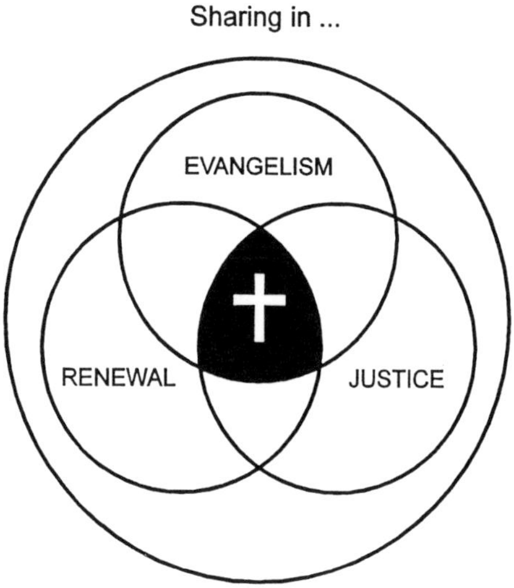

Sharing in ...

EVANGELISM

RENEWAL   JUSTICE

Figure 5 The logo of the Church Mission Society.

different emphasis from ours, or come from a different culture). This why, in the CMS logo, there is a big circle outside the three small circles, to indicate 'sharing'. The middle of the logo shows that the cross is central and is itself love, evangelism and service for justice.

PRACTISING THE EUCHARIST TODAY

The problem is, as one scholar has written, that 'the Church which is born out of the mission of Jesus no longer sees in Jesus' eucharist the mission of Jesus which is the heart of its being; it prefers instead to see in its eucharist its own self-sanctification.' Mission and Eucharist are divided from one another. The Eucharist has become the private property of religious people.

The Church's Eucharist is often all about 'our salvation', but Jesus' Eucharist was all about welcoming the poor, sinners and outcasts. The following are some ways in which we might return to the model which Jesus gave us:

(a) At the Eucharist we must listen to the story of Jesus which is *our* story, for only this story gives us a sense of purpose.

(b) At the Eucharist we must welcome outsiders as Jesus did— and give them a chance to become His followers by inviting them to

55

be baptized. If they have already been baptized (perhaps without understanding it), then we could invite them to hold out their hands for the bread and cup and so receive Jesus in a personal way. This would be a better thing to do—and more biblical—instead of inviting them to 'hold up their hands' in a special meeting, to 'sign on the dotted line' or to 'come forward'. Why invent our own signs or sacraments, when Jesus has given us His? Unfortunately, many Churches keep outsiders away from the 'Holy Table' in order to defend their own purity and holiness. But a Table which is guarded so fiercely may not be the Lord's Table after all but only the Church's table.

(c) At the Eucharist we must share and rejoice in the gifts which the Spirit gives not just to one person but to the whole Body to use for the good of all. And we must share equally in the suffering of all the members. This sharing is shown when we share 'The Peace', but we may deny it if we say that only special people (e.g. priests) can celebrate the Eucharist (which Jesus told *all* of us to do). There may be so few of these special people that some congregations can only receive communion on very rare occasions (see the discussion on p. 177). Note how 1 Corinthians 11 is followed by chapters 12–14. Jesus was made human, and instituted the Lord's Supper, so that *everyone* could see God and come to Him. The Church, however, has often made the Eucharist into a mystery which keeps ordinary people away from Him.

(d) At the Eucharist it is disgraceful when a Christian community, after receiving the one bread and one cup, then goes out and behaves as if social and economic differences (which really do exist) do not matter. Christians are 'all one in Christ', but this unity has to be demonstrated in practical ways, especially through sharing. The fact that we can *look forward* to perfect unity in the future can never be an excuse for not working for it now.

(e) At the Eucharist we hear about Christ's death, and we must go and fight against the sort of injustice and political plotting (John 18.14) which caused His death. We hear about God's love for the world and we must imitate it by living in and for the world—to stay in church is to reject the Eucharist of Jesus.

One of the problems about the Eucharist is that very often the Church has made it into a mystery which is difficult to understand. Sometimes the Church has suggested that only special people, such as priests, can understand it. But this was not what Jesus intended. He intended the Eucharist to be very simple. He used the ordinary food and drink on the table in front of Him as simple signs of the meaning of His death on the cross. The following story is a parable, or picture, of what Jesus did at the Last Supper.

There was once a class of theology students who were very dull. They could never understand their teachers' lessons, not even the simplest ones. The assignments they wrote were handed back to be rewritten, their preaching left people either asleep or confused, and at the end of the year their external examiner said they must repeat their year of study. But the second year was not much better. The Principal of their college wrote to their Bishop to say they were too dull to be pastors, but the Bishop replied that he was facing a crisis—the Church was growing so fast that he needed the students immediately. In despair, the Principal decided that the only way to teach them some basic theology was by means of something which was so ordinary that they used it every day of their lives. So he gave them one final lesson; he took ordinary food and ordinary drink from the table, and made it into a sign of the Gospel which the Bishop was sending them out to preach. That way, they could never forget; and wherever they went they would find ordinary people eating ordinary meals—and there was their message, all ready for them to proclaim. Even an idiot could do it!

Note

The diagram which follows is an expanded version of the simple chart on p. 54. It shows the three different ways in which the Eucharist speaks to us about the mission of Jesus and His Church:

PRESENT	**PAST**	**FUTURE**
The presence of Jesus	The death of Jesus	The coming of Jesus
Luke 22.15; 24.30, 31	1 Cor. 11.24–26	Luke 22.16, 18
Acts 1.4; 2.42, 46	1 Cor. 10.16	1 Cor. 11.26
1 Cor. 11.29	John 6.51	
Renewal	Proclamation	Service
God's gifts	God's love	God's promise
Living Jesus	the cross	Christ's glory
community	salvation	action
love/thanks	faith	hope
sharing His	remembering His	imitating His
sacrifice	sacrifice	sacrifice

1. Some Bible texts and liturgies emphasize that Jesus is now *present* with His people as they gather at His table, rejoice in the many gifts of His Spirit, and share in His offering of Himself to God.

2. Other texts and liturgies emphasize the sacrificial death of

Jesus as a *past* event in history which we solemnly remember and proclaim to the world because He died for all humankind.

3. Yet other texts and liturgies help us to look forward into the *future*, to the glory of the Second Coming of Jesus and the new heaven and new earth which He promised, where there will be justice. These texts and liturgies also remind us to serve and work for a better world, as He did.

STUDY SUGGESTIONS

WORD STUDY

1. What do you call the Eucharist in your Church, and what is the meaning of the name you use?

CONTEXTUAL APPLICATION

2. Which of the three aspects mentioned on pp. 48, 49 and 50 is most important to Christians in your Church? Which one is emphasized in your liturgy? What do people find are the most helpful things about the Eucharist?
3. What special significance, if any, do meals have in your culture? What significance did they have in Jesus' time?
4. In the Eucharist, do you see yourself as a passive and grateful receiver from God, or as actively offering yourself to God? What are the different theological arguments in favour of each position?
5. Why do you think that the poorer Churches of the South have rediscovered the future dimension of the Eucharist, rather than the richer Churches of the North? How could your Church be helped by Christians of another culture to understand better some aspect of Christian faith or life?
6. How should Christians respond to God's promise to renew the whole created order (a) in worship, (b) in relating to other people, (c) in relating to the environment?
7. The suggestion (p. 55(b)) that we should invite people who are not practising Christians to receive Christ at the Eucharist may be rather controversial. What are the arguments for and against doing this? What would be the dangers and the benefits?
8. Do you think that the children of Christian families should be able to receive communion at the Eucharist? Give reasons for your answer. What is your own Church's practice about allowing children to receive communion?
9. How could the Church solve the problem of people who cannot

'do this' as Jesus intended and cannot receive communion very often because of a shortage of ministers (p. 56)?

10. How was the action of Jesus at the last supper (a) like and (b) unlike the action of the Principal in the story on p. 57?

11. In what ways can we see mission in each one of the three different aspects of the Eucharist shown in the diagram on p. 57?

6. Mission and the Kingdom of God

If we search the Gospels for the most important ideas used by Jesus in connection with His mission, we are constantly brought back to the theme of the Kingdom of God. The mission of the Church continues the mission of Jesus, and the Gospels were written primarily to help missionaries in their witness to Him. Therefore we today should also make the Kingdom the most important theme of our mission. But to do this, we need to understand what Jesus meant by the Kingdom. We considered some aspects of this on p. 26.

BACKGROUND

Jewish theologians at the time of Jesus did not say very much about the Kingdom of God. Sometimes, however, they used the phrase 'the kingdom of God' to describe the coming new age when God would intervene in the world to give victory to His people and judge their enemies. The Book of Daniel says that God reigns for ever (Dan. 4.34), but also that He *will* reign one day in the future (Dan. 2.44). The problem is that God's present rule is hidden. This is (1) because His people are unfaithful and (2) because they are ruled by the heathen. One day God will put this right by saving His sinful and helpless people. Different Jewish parties held different theories about how this was going to happen. Zealots, for example, thought that God would act through the armed struggle. Pharisees thought that God would intervene in response to Israel's obedience to the law.

Thus Jewish thinking shows that the Kingdom of God is not a place (as the United Kingdom of Great Britain or the Kingdom of Lesotho are places) or even a fixed state. The Kingdom of God is a developing (or 'dynamic') situation and we should translate it as 'the Rule, or Reign, of God'.

THE TEACHING OF JESUS

God's Reign was the central theme of Jesus' message: 'It has come near', He said (Mark 1.15). Although He shared the Jews' hope for the coming of the Kingdom, Jesus also declared that it had already arrived—just as He had arrived. He *is* the Reign of God (Matt. 12.28, 41). The Jews knew that the chief characteristic of the new age would be the presence of the Spirit. Jesus said that in Him the Spirit was here (Luke 4.18, 21), and by this he meant that the future had already arrived. He demonstrated its arrival by signs and wonderful works, as the Jewish nation had always expected would happen one day (Luke 11.20; 10.24; 7.20–22). The power of the rule or reign of God could be clearly seen in what Jesus did and said. It is important to notice that Jesus did not distinguish between different kinds of activity: He preached to the people who came to Him, He cared for them, healed them and forgave them, whoever they were, according to their needs. See p. 27(d). Very often He surprised people by doing something for them which they did not expect or ask for (e.g. Mark 2.5). The Holy Spirit enabled Him to discern their needs and help them (John 3.34).

Although the new age of the Spirit had already arrived and Jesus brought Good News here and now, He also taught that there was even more to come. Many people could not see God's Rule in Jesus, and many resisted it, so He taught His followers to pray 'Your kingdom come'. See also Luke 22.18. God's Rule was both revealed in Jesus and hidden, for two reasons:

1. Jesus not only showed God's power; He also shared human weakness: people could reject, persecute and even kill Him. He often told people to say nothing about His miracles, He used obscure parables to teach them, and He called Himself 'Son of Man', a title which was not usually used for the Messiah and which people did not understand clearly. See p. 31. Jesus wanted to be sure that people would not regard Him as a worldly king (see John 18.36) whose arrival would start a revival of national power. He avoided proclaiming God's judgement on the nations (even though He warned religious leaders that they would be judged). He wanted to show the power of love which could bring salvation to all people.

2. God's Rule is 'not yet' because Jesus has not yet come for the second time. His second coming will be the time of final judgement, when His power will be clearly revealed to everyone. All this is still true for the mission of the Church today, just as it was true for the mission of Jesus.

Jesus was rejected by most of the leaders of His day, and He came especially to bring the Rule of God into the lives of those who were also rejected, e.g. poor, excluded, uneducated, irreligious and even immoral people. He reflected the teaching of the Hebrew Scriptures that God was biased in favour of those who were oppressed by their fellow human beings (Psalm 146.5–10; see Luke 1.52, 53). Oppression of the weak is, after idolatry, the sin most often condemned in the Bible. Jesus crossed all the barriers erected by the Jewish religious leaders to bring salvation to outsiders. See pp. 26, 29. For this reason He told people to act justly in their personal, social and political life, and to repent, do good and love all their fellow-humans and especially their enemies. This shows that Jesus thought that justice (a word which Christians often mistakenly translate by the religious word 'righteousness') was more important than religious observances. Justice is an essential part of the Kingdom (see Mark 12.32–34). If Jesus returned today, would 'sinners' perhaps give him a warmer welcome than the religious leaders amongst us? He would certainly disturb the Churches.

It is always God who establishes and builds His Reign, never human beings: it is His gift (Luke 12.32; Matt. 21.43). We humans can only wait for it, seek it, pray for it, receive it, enter it, inherit it. But we never do this alone, for everyone who accepts the Son of Man at once becomes a member of His community and shares His Rule. In Daniel 7.14 and 7.27 it was not only the Son of Man but also 'His holy ones' who received the kingdom (Luke 12.32). Jesus founded a community to share His death and risen life and so to witness to His Rule.

Sometimes the Church seems to be the Kingdom, but this cannot be true, because people within the Church often do not accept the Rule of God in their lives; and at times He seems to reign in the lives of some people who are outside the Churches. So the Rule of God is often much wider than the visible Church, and sometimes God's Rule seems to be smaller than the Church. We need to remember this, because most people find Jesus much more attractive than the Church. But the Church is meant to be a sign of God's Rule and a witness to it. So Christians always need to ask themselves how well they truly reflect God's Rule, and ensure that when the Church fails to do this they work to reform it.

Therefore, although only God can build His Kingdom, human beings still have a part to play (as liberation theology reminds us). The works of Jesus showed that Satan was already on the way to final defeat, and His followers can share in His works of the Kingdom. As they do this, the Kingdom becomes a reality now and its future fulfilment is also foreshadowed. Christians need to ask not only the theoretical question 'Where is the Kingdom of God present today?' but also the practical question about mission 'How can I participate now in the coming Rule of God?' (see question 7 on p. 74).

LIVING THE KINGDOM

One way of reforming the Church is to make sure that it holds in balance the different elements of the Rule of God. The Three Circles diagram (Figure 6) can help us to check that the Church's

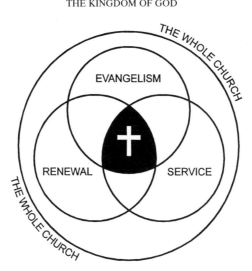

Figure 6 The Three Circles diagram.

faith and life are healthy in all three areas of renewal, evangelism and service. If they are healthy, then the Church has a 'holistic' ministry, i.e. a ministry that is as wide in its scope as the ministry of Jesus was, and is concerned with every aspect of human life. This means reflecting Jesus' teaching about the Kingdom of God in the following ways:
1. Having Jesus at the centre of our life and preaching.
2. Announcing good news for all people *now*.
3. Being open to all the gifts and powers of the Spirit.
4. Admitting our sin and weakness and our need for help.
5. Looking forward to the growth of God's Reign on earth.
6. Praying that God will work and rule amongst us.
7. Showing love to all, especially the poor and outsiders.
8. Welcoming *all* sorts of people into God's family.
9. Being ready to suffer and to keep on loving.
10. Working for justice in our own community and nation and in all the world.
11. Repenting of sin and living pure and holy lives.
12. Expecting God to change things in surprising ways.

WHAT IS MISSION?

For the past one hundred years, theologians have argued about the chief priority of mission. Some theologians have said that the priority is to evangelize; others have said that it is to show love to our neighbours; others, to worship; others, to find out what God is already doing in the world and to work with Him in those ways. Some have said that the Church as a whole should be involved in both evangelism and social action, and that it is the calling of some Christians to evangelize and some to undertake social action.

However, none of these views gives a true picture of how Jesus worked. He did not limit His ministry or set priorities in it. Guided by the Spirit of God, He mixed up His ministry in ways which we must admit were very untidy—but then, the world is mixed up and untidy, and His missionaries must do the same. 'What is the connection between the Gospel and giving food to the hungry?' someone asked. The only answer to this question must be, 'If you are hungry, food *is* the Gospel, the Good News.' But it is important to work out principles for our witness to Christ.

For example, if an evangelist is called to tell people the Good News of Jesus by word of mouth, he or she cannot be content just to speak, for a message can only be good news if it relates to the real life-situation of the listeners. In other words, it must be *contextual*. The Gospel cannot be good news to the Dalits of India unless it offers them a way out of the social discrimination they suffer. The Gospel cannot be good news to an orphaned girl unless it offers her love and a place to belong. The Gospel cannot be good news for black people unless it is also working for racial equality. No-one will ever listen to those who do not themselves listen to what other people say. We must love people as they are, as Jesus did. It is difficult to do this in some countries (e.g. Singapore) where the government discourages the Church from speaking about economic, social and racial injustices.

On the other hand, some countries (e.g. Malaysia) forbid Christians to proclaim to everyone the Gospel of faith in Christ. Therefore, the only way Christians in these countries can witness to Jesus is by caring for people in ordinary ways—but care alone is never enough, just as words alone are never enough. A Christian woman, for example, works as a midwife in a Muslim country in North Africa. At any time of day or night she responds to the needs of pregnant Muslim women, who often ask her why she does this for them. In reply, she has to tell them that she does it out of love for Isa Masih (Jesus the Messiah), and in gratitude to Him for what He has done for her.

So the evangelist is also deeply involved in social action and the Christian social worker is also an evangelist. The two tasks are inseparable parts of God's Rule in the world and they have to be reflected in the lives of all disciples of Jesus. There are more tasks than just preaching and caring, however, as the above account of the Kingdom ministry of Jesus shows. No Christian can be exempt from any of them. Because there is so much disagreement about this missiological topic, we must give it a little further thought.

CONTEXTUAL EVANGELISM

Although evangelism is one of the Church's vital tasks, it always comes second to the rule of God in the Church and in the world. Although the first Christians rejoiced when large numbers of people came into the Church, their first concern was to announce that God had broken into history in Jesus of Nazareth, to witness to Jesus' rule in the Church and to pray and work for His rule over the whole of creation. It was God's work to make His word effective to unbelievers: it was the Church's task to make His rule effective in the Church. This is why the New Testament writers were more interested in how God fulfilled His will in the Church and in the world than in how many new people became Christians. Their evangelism therefore took different forms in different human situations, i.e. it was always in the 'context' of the rule of God in human life (see chapter 9 for further discussion).

It is said that since New Testament times there have been 788 global plans to evangelize the world. We can be sure that the people who promoted each of these plans were convinced that they had at last discovered the big secret of how to make the world Christian. But each plan can only be used in a limited way. John Wesley said that revivals of religion cannot last long, because people who become Christians soon adopt better life-styles. They grow prosperous and finally become more concerned for material values than for spiritual values. God does not often build His kingdom in ways which we expect or for which we have planned—and this means that the Church can never be self-confident or triumphalist about its evangelism. Indeed, if we are honest we will admit that we do not explain, or even understand, the Gospel very well. On the other hand, God will not allow us to fall into despair or pessimism about our evangelism. He continues to do His work in spite of the many mistakes we make; in fact, we are usually the spectators, rather than the actors, in God's drama of salvation.

ATTRACTIVE SERVICE

There are many ways of being God's servants in the world. One way is to provide immediate emergency relief for those who are suffering in, for example, floods in Bangladesh. Another way is to work on long-term development projects in the area so that there will not be floods in the future. Both these kinds of activity may be called *social service* and both are needed. Very often, however, we need to take action to prevent governments from doing things which will increase poverty or suffering, or to persuade them to pass laws which will alleviate suffering. This is much more difficult, and it can be called *social action*. Social action of this kind, done by Christians and others, finally forced the white South African government to repeal its apartheid laws. In the case of Bangladesh, the floods were made worse by cutting down forests in the hills of Nepal for hydro-electric schemes—so in this case international political action was needed to change the policy of Nepal—and the policy of Norway which was paying for the hydro-electric projects.

This sort of action often arouses opposition and controversy, even among Christians. For example, the Church of England has opposed the fur trade, in the belief that the trade in animal skins damages wild life and the environment. The Bishop of the Arctic, however, points out that the Inuit people live by the fur trade, just as many Europeans live by herding sheep and cattle. To stop the fur trade will ruin their way of life and drive many of them either to commit suicide or to fall under the influence of the drug and alcohol trade from Canada. Therefore, the full facts need to be understood before decisions are made.

There are two kinds of mistakes which Christians often make in service of this kind.

1. They try to do things *for* the poor instead of *with* the poor. As a result, the rich Christians may feel good about what they do, but their action may not be what the poor either want or need. When the rich people leave, the poor have not been empowered at all. They are even more powerless than they were before, and they simply become dependent on the rich and start asking for more and more free handouts. See p. 175.

2. Christians can stir up opposition and controversy. At times this is unavoidable for true followers of Jesus (Matt. 10.34), but it is always better—and more difficult—to change people so that they will co-operate with you rather than to antagonize them so that they will oppose both your aims of justice and the poor you want to help. For an example of this, see p. 203. Jesus loved not only the poor but also the powerful and rich (Mark 10.21). Like the first believers (Acts 2.47), our service should attract, rather than repel, people.

There is one particular problem which faces wealthy Christians. Unlike most of the first Christians and probably most Christians in the world today, wealthy Christians belong to two traditions at once—the tradition of the Pharisees because they are religious and not poor; and the tradition of Jesus because they want to serve God

These people in Manilla in the Philippines live on this rubbish heap and sell whatever they can find to buy food. The help which the Churches try to give to them and other people in need may be called social service. Why is such social service part of the mission of the Church?

and identify with the poor. Jesus understood clearly that the Kingdom of God is harder for these people than for anyone else (Mark 10.23). But God's blessing *can* come to people who are not poor, provided that they receive it through the poor. Wealthy Christians also have to undertake the spiritual struggle which is necessary to ensure that the tradition of Jesus always challenges and triumphs over the tradition of the Pharisees, even though the whole of their environment pulls the wealthy in the opposite direction.

SIGNS OF THE SPIRIT

The Church in many parts of the world is being renewed because it is rediscovering many of the gifts of the Holy Spirit which were familiar to writers of the New Testament. People who discover such gifts naturally want to share them with their fellow-Christians, who then discover the power of God in new ways. As they do this, however, they need to test their new discoveries by what Jesus taught about the Rule of God. For a fuller discussion of this in relation to the healing ministry, see chapter 12.

Jesus used His gifts more in His mission to others than for His own benefit. He used his gifts especially on the frontiers of faith, i.e. amongst Gentiles, the poor and the sinful. Christians should therefore not simply 'enjoy' these gifts amongst themselves. The coming of Jesus from His heavenly home to be born as a very ordinary human being is known as the Incarnation. This principle of incarnation, of identifying with human beings, should guide Christians in their mission. This does not mean that Christians should be human (for we cannot be anything else!), but that they should go down rather than climb up, and identify with people in every kind of need. They should get involved with them in the ordinary things of life—not just in religious matters. In fact, the test of every spiritual gift is not whether it brings new excitements and experiences into our Church services, but whether it shows more clearly the Rule of God in the world. Gifts will therefore not be limited to healings, tongues, prophecy, faintings, etc. They will also reveal themselves in love to others, fellowship and joy, together with welcoming and attractive worship. This means that the signs of the Spirit and attractive service are closely connected. Those who serve need the gifts of the Spirit in order to serve, and those who rejoice in spiritual gifts need to show that these gifts are relevant to 'these little ones' and the 'sinners' for whom Jesus came.

MODERN OPPOSITION

Today many people strongly resist these forms of Christian mission, especially in countries where the 'Western' way of life has been adopted. This resistance can be found as much within the Church as outside it. It can probably be found even within ourselves, the writer and the readers of this book.

First, if we are comfortable and well-off, we shall prefer not to disturb either ourselves or other people. But the coming of Jesus disturbed people greatly—and it disturbed Jesus Himself most of all. The justice and human well-being which God wants is absent from much of His creation, and we are in part to blame. This should disturb all who want to follow Jesus. 'Peace at any price' is not one of the blessings promised in the Gospel. If we try to live as Jesus lived or try to alter the values of our society, we shall make enemies. We shall even find that the struggle is taking place within our own minds and consciences. This is spiritual warfare, and it is just as real and as authentic as the battle which is experienced by anyone who exorcises an evil spirit. This warfare was experienced by Archbishop Oscar Romero, who led a comfortable and respectable life as leader of the Catholic Church in El Salvador until God opened his eyes to see the oppression of the poor and he began to denounce the oppressors. In spite of many warnings, Archbishop Romero refused to keep quiet and he was murdered in 1981 in his own cathedral while celebrating Mass.

Secondly, the Western world-view has encouraged the idea that science can give a rational explanation for everything. Even though not many scientists today would make such a claim, the idea still remains in the minds of many people. They therefore dislike the idea of God breaking into human life in supernatural ways. They would prefer the Church to be free to believe, live and preach its own faith. They would like other people to be free to accept the Christian faith if they wish—but to do this privately. They do not want the Church to cause public disturbances through wonderful signs of the Spirit. This would imply that the teaching which goes with such signs is more than a personal faith. It is something which makes demands on the lives of every man, woman and child on earth. God broke into public life through Jesus of Nazareth so that everyone could see and accept His Rule. If He demonstrates this here and now, then the Christian Gospel is far more than the private concern of those people who choose to believe. It must disturb and challenge everyone. For further discussion of the problem of Western culture, see Special Note E, p. 152.

To summarize this chapter, the concept of the Rule or Kingdom

Oscar Romero, the Archbishop of El Salvador, was murdered in 1981 while celebrating Mass, because he criticized those who oppressed the poor. He still inspires social action. This woman, holding his picture, is speaking at a protest rally held in El Salvador on the ninth anniversary of Romero's death.

of God seems to be a specially useful model for us as we think about mission, because

1. It is Jesus' own message and he is the centre of it;
2. It is a process which involves us in making it happen;
3. It includes social and political issues in the Gospel;
4. It challenges our personal and social self-centredness.

Special Note B

DEFINING MISSION

As we saw in the last chapter, the Mission of God which is entrusted to the Church consists of a number of different parts—for example, evangelism, social service, social action, exercise of spiritual gifts. Because these parts have been emphasized in different ways, Christians have produced very different definitions of mission. Here are some of them. You may want to add to this list other definitions which you have heard.

We begin with two extremes which are completely opposite to each other:

1. The mission of the Church is evangelism alone: 'This world is a wrecked vessel. God has given me a lifeboat and said to me, "Moody, save all you can".' (D. L. Moody)

2. God's mission for the establishment of *shalom* is going on throughout the world, and the Church's mission is to discover what He is doing and enter into partnership with Him in the renewal of society. (World Council of Churches [WCC], Uppsala, 1968)

3. Mission is the proclamation of the Gospel to all nations so that the end may come. (Protestant, based on Matt. 24.14)

4. Christ has a kingdom, and His kingship must be proclaimed to all men who have been redeemed by Him. (William Carey)

5. Mission is the planting of the Church in every country and among every people. (Roman Catholic approach)

6. Mission is the Church's obedient participation in that action of the Spirit by which the confession of Jesus as Lord becomes the authentic confession of ever new peoples, each in its own tongue. (Lesslie Newbigin, 1978)

7. Mission is the witness of the Church given by proclamation, fellowship and service. (WCC, Willingen, 1962)

8. Mission is the common witness of the whole Church, bringing the whole Gospel to the whole world. (Commission for World Mission and Evangelism, 1963)

9. Mission includes everything God's Church continues to be and to do in the world, and must be rooted in the character and purpose of God, its source and sustainer. (Ray Bakke, 1987)

10. Mission in Christ's way is God-centred, joyfully entering, through thought and action, into God's ceaseless, sacrificial, loving activity to reconcile all He created to Himself. (British Council of Churches, 1989)

11. Mission arises from God's nature reproduced and reflected in the whole Church through its conformity to Christ and in its participation in the Holy Spirit's work in the world of proclaiming the good news, seeking reform of human society and exercising the gifts of the Spirit so that all creation may be reconciled to God. (Roger Bowen, 1993)

Finally, we must not try to define mission too accurately. We shall do better if, instead, we use images, symbols and events, in particular the great New Testament events of the incarnation, the cross, the resurrection, the ascension, Pentecost and the Second Coming. The Church must live in the light of the cross and always renew and rediscover the mission which comes from God.

> Looked at from this point of view mission is, quite simply, the participation of Christians in the liberating mission of Jesus, looking for a future that seems impossible. It is the good news of God's love, incarnated in the witness of a community, for the sake of the world.
>
> (David Bosch, *Transforming Mission*, 1991)

Therefore how we define mission is less important than how we put it into practice as we relate to God and to our fellow human beings. A good model of how to do mission is this five-year plan drawn up by Kabare parish, in Kenya, which has four congregations numbering 1800 people:

PARISH PRIORITIES 1986–1990

PASTORAL CARE

1. Visit the sick and elderly with Holy Communion
2. Home visitation
3. Appoint two clergy for four secondary and primary schools
4. Continue school visitation

EVANGELISM

1. Appoint a new evangelist to make a total of four
2. Plant four new congregations

3. Consider proposal to divide the parish by 1990
4. Strengthen link with Diocesan Missionary Association

TEACHING

1. Improve music and start church choirs
2. Teach Youth and Sunday School leaders
3. Start relevant Youth and Sunday School programme
4. Strengthen Mothers' Union
5. Strengthen work of Theological Education by Extension
6. Teach Family Life, Family Planning, Stewardship

HEALTH

1. Strengthen Health Committees
2. Add six Community Health Workers also working as evangelists
3. Renovate the old Dispensary
5. Make it a small-scale chemist's shop

AGRICULTURE

1. Start local Agriculture Committee and include women in it
2. Increase production of grain (nine varieties), vegetables (two varieties), fruit (four varieties)
3. Plan agricultural seminars and teaching tours

SOCIAL WELFARE

1. Start social welfare local committees
2. Help aged, disabled, orphans, widows, single parents with clothing, education and housing
3. Run Community Hall, with canteen, telephone, film show, etc.
4. Run Youth Polytechnic, to bring people together

EDUCATION

1. Develop the existing girls' boarding primary school
2. Appoint Chaplain for this institution

COTTAGE INDUSTRIES

1. Build factory for threshing millet and processing vegetables
2. Encourage small-scale businesses

COMMUNICATION

1. Build an Access Road to Rukenya

CONSTRUCTION

1. Complete two church buildings

2. Build Curate's houses for two congregations
3. Supply clergy houses with adequate office equipment.

STUDY SUGGESTIONS

WORD STUDY

1. What is a better translation of the Greek words for 'Kingdom of God'?
2. What is the meaning of the following words:
   (a) missiological
   (b) contextual?

BIBLE STUDY

3. Which of the following verses say that God's Kingdom is here already; and which say it has not yet come?
   Matt. 12.28; 25.1; Mark 4.32; 14.62; Luke 7.22; Acts 14.22; 1 John 3.1, 2
4. How was the rich man in Luke 12.16–21 harmed by his wealth? How could he have escaped that danger?

CONTEXTUAL APPLICATION

5. Why is the Kingdom a good model for Christian mission?
6. In what ways is the Church's power hidden, as Jesus' power was hidden?
7. What is the connection between the Kingdom of God and (a) Jesus, (b) the Church?
8. Is your Church doing the twelve things listed on p. 63? Can you give definite examples of what is being done?
9. In which of the three circles in Figure 6 on p. 63 (Evangelism, Renewal and Service) does each one of these twelve points properly belong?
10. Some people say that because Jesus was unique, it is too difficult to use him as a model for our ministry. Do you think that every individual Christian should follow Jesus' model of a holistic ministry? Or is it good enough if this is done by the local congregation together (as in the example on pp. 72–74), or by the whole national Church?
11. Give examples of any evangelism you know which is careful to relate well to people's real needs.
12. Give examples of any Christian social work you know which also attracts people to Jesus.
13. Give an example of God extending His rule in unexpected

ways, in situations where Christians watched as spectators rather than taking an active part.

14. How did Jesus empower people rather than make them dependent? How can the Church ensure that it empowers people?

15. What principles for mission can we learn from the Incarnation?

16. How could Archbishop Romero have escaped danger? How could Jesus? How were Archbishop Romero and Jesus alike, and how were they different?

17. What sort of opposition do you think the 'signs of the Spirit' could provoke?

18. Consider again the different definitions of mission given on pp. 71–72. Which definitions do you find inadequate, and why? Write your own, brief definition of mission.

19. Divide the different activities of Kabare parish into different categories (evangelism, social action, social service, etc.). How does this plan compare with your Church's mission programme?

PART 2
MISSION AND CULTURE

7. Bridging the Gap

The modern missionary movement has been in progress for over two hundred years. It has usually looked like a movement 'from the West to the rest', and evangelism has been accompanied by literacy, education, medicine, agriculture and technology of many different kinds. In many parts of the world the Church has been connected with 'Christian' colonial powers (see p. 9). The missionaries brought their culture with them, and mission was often seen as getting rid of paganism, and encouraging civilization, reading, education or economic advancement. Sometimes these benefits were given to the local people by force, whether they liked it or not. Christianity 'went forward on the wave of Western prestige and power'. But mission had not always been like this.

HISTORICAL BACKGROUND

The first Christian missionaries were Jews. Naturally, they brought their culture and history with them, as it was recorded in their Scriptures, but much of our New Testament tells how these first missionaries struggled in order to *avoid* imposing their culture on their converts. In some ways it was easy for them to leave their culture behind, because not many people wanted it anyway! Although some people were attracted to the Jewish faith, very few people wanted strict Jewish rituals like circumcision, food laws and sacrifices, and no one wanted to learn the Jewish language or share the poverty and general unpopularity of the Jews.

As the Church expanded into the Gentile world, Christians remained a persecuted minority in a hostile world. It was the *faith* of Christians which attracted people, certainly not their culture or social standing. But then the Emperor Constantine was converted in AD 312, with the following results:

1. The Christian faith became not only fashionable but necessary for social advancement. People had new reasons for joining the Church, and often they had no loyalty to Christ.

2. There was no longer any difference between the Church and

society: the Emperor was Head of both, and it was no longer easy to see the boundaries between the two.

3. The Church lost its sense of mission. It handed over leadership to the State, and its mission was taken over by 'Christendom' (all the nations which considered themselves Christian). The Church became tame and obedient.

4. The Church became an organization of the State, instead of an organism driven by the power and freedom of the Spirit.

During the Middle Ages in Europe (between about AD 500 and 1500), and even after the Reformation in the sixteenth century, Christians were taught that the words of Jesus in the Great Commission (Matt. 28.18–20) did not apply to them, but only to the apostles who heard and fulfilled them. Mission was the responsibility of the State, whose rulers were like the Kings of Israel. The Church's responsibility for teaching people about Christ only extended as far as the State's power extended. Therefore when British rule extended into India in the seventeenth century, the Church of England included in its new 1662 prayer book, for the first time, a Service for the Baptism of adults, 'which may always be useful for the baptizing of natives in our plantations'. The Protestant Churches never thought of leading the way into new regions where unbelievers might be found and evangelized.

In the nineteenth century four new ideas emerged which made Christians think about mission in a new way:

1. *Commission* In 1792 William Carey wrote his famous book *An Enquiry into the Obligation of Christians to Use Means for the Conversion of the Heathen*. This book was based on the need for Christians to take seriously the Great Commission of Jesus, and not to leave everything to the sovereign act of God. When Carey made this point in the Baptist Church where he was minister, one of the elders called out, 'Sit down, young man; when God is pleased to convert the heathen He will do so without consulting you or me!' (It is interesting today to notice that Carey was not concerned only with evangelism. His book also called on English people not to buy West Indian sugar because of the inhuman working conditions of the natives on the plantations.) Carey's book prepared the way for the voluntary societies which began the modern missionary movement. Many Church leaders of his time did not approve of this movement.

2. *Colonialism* The East India Company appointed Chaplains for service in the areas where it had influence, but the Company declared that the work of the chaplains did not include evangelizing the Indians. Eventually, however, the colonists encountered the non-Christian world and this made many Christians want to evangelize.

3. *Compassion* David Livingstone saw 'commerce and Christianity' as the only way to end 'the abominable traffic' of the slave trade which, he believed, stood in the way of both evangelism and civilization.

4. *Civilization* When H. M. Stanley had met Livingstone and, later, King Mutesa of Buganda, he wrote to *The Daily Telegraph* newspaper in London in 1875 that this 'enlightened and progressive ruler' relied upon Christianity to bring light and hope to his country and called for a 'pious and practical missionary'.

CULTURE SPEAKING TO CULTURE

Communication often fails because a speaker may think that he or she has said one thing, but the people he is talking to hear or see something different. Figure 7 provides an example. Two people may look at it, and one of them may see a young girl, and the other

Figure 7 A young girl or an old woman?

may see a very old woman. Each of them will find it difficult to see what the other sees—but they are both looking at the same picture.

A good example of misunderstanding occurs in Acts 14.7, where the people of Lystra totally misunderstood Paul's message. And if Rev. 3.20 is read in Africa, it might sound as if Jesus was a robber, because only someone up to no good would knock on the door instead of identifying himself with an honest shout 'May I enter?' So a literal translation of the Greek words must be avoided here. In the same way, the Inuit people of the Arctic know nothing about grazing animals, and to them the description of Jesus as the 'Lamb of God' is meaningless. In their Bible, therefore, He has become 'the Baby Seal of God', for the seal is an animal they understand and depend upon for food, clothing and fuel—it is their life.

Translating ideas across cultures in this way is called 'Dynamic Equivalence' by translators, i.e. they do not translate every word, but they translate the *meaning* of the words. The same principle should be followed by anyone trying to communicate new ideas. For two examples of this, see p. 44. Below are some more examples.

Bishop David Gitari of Kenya tells this story:

> Some missionaries went to a village in West Africa and started to preach the Gospel to the chief. He was responsible for a whole tribe. He was very impressed by the Gospel, and said he wanted to become a Christian. He was told the way to do this was through baptism, but 'We cannot baptize you because you are a polyga-mist. You have to send away all your wives except one.' So the good news became bad news, and he expelled those missionaries saying 'I do not want to see you here again'. A few weeks later, Muslims came, preaching Islam and told him he could keep his wives. So the chief, his family and the entire tribe was lost to Christianity.

It does seem strange that missionaries should have condemned the 'sin' of polygamy (which of course they did not really understand because they had never experienced it), yet have encouraged the chief to divorce his wives—which is the greater sin in the teaching of Jesus.

In another place missionaries came with the 'good news' of forgiveness and eternal life in heaven. The first question the local people asked was,

'Are my mother and my grandparents in heaven?'

'Did they trust in Jesus Christ?' asked the missionary.

'Of course not,' was the reply, 'they had never heard of Him.'

'They will not be in heaven, then,' said the missionary, 'but I will, and everyone who has turned to Jesus.'

Missionaries today are more likely to live and work among their own people, like this Tanzanian.

'Well, I don't want to go; I'd rather be with my ancestors than with you and yours.'

Here again what was intended to be good news sounded like bad news in the local culture.

When the first missionaries came to Uganda in 1877, people noticed their great skill of reading and writing more than they noticed the good news of Jesus. A Christian going to Church did not say he was going to pray or worship, but 'to read'. Prayer and worship they already knew—indeed, many African theologians would go so far as to say that they knew God and the possibility of salvation. Reading, however, was the dramatic new feature of the new religion—so there was a lot of confusion between what was the Gospel and what was the culture brought by the missionaries.

A Gospel which brings peace of heart, purpose in life, and fellowship may be attractive to comfortable people in the North. It is not good news for poor people in shanty-towns in the South whose first need is justice.

In Britain churches are open to everyone—but the Christians inside many of the churches wear suits, own cars and use a worship book which has 1300 pages—so not everyone can feel at home there.

A church in London realized that it was failing to reach the local people, many of whom came originally from India and Pakistan.

Figure 8 The poster.

Wanting to welcome them, it therefore advertised for an Asian Christian to come and work for the church. To show that it was in earnest about wanting to welcome people, it produced a poster. See Figure 8 on p. 81 and Question 7 on p. 93 below.

THE NATURE OF CULTURE

The simplest definition of culture is that it is 'the patterned way in which people do things together'. A more accurate definition is that culture is 'the integrated system of learned patterns of behaviour, ideas and products characteristic of a society'. Culture involves the beliefs, values, customs and institutions which bind a society together with a sense of identity, value, security and continuity. Culture is both a bridge which links different generations of people to one another, and a wall which separates people from others who want to invade or change their culture. People cannot escape their own culture because it is within them; but they can defend themselves against another culture, or they can deliberately enter a new culture as the Son of God did when He was born as the man Jesus.

If we look at any culture in the light of the Gospel, we shall see that it has some features which are praiseworthy, some features which are intolerable, and some which are tolerable. Bishop Gitari, for example, praises one tribal culture for its family values and shared way of life. He condemns it for its custom of putting new-born twins to death; and regards its practice of circumcision as tolerable.

When different cultures meet, there can be four possible results:

1. *Conflict* This happened when Simon Kimbangu was called by Jesus to preach and heal. The missionaries rejected his African ministry as not Christian—and some of them still do (see p. 139).

2. *Co-existence* Hindu, Jewish, Zoroastrian, Christian and Muslim communities lived together as good neighbours in Kerala (and in many other Indian states) for many years until the Hindu–Muslim conflict began in the struggle for self-rule in the early twentieth century.

3. *Competition* The philosopher Hegel thought that in Western Europe human beings had reached maturity and 'the end of history', because Westerners ·had competed against all other cultures and had triumphed.

4. *Cross-fertilization* In 1913 Bishop Lucas introduced Christian sacraments into the rites of Tanzanian Traditional Religion. He did not do this in order to abolish existing African society but to baptize it for Christ. According to Romans 9–11 different cultures can learn

from each other and support each other precisely *because* they are different. So each culture gives something to the other, as plants cross-fertilize each other, and each culture can praise God for the differences.

The last of these responses to a different culture—cross-fertilization—should be the aim of Christian mission. People usually react to a different culture by disliking it at first, then questioning it, and finally appreciating it in terms of its own values and world-view, and realizing that they can learn a lot from it. This was the experience of Timothy Richard, a Welsh missionary in China in 1900. He wrote:

> Ancestor-worship has undoubtedly been carried to excess in China, but it is the powerful bond of family and clan as well in this life as the next. To abolish it will destroy Chinese society as we know it. There is much that is beautiful in this custom, and change should be constructive rather than destructive. Missionary tracts against it have led to riots, not because of the wickedness of the Chinese but because of the ignorance of the writers, who were charging the natives with sin where there was no sin. When I first came to China, a missionary friend brought me in triumph the ancestral tablet of a native Christian which the owner had consented to burn. I said to him, 'When he burns his tablet, I suppose you will at the same time burn your parents' photographs?'

In the modern world, when should a country be called 'backward'? When it is heavily in debt (like Brazil)? When most of its people are illiterate (South Africa)? Or when private gain at the expense of others is rewarded (Britain)? We must learn about cultures before we can answer these questions.

CROSS-CULTURAL COMMUNICATION

The Church faces two dangers in its inevitable encounter with culture. One danger is that its life and teaching may be so *similar* to the prevailing culture that the Church is no longer the bearer of God's judgement and promise. It becomes simply the guardian of the culture and fails to challenge it. Indeed, the Church cannot challenge the culture because it is like a mirror, which simply reflects the culture. The other danger is that the language and life-style of the Church is so different from the culture that it becomes the language and life-style of a ghetto which makes no contact with the culture. When the Church tries to preach the Gospel to people of another culture, how does it find the proper path between fitting in with the culture so much that the Gospel loses its power to challenge traditional ways of life, and attacking the culture so strongly that the Church either fails to communicate altogether or else it cuts off its converts from their own culture? This is a question which all missionaries must ask. Some Western missionaries in the past did not ask this question and so (a) they failed to challenge their own Western culture with the Gospel and (b) they made their converts devalue their local culture.

There are four ways in which the 'Sender' of a message can try to communicate with the person who receives the message, the 'Receptor' of it (see Figure 9):

1. *Isolation* The Sender and the Receptor remain in separate worlds, and the Receptor simply fails to understand. This is, of course, an example of non-communication, but it is very common. It is what happens in much television evangelism.

2. *Extraction* The Receptor enters the Sender's world. This happened when converts were taken into the mission compound, and became evangelized *islands* rather than *bridges* of witness into their community. It was the converts (the Receptors of the Gospel) who had to carry the burden of learning a new language and culture.

3. *Identification* The Sender enters the Receptor's world, and understands the language, culture and world-view. Here it is the Sender who carries the main burden of learning new things.

4. *Reciprocation* Mutual exchange of the Sender/Receptor roles, where both learn from one another (see p. 108).

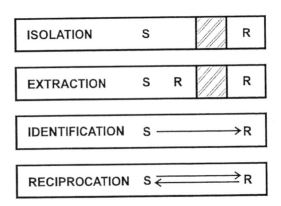

Figure 9 Communication between Sender (S) and Receptor (R).

An illustration of the wrong sort of communication is the story of the monkey who one day almost drowned in a river. A day or two later, when he was walking beside a stream, he saw several fish leaping about in the water. Remembering his own dreadful experience, and feeling sorry for the fish, he put his hand in the water, rescued them and tied them to the branch of a tree. Nothing could be better news than that—if you are a monkey. But not if you are a fish! They could not, of course, live in the tree—and yet the Church has often expected people of different cultures to welcome and follow its own strange and unfamiliar customs.

An example of reciprocation or mutual exchange occurs whenever the Receptor receives the Bible from the Sender and is then free to read it in a fresh way and interpret it *against* the tradition held by the Sender (e.g. in allowing polygamy [see p. 101], or encouraging corporate baptisms [see p. 108]). The Church in Kenya has adopted the local custom of 'harambees', i.e. meetings where people are encouraged to give donations in public for the work of the Church. This custom was opposed by some Europeans on the biblical grounds that giving should be private (Matt. 6.3,4), but Africans defended it on the equally biblical grounds that people should encourage one another to give more generously (2 Cor. 8.1–7; Heb. 10.24).

AN INDIGENOUS CHURCH

Roland Allen complained in 1912 that mission Churches in most parts of the world were

(a) *not indigenous*, i.e. not rooted in the local culture;

(b) *dependent* on parent Churches for money, ideas and leaders;

(c) *all alike*, so failing to reflect the God-given riches and differences of China, or Kenya, or Brazil.

Allen noticed that most of the mission Churches he saw used buildings which were like the buildings he had seen in Europe. They worshipped God with European liturgies and tunes, followed European behaviour and rituals, and relied on foreign leadership. These mission Churches gave no sign that they belonged to the culture around them.

However, Allen says that a truly indigenous Church is

a group of believers who live out their life, including their socialized Christian activity, in the patterns of the local society, and for whom any transformation of that society comes out of their felt needs under the guidance of the Holy Spirit and the Scriptures.

People need to use this bridge to cross from Penang Island to the mainland of Malaysia. People who live on an island need to adjust to a different way of living on the mainland. What bridges exist between your Church and the people to whom God sends you in mission? What sort of bridges do you and your fellow-Christians build? Do people cross these bridges into the Church?

Allen and others taught that this type of group has the following characteristics:

1. The Church often begins independently, without the work of missionaries.

2. The Church is not founded, but it is *planted* in the soil of the local culture.

3. New converts are taught simply and clearly, so that they can easily translate teaching into living and doing.

4. Christians take responsibility for one another and for the good order of the Church. They do this in ways which make sense in terms of their own local culture.

5. The Church should use its own financial resources and discover its own spiritual gifts to strengthen its life, to discover new revelations, new aspects of the Gospel, and new forms of Christian living, in direct dependence on the Holy Spirit.

6. The 'parent' Church often does not recognize the indigenous Church; instead, it disowns it.

This pattern can be seen in the story of Peter and Cornelius in Acts 10. This episode is sometimes called the conversion of Cornelius—but it could equally be called the conversion of Peter. A similar pattern has been repeated thousands of times in the history of mission. The Church never possesses the Kingdom of God, and it does not advance by its own strategy (Acts 10.28), but rather by the work of the Holy Spirit who opens someone's mind to the Good News (10.3–6), perhaps through a visitor, a preacher, a Bible text, a dream, a prayer or a deep experience of joy or sorrow. Christians do not plan or even know about this beforehand. They just have the privilege of seeing it happen as God goes before His Church (see p. 125). And, like Peter, Christians can usually find good reasons for refusing to follow (10.15–17; 11.3). But they must follow if they are to be faithful. For the mission is not theirs, but God's.

FORM AND FUNCTION

Anthropologists distinguish between Forms and Functions in human cultures. The Function (or Meaning) of any practice or ceremony is its purpose. For example, people may have a ritual to recognize the end of a person's life on earth at death and send him on his way to the next stage of life. They may have a custom which relates to the worship of God, or a ceremony which tries to anticipate and ensure a good harvest. Functions like these are shared by most peoples in the world. The Forms they use, however, are not the same; they vary from culture to culture. Christians are called to discern which Forms of traditional culture in their society can be 'baptized' in the service of the Gospel, and which Forms are incompatible with the Gospel. Missionaries (e.g. Bishop W. V. Lucas, see p. 149) have often tried to discern this themselves, but it is better to leave decisions like these to the people who belong to the culture and understand its Forms and Functions best.

Three examples can help us to understand this important process. The first comes from Jesus Himself. He said to the Jews, 'Destroy this temple and in three days I will raise it up.' They thought he was speaking about the Temple built by Herod, but he was speaking of the temple of His body. This saying occurs three times in the Gospels and was remembered by both the followers and the enemies of Jesus (Mark 14.58; 15.29; Acts 6.14). However, the first Christians only gradually came to understand the meaning of this saying, as they realized that the old Temple building would be replaced by the new people of God through the resurrection of Christ from the dead. This, said James in Acts 15.14–18, was the meaning of the words of Amos 9.11, 'I will rebuild the fallen house of David'. The Church is now the new Temple (1 Cor. 3.16) where spiritual sacrifices are offered in the true worship of God (Heb. 10.20; 13.15; 1 Pet. 2.5). The Function has not changed: it is still to worship God. But the Form has changed: it is the people who are important rather than the place—though the old name for where God dwells, the Temple, is still used to describe the people. So we see that Jesus maintained continuity with the former culture by using the same name, but altered its Form in order that all peoples could fulfil the Function of worshipping God in spirit and truth.

The second example is a simple one taken from some modern healing practices. Some of John Wimber's followers, when they pray for God's healing, have been taught to position their hands about an inch away from the sick person, not actually on him or her. Of course, it is the Spirit of God who heals, not human hands. The hands are the Form; the healing is the Function. Forms usually differ from culture to culture, but the Function is based on God's revelation of Himself in Christ as the only source of wholeness and healing. Most aspects of worship and ministry provide many similar examples.

The third example of the difference between Form and Function comes from the Shona people of Zimbabwe. They had a traditional rite known as *kurova guva*, connected with burial of the dead. The Form of this rite involved divination, medicines against witchcraft, a libation of beer and a feast of roast meat beside the grave. The Function of this rite was to release the deceased person from the land of isolation and bring the ancestral spirit back as guardian of the family. This rite was opposed by Roman Catholic missionaries, but the Shona people were totally committed to it. In 1969 a Church Commission was set up to solve the problem and this Commission composed 'The Zimbabwe Liturgy for Second Burial'. This service kept most of the traditional Form of the rite, but made the following significant alterations:

1. Traditional medicines were replaced by holy water;
2. The animal killed for the feast became a symbol of Christ's sacrifice;
3. The ancestral spirit was not invited back to its former home on earth but welcomed into a heavenly home;
4. The whole rite is dominated by repeated prayer to the God and Father of our Lord Jesus Christ. (W. V. Lucas would probably have wanted to incorporate the Eucharist into the feast of roast meat beside the grave.)

In this example, both the Form and the Function are changed when they are given a Christian meaning, but the value of the traditional meaning is not denied. The Function of meeting the felt needs of both the deceased and the bereaved community is still achieved.

JESUS AND CULTURE

Jesus both identified with the culture of his day and challenged it. He did not deny the existence of demons—but He defeated them. But His challenge is two-edged. On the one hand Jesus challenges the fear of demons which grips many traditional societies and offers liberation. On the other hand, Jesus also challenges the European world-view which denies spiritual and supernatural realities. Many missionaries in the past had nothing to say about the spirits, demons or ancestors which dominated people's lives in Africa (and elsewhere). Because they had made Jesus a comfortable part of their own Western culture ('domesticated' him—see p. 96), the Jesus they proclaimed could neither question their own culture nor set free the Africans. True liberation could come to both sides only through 'Reciprocation', i.e. learning from one another.

The Churches of the North use enormous energy to write and speak about the spread of Christianity in the world today. They have the biggest resources of money and management to undertake the task of world evangelism. However, they are culturally less suited for this task than any other Church because they have become so expert and self-confident that they find it difficult to listen to other cultures and understand them.

Americans are particularly skilful at wrapping up or packaging goods for a consumer society. The Churches of the USA reflect their own culture. They have taken insights from many parts of the world Church, and then made people feel that they need the growth, success, healing, etc., that the American Churches advertise. The Americans use marketing techniques through Centres, Conferences or TV to make these 'commodities' or good things popular and, finally to sell them. This has happened in the case of the Church Growth Movement, the Charismatic Movement, the Signs and Wonders Movement, and many others. The goods being offered seem to fit certain stated needs, but they often prove inadequate in new situations. But the Jesus of the Gospels constantly identified with a variety of cultures (priests, peasants, rabbis, Gentiles). And He constantly challenged people's expectations of Him, by doing the unexpected: forgiving the paralytic, raising the widow's son, eating with Zacchaeus, etc. (see p. 27). A pre-packaged Jesus, 'packaged' for one particular culture (e.g. American) can never do this. By doing this to Jesus, we restrict Him to our own agenda or ideas and aims and He will never surprise us.

CHURCH AND CULT

The first Christians knew that many religious cults existed in their world. Two examples of popular cults were the worship of the Egyptian goddess Isis and the worship of Mithras, a god of light who was particularly popular with soldiers. These cults were generally protected by the State because they were forms of personal, private religion. They did not call everyone to accept them and join them. But when Christians began to follow 'The Way', they did not use one of the many words commonly used for a religious cult (e.g. *thiasos*). They used the word *ekklesia*, which was a concept from civil life used for a public meeting when the town clerk called all the citizens together to decide affairs of state, as in Acts 19.39. The difference between *thiasos* and *ekklesia* can be set out as follows:

Thiasos was the word for a private cult, devoted to a mythical hero-redeemer, Its aim was the personal salvation of its members, and it required strict adherence to dogma, ritual and language. It engaged in propaganda so that it would produce carbon copies of itself.

But the *ekklesia* was the assembly which God calls into the public market-place of the world. It was based on a historical Lord who engaged in mission in order to extend his kingdom and bring to birth the children of God. These children are the image of their parent rather than the image of the missionary who evangelized them and acted as a 'midwife' at their rebirth.

Thiasos	Ekklesia
private religious group	public assembly of God
for members' salvation	for the world
mythical redeemer	historical Lord
strict ritual	contextual
propaganda	mission
carbon copies	children of God

Ekklesia is therefore a word which belongs to local culture and also challenges local culture. It acknowledges God's authority over all earthly powers, and calls on the whole world to do the same. For this reason totalitarian governments tolerate private religious cults but oppose the Church when it makes public claims. But see Question 16, below.

HOW OTHER CULTURES CAN HELP US

There is no reason why we should imitate strange cultures, because we have to accept our own culture. We must, however, allow the Gospel to criticize our culture. Often, the best way of doing this is to see our own culture for a period through the eyes of another culture. When a new missionary was in a bus crash in India and had both legs broken, he asked 'Why has this happened to me?' A Hindu replied, 'The *karma* of your former lives has caught up with you'; an African would have said, 'An enemy has put a curse on you'; the Indian pastor said, 'It is the will of God'; a European said, 'There was no brake fluid in the brake pipes'. Which was the best answer? Each answer represented a different world-view and each world-view can contribute much to our understanding of the world and the Bible. This is why *all* Christians need to meet people of other cultures, even if they live in a place where everyone belongs to one culture. If we hear the voice of only one culture we may miss the word of God altogether. T. S. Eliot, a British poet, put it like this:

> We shall not cease from exploration,
> And the end of all our exploring
> Will be to arrive where we started
> And know the place for the first time.

Sometimes Christians have been tempted to look for a form of the Gospel which is above all cultures, and which all cultures should therefore accept. Some people have tried to find this 'super-culture' in the Bible. However, the New Testament itself is multi-cultural and offers no example of a super-cultural model of the Gospel. Peter (and the faith which Peter held) needed to receive the strange culture of the Gentile Cornelius equally as much as Cornelius needed to receive the faith of Peter. The events of Acts 10 give a message to the evangelizer (Peter) as well as a message to the evangelized (Cornelius) and the Church at that time was humble enough to recognize its Master's voice when He spoke from another culture. The Church was humble enough to reflect on its encounter with 'otherness' and even to rethink the way it expressed its own message in the light of this encounter.

This process of rethinking is called 'inculturation'. Inculturation means stating the message of salvation in a different way and describing Christian life and doctrine in the thought patterns of different peoples. The aim of inculturation is 'to make Christianity feel truly at home in the cultures of each people'. There are four principles of inculturation:

1. The message must be relevant to the cultural context;
2. The message must be stated simply;
3. The message must be interesting and attractive;
4. The message must be in language familiar to the people.

The New Testament witnesses very clearly that the Gospel can be expressed in terms of an infinite variety of human cultures. It therefore provides a better authority and a better model for mission than, for example, the Western Church, which has often taken for granted the superiority of its own culture and 'the universal significance of Christian thought as it has evolved in the West' (Cardinal Josef Ratzinger).

Other people have thought that as Christians work together and appreciate the world's many different cultures, they will be able to put the 'essential' Gospel into a form which does justice to all cultures equally. This, however, would be a barrier to inculturation, rather than a means of obtaining it. Faith needs to become culture, and culture to be 'baptized' to become faith (see p. 83). 'A faith which does not become culture is a faith which has not been fully received, not thoroughly thought through, not fully lived out' (Pope John Paul II). This is why some Christian missionaries worked so hard to preserve traditional culture. Faith and culture support one another.

STUDY SUGGESTIONS

WORD STUDY

1. What is the meaning of the following words:
   (a) Christendom
   (b) Form, and
   (c) Function
   (d) Inculturation?

BIBLE STUDY

2. What evidence can you find in the following passages that the first missionaries tried not to impose their culture on their converts?
   Acts 15.6–29; Acts 17.22–31; Gal. 2.3–5, 11–14; 1 Cor. 9.19–23.
3. In Romans 9–11, what could Gentiles learn from Jews, and Jews learn from Gentiles?

CONTEXTUAL APPLICATION

4. Why did the Church become less concerned with mission after the conversion of Constantine than it had been before? Do you think a close connection between Church and State today would help or hinder the work of mission? Give reasons for your answer.
5. Which of the four motives for mission mentioned on pp. 77–78 are most relevant today? What other good reasons for mission can you think of?
6. What mistakes were made in each of the four examples of cross-cultural mission given on pp. 79–82? How could the good news have been communicated better?
7. Why do you think the poster on p. 81 was unsuitable?
8. In this chapter and the next chapter, there is much criticism of modern Western culture. Has Western culture also brought positive benefits to other countries, especially in the area where you live? (You might think of health, education, technology, etc.)
9. In the light of the Gospel, what elements of your culture do you feel are (a) praiseworthy and (b) intolerable?
10. What is there in your own society and culture that the Church (a) values and tries to preserve and (b) challenges and tries to change? How successful is the Church in communicating this to people?
11. What examples of Isolation, Extraction, Identification and Reciprocation have you noticed in mission activities?

12. Has any part of the Bible ever made you question any Christian belief or practice which you have been taught? If so, how?

13. Fifty years ago Anglicans used to boast that the Anglican Church's worship was the same all over the world. Why should they have been ashamed of this rather than proud of it?

14. Can you see the six characteristics on p. 87 in your Church? How does your Church reflect these signs and features?

15. In his encounter with Cornelius, how was Peter like Jonah (see p. 19) in his encounter with Nineveh? How was he different?

16. What features of (a) *thiasos* and (b) *ekklesia* are present in your Church? In what ways might your Church need to change in order to be more clearly an *ekklesia*?

17. Has another culture helped you to 'know your place for the first time'? If so, how?

18. In the story of the bus accident in India (p. 91), what question was the missionary really asking? Who gave the best answer? Give reasons for your opinion.

8. The Missionaries

Missionaries of the past made us Africans ashamed of being ourselves because they so often tried to 'circumcise' us into Europeans before allowing us to become Christians . . . Yet these people from overseas brought us something too wonderful for words (as a result of which the liberation struggle was well and truly launched), even if they brought it wrapped in Western swaddling clothes. It must be the task of African Christians to share this priceless treasure with others and to ensure that it does not remain an alien thing.

Archbishop Desmond Tutu

As we saw in the last chapter, it is true that many of the first missionaries could not distinguish between the Good News of Jesus and the Western culture in which the European Churches had wrapped it. They also failed to grasp fully the culture of the people to whom they came. This was not deliberate sin; it was just normal human foolishness and weakness. Some missionaries, however, were well aware of the gap between cultures. In this and the next chapter we shall discover how some of these missionaries tried to bridge that gap.

INDIVIDUAL CONVERSIONS

For many years Western Christians did not do very much about taking the Gospel to the rest of the world (see p. 77). But European Christians in the eighteenth century who had been influenced by the Pietist movement were eager to share with people all over the world the joy of their own personal experience of salvation in Christ. The Moravian Brethren were especially active, sending missionaries to twenty-eight countries over a period of twenty-eight years. Their aim was not to plant the Church but only to convert individuals who could then form small fellowships. They were the 'first fruits' of the full harvest which would be reaped later. The Moravians did not think that these converts would change their society—they were simply 'islands' of spiritual light.

THE MISSION COMPOUND

The new mission agencies created in the nineteenth century moved from the idea of individual conversion to the founding of local Churches which were similar to the sending Churches. The only way this could be done was to announce what God had done in Jesus and to set up Christian settlements for those who wished to respond and learn more. Those who entered these settlements or mission compounds often had to be protected—both from their enemies who wanted to make them slaves, and also from their friends who wanted to keep them within their traditional culture and religion. But in the mission compound they could learn to be Christians. This involved learning to read, so that they could read the Bible. After three years, they might be baptized.

The people who came to the mission compounds learnt not only the Bible but the dress, the worship, the music and the customs of 'Christianity' as the missionaries understood it. European musical instruments (e.g. harmoniums) replaced local ones; this often happened because the local Christians insisted on the change, not only because the missionaries requested it. Ever since those far-off days it has been difficult to reverse this trend and rediscover local forms of culture.

The founding of local Churches which were self-governing, self-supporting and self-propagating, required the training of local leaders. This did not, however, make the Church any more indigenous, because the leaders (like many a 'Brown Sahib' in Indian secular life) were simply those people who had become expert in the theology and organization of the sending Church. Apart from their nationality, they were no different from the foreign leaders whom they replaced.

GUSTAV WARNECK (1834–1910)

Gustav Warneck has been called the founder of the Protestant science of missions. He believed that European colonial expansion could open the door for missions, but that the missionary task should always be independent of colonialism. Warneck's vision for mission had three stages:

1. Individual conversions through preaching the Kingdom of God and the 'divine process of mission as education'.

2. The creation of indigenous 'people's churches' which could take responsibility for organizing their own life.

3. The Christianization of whole peoples, when paganism is finally overcome and the people all live in such a Christian atmosphere that everyone knows the truth and can experience salvation. In this way 'the Christian faith does not destroy but transfigures the particular character of a people.'

In theory Warneck wanted indigenous Churches, but his emphasis on education meant that these could not really exist—they

96

could only be based on what the indigenous Christians had been taught by the missions.

BRUNO GUTMANN (1876–1966)

Bruno Gutmann, a German Lutheran missionary, took Warneck's theory a step further by applying it thoroughly among the Chagga people on Mount Kilimanjaro. Because of his strong theology of creation, Gutmann believed the following ideas.

1. God has already given people social systems which missions must respect and build upon. This meant that 'blood and soil' were God's sacred gifts to the Chagga—in particular (a) their ancestry, (b) their land and (c) their age-group fellowship. The Gospel of Christ must fit into that basic framework and not destroy it.

2. The clan is the basic unit of society. People are not converted as individuals by leaving one group and joining another, but by joining the holy clan—which had no pastors because Chagga society had no religious officials of that kind.

3. God has created human beings to depend on one another. The African systems of dependency are better than European systems, so they must be preserved. Therefore the leader's task is to build and preserve relationships between human beings.

At Moshi, Gutmann built his model congregation. He did not lead it but was himself under its authority. The people loved him, but few of them followed him. The simple reason for this was that the Chagga were the most progressive tribe in East Africa. They wanted to receive the new ideas and technology which the Europeans were bringing more than they wanted to preserve their old traditions. Gutmann wanted them to preserve their traditions because he believed that they were God's revealed truth, like the Gospel itself.

This is a problem which the Church always has to face in its mission. Should it bring in new ideas which young people will welcome because they are impatient with the old tradition? Or should it 'accommodate' or 'inculturate' its message to the old tradition (an action which many people resent because it holds them back from progress)?

Gutmann's colleagues laughed at him for 'fellowshipping with the natives in a hopeless attempt to be St Francis among the birds'. More seriously, Karl Barth opposed Gutmann's 'natural theology' because, said Barth, 'The starting point of mission is not creation but God's revelation in Christ'. Barth also felt that in the 1930s 'blood and soil' sounded too much like Hitler's Nazi doctrine of preserving the rights of a sacred race, a doctrine which was tearing

The old style of mission insisted that new Christians left their family and their own culture and came to live with the missionaries and other Christians in the mission compound, like this one in Borneo.

the whole of Europe apart at that very time. 'Blood and soil' could encourage ethnic cleansing and tribal conflict.

But today we probably need to rediscover Gutmann and his theology of creation. For too long evangelists have brought a 'new' Gospel which does not connect with the daily life and concerns of the people. Gutmann, like Paul at Athens (Acts 17), understood and respected the culture of his hearers, and made specific connections with it so that the Gospel could take root and become truly theirs, not a foreign import. This is as important in modern urban mission as it was in the old rural mission field (see p. 108).

COLONIALISM AND MISSIONS

By the time of Gutmann, the golden age of missions had dawned, and people were as optimistic as Warneck had been that the whole world would soon be Christian, as Europe was Christian. The slogan of the World Missionary Conference at Edinburgh in 1910 was 'The Evangelization of the World in this Generation'. No one questioned the view of the German philosopher Hegel that world history had moved from the East (where human beings were like children) to the West (where they had become mature adults) and that countries like 'Chile and Peru have no culture of their own' and 'Africa is characterised by . . . absolute inflexibility and an inability to develop'. Since, according to Warneck, it was 'the Gospel which had made the Western nations great', the West had the right to impose its own image on the entire world, and make people 'English in their language, civilized in their habits and Christian in their religion'.

But two terrible world wars caused by the so-called Christian West changed all these ideas (together with a number of other factors—see p. 2). The word 'missionary' has become as unpopular as the word 'colonialist'. Most Western mission agencies have chosen new names for themselves which do not include the word 'missionary'. This new view is reflected in the titles of some books published since 1960, e.g. *Missions in a Time of Testing*; *Missions at the Crossroads*; *Christian Missions and the Judgment of God*; *The Unpopular Missionary*; *The Ugly Missionary*; *Missionary Go Home*; *End of an Era*. In the end, this may not be a bad thing for the Church's mission. The Church has always needed apparent failure and suffering in order to become aware of its mission. The Church is always in a state of crisis but only occasionally does it know it. Now, under criticism, true mission can go forward, for the word 'crisis' means a turning-point, an opportunity.

But what is the truth about the relationship between missions and colonialism? A simple way of looking at this relationship is as follows:

1. In some places (e.g. India) colonial authorities were there before missions. They opened the door for missions, but did not do this deliberately. In other places (e.g. parts of Africa) the missionaries arrived there first.

2. Naturally there was a relationship between the colonialists and the missionaries, often based on nationality and language. At times, the colonialists and missionaries agreed, but not often for very long. Conflicts were much more common than agreements.

3. Missionaries often began their work by planning to make the natives 'civilized, peaceful and obedient' to both Church and State. Livingstone's stated aim, for example, was to bring 'commerce, civilization and Christianity' and he wrote secretly to a friend to say that he planned to discover and to exploit the natural resources of Africa for Britain. His experiences and friendships with Africans, however, changed his attitude to one of respect and support for the African peoples who were already threatened by Arab slave traders and who would soon be exploited by Europeans. In clear contrast to people like Stanley and Rhodes, Livingstone encouraged African hopes and African leadership. His African friends (whose opinions must be respected) knew this and loved him for it.

4. Many missionaries changed as much as Livingstone, for four main reasons:

(a) They became students of the language and culture of the place where they worked. William Carey became Professor of the Sanskrit and Bengali languages, laid the foundations of modern Bengali literature, and classified Indian plants in botanic gardens. Henry Martyn's translation of the New Testament into Urdu, completed in 1810, is the basis of the version still used today. In the beginning the missionaries used local languages for the sake of the Gospel, but then they went into partnership with (for example) the Zulus in a new revival of the culture and history of the people. The missionaries developed a wide interest far beyond religious matters.

(b) In the light of the local wisdom which they discovered for the first time, some of the missionaries became acutely critical of themselves, and even of their own culture. For examples, see point 6 below.

(c) Although the missionaries began teaching the people to read in order to read the Bible, they gradually realized that, 'in fact if you teach people to read, even if you only intend them to read the Bible, you have started something which it is not in your power to stop'. Reading, thinking—the Bible itself—gave ordinary people a sense of self-worth, dignity and power which revolutionized their countries.

(d) Some of the missionaries became aware of the cruel exploitation of the countries where they served and stood with the native people against both the colonial government and European settlers (when there were large numbers of settlers, they created bitter conflict and bloodshed). It was often only the missionaries who could begin to see life from the point of view of the native people. For this reason, missionaries in Africa were rarely harmed by the Africans in the conflicts which arose.

5. The colonial rulers often bitterly opposed missionaries. We see examples of this in Tanzania, when the Anglican Church appointed Yohana Omari as its first African bishop in 1955; and in Kenya in 1908, when the Kenyan government tried to force Africans to work on settler farms—where the missionaries knew they would be badly treated.

6. New converts often showed that they were wiser than their teachers. A South African polygamist refused baptism, telling the missionary, 'Many who have become Christians have driven away their wives and children like so many things of no value; although I might live with only one wife, yet I like the others, and I could not think for a moment of driving away my children.' As a result of local arguments like this, Bishop Colenso of Natal wrote, 'How can you justify asking polygamists to commit the sin of divorce to remedy the offence of polygamy?' One South African chief showed the missionaries he knew more about Christian strategy than they did when he commented on their mission compound, 'Why is it that you call the believers of my people all to live in one place? Is it God who tells you to do so? I do not like your method of breaking up the kraal. Let the believing kaffir look to his own countrymen, and not go away, but teach others.' (See p. 96.)

7. An African scholar has exposed a major weakness in this debate about the effect of missions and colonialism: both sides in the argument tend to assume that the 'natives' were just passive objects whom foreigners could shape, help or exploit as they wished. But that was never the case. We are talking about human beings who knew their own world and were well able to think for themselves and make their own decisions about what was good and what was not good for them and their people. When they made their own response to the Gospel, Christians of the younger Churches proved that they could not only shape their own future, but also radically influence the future of the world Church.

(An Indian friend points out that some of the natives may have acted as I have described in the above paragraph. Nevertheless most of them were not free to make their own objective choices. They were in such bondage to the values of the colonialists that they could not avoid asking 'How can I get the best deal for myself and my family in this situation?' and would often answer 'By becoming a Christian and by accepting the education and culture which my colonial masters value.')

ROMAN CATHOLIC MISSIONS

The above survey does not take sufficient account of Roman Catholic missions. Their history was very different. The Protestants of the Reformation did nothing about world mission because they used all their energies to organize their own Churches as they began to emerge. At the same period (the sixteenth century) Roman Catholics knew they held a dominant position in Europe. They felt confident, therefore, about expanding the Church all over the world. For them, the Church was the same as the Kingdom of God. It was like a shop, stocked with a supply of heavenly graces which priests could hand out to consumers.

One of the greatest missionaries at this time was Francis Xavier (1506–1552). He was one of the first six members of the Society of Jesus, the Jesuits, and a friend of their founder, Ignatius Loyola. He travelled through Asia for eleven years. At the start of his travels, Francis Xavier opposed all non-Western customs, but when he reached Japan he learnt to value Eastern culture. Like most Catholics of his time, he thought it was the duty of the Christian kings of Portugal and Spain to force their subject peoples to convert to Christianity. At other times, however, Francis Xavier protested against the cruel and sinful practices of European government officials which discredited the Church to which these officials belonged.

In 1622, the department of the Vatican called *Propaganda Fide* ('Extension of the Faith') was founded in order to take the task of mission away from kings and give it back to the Church. *Propaganda Fide* advised missionaries not to force people to change their customs, because

> What could be more absurd than to carry France, Spain, Italy, or any part of Europe into China? It is not this sort of thing you are to bring but rather the Faith, which does not reject or damage any people's rites and customs, provided these are not depraved.

This debate about how far the Christian faith should change or even abolish traditional local customs continued until the Church finally gained control of missionary work in the nineteenth century. The most effective missionary work was done by Jesuits. One example was Matteo Ricci (1552–1610), who worked in China. He did not receive permission to enter the Imperial City of Peking (now Beijing) until he had been in the country for seventeen years. He then addressed the Emperor

> with respect in order to offer gifts from my country. Your Majesty's servant comes from a far distant land which has never exchanged gifts with the Middle Kingdom. Fame told me of the remarkable teaching and fine institutions with which the imperial court has endowed all its peoples. I desired to share these advantages and live out my life as one of your Majesty's subjects, hoping in return to be of some small use.

Ricci used his skills as a clock-repairer and map-maker, and soon became a Chinese scholar and linguist. He tried to make Christianity as Chinese as possible and to find Chinese equivalents for Christian terms. He wrote in a Catechism:

> Those who adore heaven instead of the Lord of Heaven are like a man who, desiring to pay the Emperor homage, prostrates himself before the imperial palace at Peking and venerates its beauty.

One of the books Ricci wrote in Chinese led to the first conversions in Korea two hundred years later. He honoured Confucius as a holy teacher, and his fellow-Catholics later accused him of adding Confucius to the Church's list of saints. He regarded 'ancestor-worship' as only respect for the great people of the past, and not contrary to Christian teaching (see p. 83). Ricci trusted the Chinese Christians themselves to make the final decisions about what they could and could not do.

In the same way Robert de Nobili (1577–1656) defended the Hindu caste system in India (although he criticized the superstitious elements in it), and he evangelized within it. A number of high-caste Brahmans were baptized, but it was de Nobili's work among the lower castes (whom he kept separate from the higher castes, just as society did) which really flourished. He lived, ate, dressed and studied like a Hindu scholar and holy man. This meant giving up meat and leather shoes and even cutting himself off from the existing Christian Church. Through his efforts, Indians could see that Christians did not have to be European. Like Ricci, de Nobili's fellow-Christians accused him of diluting or watering down the Gospel through fear of opposition from Hindus.

Because of the work of Ricci and de Nobili, the Church had to debate the great controversy about 'Accommodation'. Can the

Matteo Ricci (left) upset the authorities of the Roman Catholic Church by adopting Chinese dress and customs in his mission work in China. What are the advantages and dangers of this sort of cultural identification?

Gospel be 'adapted' or 'accommodated' to local situations, or must it always arrive as a foreign import? Can it be presented as fulfilling the local people's own hopes and dreams, or will that deform the Gospel by connecting it with religious ideas which are anti-Christian (a process called syncretism)? In 1744 this controversy was settled by a papal bull of Pope Benedict XIV. This written edict prohibited any adaptation of Christianity to local culture, except in very trivial matters. All missionaries were required to submit to this bull (which was not repealed until 1938) and were not allowed to discuss the subject. Thirty years later all Jesuit missionaries were recalled from their missions.

Since the Second Vatican Council in 1962, there has been a revolution in Roman Catholic thinking about mission. For the first time the Church is not centred on Europe. It is global, though it still has to change a lot of its thinking—the 1994 African Synod of Bishops, for example, did not meet on the soil of Africa but in Rome, and the bishops were not allowed to bring their African theologians with them! The Church is now presented as a Servant and a sign of human fellowship with God, rather than as a dominant master. A Roman Catholic document published in 1982 said that 'the Christian faith must be rethought, reformulated and lived anew in each human culture'. This is called 'inculturation'. Roman Catholic and Protestant missiology are more alike than ever before. Since they now speak the same language about mission, they can increasingly help one another.

Special Note C

CHRISTIANITY REDISCOVERED

Christianity Rediscovered is the title of a book written in 1978 by Vincent Donovan, a Roman Catholic priest working among the Masai people of Northern Tanzania. Its sub-title is 'An Epistle from the Masai', because it tells what happened when a group of Masai discovered the story of Jesus. They not only received the Good News, they also contributed to it, out of their own cultural way of understanding it. The book has become a bestseller in Britain and North America. It is one of the best modern examples of how the Gospel and culture can interact in Christian mission.

Donovan noticed that the Church had many centres of medical, educational and rural development work among the Masai. These social ministries had two effects: (1) either they detribalized the

Masai by cutting them off from their traditional, tribal roots, or (2) these social ministries made the Masai dependent by simply providing material benefits in time of need. These ministries did not, therefore, make any real connection with the Gospel. But Donovan had found an old book by Roland Allen called *Missionary Methods: St. Paul's or Ours?*, published in 1910. In this book Allen pointed out that Paul spent time in a place telling people the story of Jesus and then he left. He did not found institutions, provide welfare or organize their finances, ministry or worship. He did not even baptize. He left the converts to lead the new Church which the Holy Spirit was planting within their culture. Donovan obtained his Bishop's permission to try the same method among the Masai.

So he arrived amongst them and asked if he could stay with them and talk with them about God. Catholic schools and hospitals had done good work in the area for twenty years, but the Masai response was startling. 'Who can refuse to talk about God?' they replied. 'If that is why you came here, why did you wait so long to tell us? Why did you not come before?'

In the months that followed, Donovan met with people from five settlements, who were called together by their chief into discussion groups. The Church grew up in this area in a form which was decided by (1) Jesus' message about God and (2) the Masai culture. For example, the Masai convey the idea of forgiveness by spitting— so their baptism service includes the symbol of spitting. A tuft of grass speaks to them of peace—so that is a new sign brought into the Eucharist. They felt that the good news of Jesus preserved the very best of their own traditions (which, after all, they believed had come originally from God). Here are just three areas where their culture helped to form their theology:

1. *Jesus* Donovan told stories about Jesus and the stories told by Jesus, and translated them into cultural terms which the Masai could understand (this was probably easier to do for them than for city dwellers in New York or Paris!). They sat around retelling the stories, because they did not read. Donovan had told them nothing about Jesus being God, or about the Trinity. But they began to ask, 'Was there ever anyone like this Jesus?' They saw Him as a real man; then as The Man who could be a pattern for all human beings; then as the Man who showed God to them. The gradual dawning of their understanding seems to have been just like that of Jesus' first followers. Why *tell* people all the Christology, the theology of Christ, and rob them of the excitement of discovering Him for themselves—an experience which set the early Church on fire?

2. *Baptism* One day Donovan thought it was time for some baptisms, and he started to tell the chief which people he thought

Ol Doinyo Lengai, the sacred Mountain of God of the Masai people in Tanzania. What did the Masai teach Vincent Donovan about missionary methods?

were now mature enough to qualify for baptism. 'She was not attentive; he missed too many discussions . . . ' But the elder rebuked him, 'We always do things together; why are you trying to break us up? You said you were bringing *good* news. When we say "*We* believe", that is what we mean.' So they were all baptized, and that was their decision—and then Donovan realized that this was the New Testament pattern too. And water is the most sacred element known to the Masai; it is, literally, their life. Their word for rain is the same as their word for God. They seem to have a better theology of baptism than any Western seminary.

3. *The Church* The Masai chose to translate 'Church' by the word *orporor*. It means 'age-group brotherhood', a Masai social group which they did not enter at birth but after a painful initiation (including circumcision). Those who were all initiated within a seven-year period were linked together for ever and given a unique name, which was never used again. It is the most sacred fellowship which exists in their culture. But now the *Orporor* of God includes not just a seven-year period but all the years until the end, and crosses barriers of sex, age and even tribe. It is the first universal *Orporor*, but it is still an age-group brotherhood—a brotherhood of the last age, the final age of God's kingdom. And it can never be thought of as a building—it is people!

This model of mission is totally different from the 'holy' mission station, separated from the bad, godless, pagan tribe outside. We should allow Donovan's experience to show us that many well-established Churches in the world are still following that old model. The Churches are institutions with a religious life which is as irrelevant to their neighbourhoods as the mission station was to the tribal life of Africa. Young people in the cities of the world have their culture and their beliefs. The Church must enter into them with respect and it must expect to find much that is valuable and even given by God. And then we must not call these young people back to where they were once, or to where we are—but we must pray for the courage to go with them to a place where neither of us have ever been before, a new place where we can 'rediscover' Jesus in a new way. This experience may be exactly the injection of new life which our Churches need. Through mission, the missionaries may receive more than the receivers!

One young Masai was a leader of prayer and festivals among his people. He seemed a born religious leader. Once he spent three days lying on the rim of the active volcano sacred to the Masai, searching with longing for God. But he did not see Him. He had to return, to more prayers, more pleading, perhaps more visits to the fiery volcano. Then Donovan met him and said, 'You think you have been seeking God, Ole Sikii, as a lion hunts its prey; but no, it is God who has been seeking you—you did not send for me, but God sent me to you. God is here and has found you. You are not the lion hunting; God is the lion.'

Donovan wrote as follows:

Every theology or theory must be based on previous missionary experience, and any theology which is not based on previous experience is empty words . . . The Gospel itself, untied to any social service or inducement, is a message filled with power and fertility and creativity and freedom. This book describes an attempt to empower a particular people with the freedom and total responsibility of that Gospel. This experience, lived out in the lonely pastoral setting of the Masai steppe, is far removed from the spreading urban-technological society in which we live. Can the experience of the one world be of any value to the other? I do not know. I can only say that the cry of hopelessness I heard then in that desert setting is not much different from the cry I hear today in the wasteland of our cities.

'Preach the Gospel to all creation,' Christ said. Are we only now beginning to understand what He meant? I believe the new song waiting to be sung in place of the hymn of salvation is simply the song of creation. To move away from the theology of salvation to the theology of creation may be the task of our time.

STUDY SUGGESTIONS

WORD STUDY

1. What is the meaning of the following words:
   (a) accommodation
   (b) syncretism
   (c) inculturation
   (d) papal bull?

CONTEXTUAL APPLICATION

2. How foreign is Christianity in your country? How indigenous is it?

3. What values and traditions from the past should Christians in your country preserve? How can they also be progressive? What are the dangers in going to one extreme or the other (too traditional or too modern)? What practical guidelines can you offer?

4. (a) What do you understand by 'a theology of creation'? What examples of it do you find in the Bible?

(b) In what ways could such a theology be important for those who plant Churches in new places? In what ways could it be dangerous?

5. What positive contributions have missions made to the life of the people of your country? What harm have they done?

6. Should people feel embarrassed or proud of the name 'missionary'?

7. Note the examples of local Christians correcting the views of missionaries (p. 101 and Special Note C). Can you give any similar examples of Church leaders being 'corrected' by lay Christians? See Acts 11.20.

8. Note the difference of opinion between the African and the Indian about the effects of missions and colonialism (p. 101). What is your opinion?

9. What good principles of mission can be learned from (a) Matteo Ricci, (b) Robert de Nobili and (c) Timothy Richard (ch 7, p. 83)?

10. Missionaries need to listen both to the word of God and to the voices in the world; this has been called 'double listening'. How did Gutmann and Donovan do this? Which people or groups in this chapter did only 'single listening' (i.e. listening *either* to the word of God *or* to the voices in the world)?

11. What aspects of Masai Christian theology do you find most instructive? How could our Churches learn from them and from any people of another culture?

9. The Church Growth Movement

Donald McGavran, an American missionary in India, asked why some parts of the Church grow while other parts do not and why some Churches grow at some times but not at other times. Like many missionaries before him, McGavran realized that new Christians should not be taken out of their own culture but should hear the Gospel within it. In this way, new Christians become *Bridges of God* (the title of McGavran's first book) rather than 'islands of faith', and the Church will multiply by groups within the culture rather than grow by individual additions. In 1965 McGavran founded the Institute of Church Growth. He defines 'Church Growth' as follows:

> Church Growth is that *science* which investigates the nature, function and health of Christian Churches as it relates specifically to the effective implementation of *God's commission* to make disciples of all nations. Church Growth strives to combine the eternal principles of *God's Word* with the best insights of contemporary *social and behavioural sciences*.

This definition shows that (a) Church growth is a complex topic which requires scientific study; (b) evangelism is a priority; (c) the Bible is the final authority; (d) sociology, psychology, etc. are essential tools for Christian mission.

FOUR DIMENSIONS OF CHURCH GROWTH

Not all growth is good, as Jesus often pointed out (e.g. the growth of leaves instead of fruit, or weeds, or plants without roots). Churches also can grow in wealth, popularity and many activities in ways which may not be pleasing to God (e.g. the Church of Laodicea, Rev. 3.18, or a Church which is racist or tribalist). Such Churches should not be helped to grow but helped to die, which suggests that numerical growth should probably not be our first objective (see p. 65). Here are four dimensions or kinds of growth which are commended in the Bible (see especially Acts 2.42–47):

Conceptual growth (Growing up to maturity, Acts 2.42, 46): Christians grow in understanding and they change, like Peter did in Acts 10, and the whole Church after him.

Organic growth (Growing together in relationships, Acts 2.44–46): Christians of different views and cultures grow in fellowship and love, as Jews and Gentiles learned to do (Rom. 15.1–7).

Incarnational growth (Growing out into society, Acts 2.43, 47a):

ACTS 2.41-47b

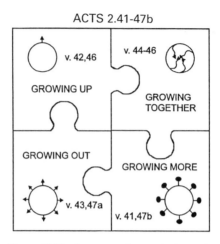

Figure 10 The four sorts of numerical growth.

Christians grow in service to the world by doing good, relieving need and changing society.

Numerical growth (Growing more in numbers, Acts 2.41, 47b): New Christians join the Church through evangelism—this growth in numbers has been the Church Growth Movement's main concern.

Ideally every local Church should have an equal concern for each of these four dimensions (see Figure 10 above), just as Jesus Himself grew in four distinct ways (see Luke 2.52). In practice, however, most Churches 'specialize' in some of them and neglect the others. One local Church in Kenya tried to get the balance right by planning the programme outlined on p. 72.

There are four sorts of numerical growth:
(a) Biological (B), when babies are born in Christian homes;
(b) Transfer (T), when people leave one church and join another;
(c) Restoration (R), when those who have lost faith regain it;
(d) Conversion (C), when people turn to Christ for the first time.

Only (c) and (d), Restoration and Conversion, represent real church growth in numbers. Figure 11 shows how two individual churches were affected by these four sorts of numerical growth.

Over a period of one year, the Church of the Holy Cross (Church A) lost three members through death, but gained four new members when church members had babies (Biological). Six

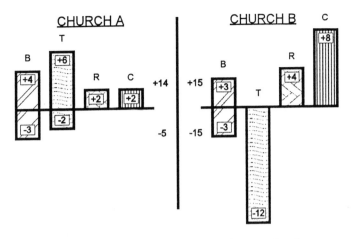

Figure 11 The effects of numerical growth on two churches.

people left other churches to join Holy Cross, but two members moved away to other places (Transfer). Two lapsed members came back into fellowship (Restoration) and two others joined after turning to Christ for the first time (Conversion).

In the nearby Zion Church of God (Church B), however, three members died and three new babies were born. Twelve people left the church to become active members elsewhere (there could be many possible reasons for this). Four lapsed members were restored and there were eight new converts. See Question 4 on p. 129.

FOUR STAGES OF CHURCH GROWTH

These stages are a way of describing the barriers the Church has to cross in its mission. They reflect Jesus' words in Acts 1.8, where He told his followers to take His message (a) to fellow-Jews in Jerusalem, (b) to the wider Jewish community, (c) to Samaritans who accepted just the first five books of the Bible; (d) to anyone and everyone throughout the world.

For Christians today the first stage would be 'Internal growth' i.e. evangelizing the baptized or church members, where there are no barriers except the barrier of personal commitment. The second stage would be 'Expansion growth', i.e. evangelizing local people who share our culture, where the chief barrier is the church door, or understanding what we are talking about. The third stage would be 'Extension growth', i.e. planting new churches in the same area but in different cultural backgrounds, e.g. one city church in Sao Paulo, Brazil, has brought hundreds of 'satellite' churches to birth in the shanty-towns round about. The fourth stage would be 'Bridging growth', i.e. crossing major barriers of culture, language and race, e.g. when Chinese reach out to their Malaysian neighbours in Singapore; when Kikuyu from Nairobi go to nomadic peoples in the northern deserts of Kenya; or when English Christians meet Pakistani immigrants in Bradford. Such meetings may not require distant travel, but they may need years of learning and preparation.

THE COMPLEXITY OF CHURCH GROWTH

When we ask what might help or hinder the Church, we always need to consider many different factors. Figure 12 opposite shows how almost every local Church is affected by factors like these. Some of the factors relate to the nature of the local or national society, and some relate to what Christians are like or how they behave. Other factors indicate spiritual issues, some of which may be good and some evil. Most of these factors come under one of the following headings:

1. *Local Church factors* These may include such problems as having no pastor for a time; immoral behaviour by a church official; or disunity in the Church.

2. *Local community factors* These may include problems such as persecution of the Church; or the presence in the locality of a large group who use a language unknown by the majority.

3. *National Church factors* These may include problems like a public statement by a Church leader questioning a basic article of the faith; or the withdrawal of financial support by a rich partner Church.

4. *National community factors* These may include the fall from power of rulers who promoted the Christian religion; the election of a Muslim President; or the national introduction of a new rural communal-farm policy.

5. *Demonic opposition* is a factor which cannot be easily observed like the first four factors, but it is often present in anti-Christian forces, and can even use Christian religious powers and institutions to oppose the true work of God. For examples, see pp. 132 and 142.

6. *The Holy Spirit* is the essential factor which enables the Church truly to grow as God wants it to. The Spirit makes the study of Church growth exciting and unpredictable, for He may do the

COMPLEXITY

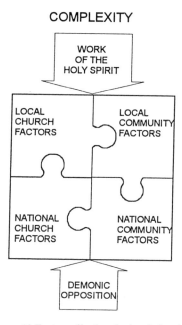

Figure 12 Factors affecting the local church.

complete opposite of what the experts expect. The Holy Spirit led Jesus into the desert to be tempted by Satan, and He led Him to Jerusalem to die at the hands of His enemies. These were both occasions when God's work *seemed* to be hindered but was in fact advanced. The following historical examples show that all the above 'problems' may actually help the Church rather than hinder it. It all depends on how the Spirit is at work.

Factor 1 Church leaders may quarrel and split apart—but the Church may benefit in the end (see Acts 15.39; and the story of Kimbangu on p. 131); or unknown lay people may overturn official church teaching under the Spirit's guidance (see Acts 11.20,21; and the start of the East African Revival in 1935 —see p. 143).

Factor 2 Bitter persecution may spread the Gospel (see Acts 8.1, 4; and the experience of Japan in 1580 when the persecuted and suffering Church went underground, and had grown to thousands of members by the year 1865 when churches were re-opened).

Factor 3 Lack of external funds and trained local leaders often makes a Church rely on the work of the Holy Spirit in all its people (see Acts 17.10 and 1 Thess. 1.4–10; and the way Madagascar Christians distributed hand-written Scriptures during the terrible persecution by Queen Ranavalona, with the result that the number of those who came out of hiding in 1861 was four times as many as those who went into hiding in 1835).

Factor 4 In one country a pagan president was replaced by a Christian one who loved to preach in churches on Sundays—but in time this Christian president proved to be corrupt, and although the Church grew in numbers it declined in morality and spirituality. In another country, Tanzania, pastors were at first dismayed when a 'communal-village' programme (Ujamaa) was imposed on the country in 1968, until they found that it made their work easier because people were all being moved into large central villages.

SEVEN AXIOMS OF CHURCH GROWTH

The Church Growth Movement sets out a number of axioms, or principles, which are to be followed if the Church is to grow. We should examine these carefully to see what lessons we can learn from them. Here are seven of these axioms:

1. *Accumulate*, i.e. numerical growth through evangelism. Evangelism should have the following four characteristics:

Presence (see 1 Cor. 9.19–23). Just as Jesus belonged to a particular place and time in His incarnation (see p. 68), so evangelists must become like the people to whom they are sent. They must listen to the agenda of those people, and relate the message of the Gospel to them. This is the foundation of all evangelism.

Proclamation (see 1 Cor. 2.2). The evangelist listens not only to the world, but also to God, and announces the message of what God has done in the context of the hearers. One of the chief tasks of evangelists is to get the right balance between presence and proclamation (see example on p. 64). This has been called 'double listening' and all evangelists need to do it.

Persuasion (see Rom. 1.5, 6). An essential part of the message of the first preachers was the call to respond by believing in Christ and also by joining His Church. Evangelism should therefore have visible results—but these are *results*. They are not evangelism itself, and they are not the aim of evangelism. The Church Growth Movement has been criticized for making membership of the Church the purpose of mission, when the purpose should be the rule of God in people's lives through Christ.

Power (see Rom. 15.19). The graces, gifts and signs of the Holy Spirit accompanied the first preaching of the Gospel. The Good News was supported by the fact that something was happening (see p. 156). Evangelists should expect clear signs from God in people's lives. These may include physical healing or speaking in tongues, or brotherly and sisterly love, or any other change which the Holy Spirit gives. See p. 165.

2. *Activate* All members of the Church should be involved in evangelism, but not all of them in the same way. Christians are not all called to be evangelists and they often need to be set free from thinking that they should be. They are, however, *all* called to be
  (a) Christ's representatives, who are present for Him in the world;
  (b) His witnesses, who are able to say what He has done for them and is doing in them.
Some people are called to be evangelists, i.e. advocates who argue for the Gospel and persuade people to respond. In a law court, witnesses are only allowed to testify to what they have seen and know—they are not allowed to go beyond that and say what they think. That is the job of the advocate, who needs to rely totally on the testimony of the witnesses. In the same way pastors and evangelists rely on the witness of all Christians to persuade people to follow Jesus.
A local church has a missionary outlook (or dimension, see p. 14) when
  (a) it welcomes outsiders and makes them feel at home;
  (b) it is more than just a group of people being cared for by the pastor;
  (c) its members are actively involved in local communities;
  (d) it is flexible enough to meet new needs and challenges;
  (e) it refuses to allow a small inner group to dictate what is done.
It is the task of all Christians to see that their Church is like this.
3. *Concentrate* A local Church should know who will probably respond to its message and take special care to be in touch with such people. In Britain it has been found that most people respond to the Gospel because of close personal friendships with Christians, not as a result of special evangelism programmes. These friendships make them ask why Christians are different. In India and Latin America people who suffer injustice often respond to a Church which is ready to support them. When people in Tanzania were moved to communal villages, many of them feared their unfamiliar surroundings, and were open to a new message from God. Chinese people want healing and freedom from evil spirits which wound both body and soul.
In general, times of change in personal circumstances (e.g. bereavement, marriage or the birth of a new baby) make people

ask fundamental questions about the meaning of life, and they are open to good news from God. But it is dangerous to think that we can calculate how near someone is to God. The work of the Holy Spirit in people's lives can be gradual or sudden, and this work often proves that our expectations were wrong.

4. *Separate or Integrate?* The Church Growth Movement says that people 'ought not to be expected to cross unnecessary cultural barriers to become Christians'. As a result of this principle, the Movement believes that local Churches should try to be 'homogeneous', i.e. all its members should come from one tribe or cultural group. If this happens, new Christians from that same group will be attracted to the Church but will not have to change their culture or behaviour too much. People from other cultural groups will then go to another Church which contains people from their own tribe or culture.

This principle has become very controversial. The following are some points in favour of it.

(a) People need to be able to worship in their own mother tongue, e.g. Welsh-speaking people in Wales.

(b) Christians need to recognize the value of their own God-given culture, and to have the self-confidence to develop their own authentic forms of Church life and worship without being 'corrected' by a dominant cultural group. (This was the reason why many Africans called for a 'moratorium', or temporary suspension, on foreign missions: see p. 150). Many Christian immigrants from the West Indies experienced domination by British culture when they came to Britain in the 1950s and were not welcomed in some British churches.

(c) Converts from other faiths, e.g. Islam or Judaism, may find it difficult to accept some aspects of Christian worship at first. They may need to worship in a separate group for a time until they can integrate.

On the other hand, there are strong arguments against separate groups, especially arguments from the New Testament. Jesus brought together people who were totally different (e.g. Simon the freedom fighter and Matthew the colonial tax-collector) and taught them to love one another. Ever since, His Church has been a fellowship of Jews and Gentiles, rich and poor, slave and free, male and female. This is not just an accident; it is part of the Gospel itself. The Good News is not a matter of individual forgiveness and salvation; the Good News is that Jews and Gentiles share together in the one Body of Christ (Eph. 3.6; see Rom. 3.29, 30). Only a Church which is in principle multi-cultural can be the Church of Jesus Christ—and unless people can see that the Church is like this,

The Church Growth Movement believes that local Churches, like this West Indian congregation in Britain, should be 'homogeneous', so that all its members belong to the same tribe or culture. Is this a good idea? What points are in its favour? In what ways could it create problems?

they cannot see the Good News. Therefore Churches of separate groups do *not* help people in their Christian discipleship and over a long period such Churches may actually hinder evangelism. We can only enjoy the variety of creation, which God has planned to enrich all of us, in mixed Churches. The opposite of this was seen in the apartheid system of South Africa.

5. *Investigate* Every local church must understand both itself and the community in which it lives. This is essential. One way of doing this is known as *Mission Audit*, which involves asking detailed questions about the sociology and world-view of the people around us, and asking similar questions about the Church. This helps us to discover how well the Church relates to its neighbourhood. Is it reaching all the people, or only a select group? Does it meet the real needs which people feel, or only the needs that the Church imagines they have? What do Church members think about the local people? What do local people think about the Church? How do the opinions of the local people and the opinions of the Church relate to each other?

One way of investigating these questions is to ask the people outside the Church. An American missionary in Indonesia found that he was not making any progress in reaching the local Muslims. So instead of telling them what he thought they needed and how Christ could meet those needs, he began to ask *them*. Their chief need, they said, was help to build a mosque for their area. His mission board in America may have felt rather alarmed to hear this, but nevertheless they did provide some funds for the new mosque, and the missionary himself started to help with the work of bricklaying. As he did so, he made new and close friendships. After a time of working together, the mosque was finished; but by that time there was also a group of Muslims meeting with a few Christians to study the Bible together. This could never have happened if the missionary had not been ready to investigate, and to act on the results of his investigation.

However, we must remember that the Church needs to grow not only in numbers but in all its dimensions. An excellent Mission Audit was done recently of society and the Church in Singapore. Unfortunately, it only suggested changes which would lead to numerical growth. For this reason, the audit decided that educational and ecumenical work was a waste of time and money (although they represent growth in incarnation and fellowship). To spend money on beautiful new sanctuaries, on the other hand, was worthwhile because these attract larger numbers of people. For a model for Mission Audit, see Special Note G.

6. *Evaluate* All Churches should set themselves an aim and

Figure 13 Specific goals all serve the general aim.

specific goals. The aim might be to glorify Christ as Lord, or to co-operate with what God is doing in building His kingdom—the aim should be general (perhaps even rather vague), and it should focus on God rather than on the Church. But it should be kept clearly in view. Then specific goals (or targets) should be set, which all serve the general aim.

Goals should be specific in five ways (Figure 13). They should be:

(a) *relevant* to the situation, e.g. do not aim to develop the Sunday School if there are no children in the area;

(b) *measurable* in amount and in time, so that you can tell when they have been achieved; e.g. not 'The choir to sing more relevant songs' but 'The choir to teach the congregation six new songs of worship every month for six months';

(c) *achievable*, so that people do not get discouraged by failing to achieve unrealistic goals; e.g. 'Form a group to pay regular visits to lonely old people in the neighbourhood', rather than 'Set up a job scheme to get rid of unemployment in the area';

(d) *significant* rather than trivial; e.g. 'Create prayer triplets of three people praying together as partners' rather than 'Buy our minister a new preaching gown';

(e) *corporately agreed* by the whole Church, not the personal wish of one particular individual.

This Tanzanian football team has achieved its aim of winning the cup, and in order to do so the players had to achieve many goals. 'All Churches should set themselves an aim and specific goals' (p. 121). What are your local Church's goals?

However, all goals must be provisional or temporary, so that the Holy Spirit has the freedom to alter them. Karl Barth said that missionaries must be humble: we cannot know the true purpose of mission, because it is known only to the Lord of the Church. He alone knows people's real needs, and our work is futile human activity unless God makes our work part of what He is doing. Many missionaries accused Barth of paralysing the work of mission. In his reply, Barth referred to Jacob who was struck on the hip by the Angel of the Lord and limped ever after, and so, for the first time, became a man God could use. 'Perhaps', said Barth, 'only a similar paralysing blow would make mission weak enough to be used effectively in God's hands.'

This does not mean that we should not set goals. We should be like sailors setting out in their boat. They hoist the sail and set the rigging, they point the front of the boat, the bows, in the right direction—but then they wait, entirely dependent on the wind and the current they are given. The Church, too, must move forward, but it must always be sensitive to the wind of the Spirit to correct its course and alter direction towards God's will. But if we fail to plan, then we plan to fail.

7. *Educate* The Church Growth Movement says that Churches should aim at making disciples (i.e. learners) of Jesus Christ as Lord, not perfect Christians. The process of 'perfecting' (i.e. changing one's way of life according to Christ's will) comes later. This also is a controversial matter.

Those who criticize this view say that the Church Growth Movement is so keen for new people to join the Church that it invites them to come to Jesus on easy terms, i.e. it offers 'cheap grace' (grace which does not cost very much), because it says little about the cost of following Christ. It does not tell new Christians that the Gospel demands a commitment to justice and morality, especially in the big issues of racism and economic and political exploitation which face the world today.

People who defend the view of the Church Growth Movement answer that the Gospel is a free gift from God. It is not offered only to those people who succeed in reaching a certain standard of justice and morality—that would be salvation by works, and it would ask people to pay too much for the Gospel, making grace 'over-expensive' (i.e. costing too much). In any case, the Sender of the Gospel cannot possibly know in advance what sort of morality and justice God will require of the Receptor, especially if his or her culture is different from that of the Sender. Only the Receptors can discover that, when together they reach a better understanding of

God's Word under the guidance of God's Spirit in their own context, as Roland Allen showed (see pp. 87 and 96).

There is something to be said in favour of both the above points of view. But both represent extreme viewpoints. The right way lies somewhere in between. It is certainly true that people should not get surprises about ethical issues after they become Christians, which they might if they are offered 'cheap grace'. But neither is it possible to tell people in advance everything which the Lord might require of them in their future discipleship. The important point is that the Church which proclaims the Gospel of grace also demonstrates *by its own life* the principles of justice and morality. The people can see this even before they turn to Christ. Justice and morality do not have to be explained in detail because they are active and visible in the life of the Church. They cannot be avoided. If they are, then a false gospel is being proclaimed, and the grace being offered is 'incredible grace', because it is irrelevant to the context and questions of people's lives.

EVALUATION

The Church Growth Movement has shown the value for mission of listening and understanding before speaking. They have thought out principles of mission and presented them clearly. They help us to think even in areas where we disagree with them. Their use of the science of management techniques which have been developed in the USA can be very helpful to those Churches which may have spent more time on developing spirituality or theology, and little time on organization.

However, the Movement has relied too much on human management skills, and not enough on theology or history which show us that God's work does not usually follow expected or predictable patterns. 'Church Growth' has failed to ask probing questions like 'What is growth?' and 'What is the Church?' It has too often assumed that growth is growth in numbers, and has not said enough about the other dimensions of growth.

The Church Growth Movement also assumes that 'evangelical' Churches ought to grow and, indeed, should 'leapfrog' over other local Churches which are not evangelizing. But clearly many evangelical Churches ought not to grow. No oppressive system (e.g. apartheid evangelical Churches in South Africa) should prosper until it has enthroned justice in its own house. The Catholic Church, on the other hand, was a God-given sign of hope amongst the oppressed people in Communist Poland for many decades. In China the Church opposed the Communists until they took power in 1948 and expelled all foreign missions. At that time there were just over four million Chinese Christians (both Roman Catholic and Protestant). Later on, in the Cultural Revolution of the 1960s, the churches were all closed. But now it is known that all this time the Church was growing rapidly among the people, and today it is said that 15,000 new people become Christians every day (although all statistics about China can only be rough estimates). In 1995, there are probably about sixteen million Chinese Christians. We have to say that Chairman Mao Zedong—though he certainly did not intend to—conferred a great favour on the Church by persecuting it, because it is now a truly indigenous Chinese Church. The return of large numbers of foreign missionaries to China would be the greatest calamity which could happen to the Chinese Church. But those who follow the principles of Church Growth are perplexed by such actions by the Spirit of God, because they cannot be fitted into any known human management scheme.

Special Note D

STRUCTURE AND COMMUNITAS

The Christian Church is both a human organization with its own plans and traditions, and also a living organism in which the Holy Spirit lives and works. Most Christians experience the Church in both these ways. The first, the human organization, has been called 'Structure', the second, the living organism, has been called 'Communitas' (a Latin word which means 'community').

Human beings need structure in all parts of their lives. It is a gift from God, and we can see it in governments and in every orderly part of society. Within this structure, certain people are given leadership and authority for the good of everybody. Structure helps us to continue past traditions so that we feel secure and 'know where we are' (see p. 82). It protects us against change which might disturb us.

But human beings sometimes want to break free of the structure and to get involved in the action, to make decisions, and express their hopes and opinions. They want to show that it is not only politicians who are important but also ordinary people. They want to have their say, and to show in reality that they are all equal and united. This deep desire for communitas is also a gift from God.

We can see the tension between these two God-given instincts in all human societies and in the Church. Perhaps the revolutionary

For many years foreign missionaries were forbidden to enter China, but the Chinese Church went underground and, like this congregation, grew without their help. What important point does this make about the work of Christian mission?

peasant movement of Mao Zedong in China against the Kuomin-
tang government showed this tension. Certainly the rise of African
prophets showed it (see p. 136). They brought a message direct
from God to set the people free from enemies that the structure was
powerless to defeat.

In the Bible, the people welcomed the Schools or groups of the
Prophets when they challenged the corrupt structure of kings and
priests of Israel. In the time of Jesus, structure was seen in the Law
and the Temple, and it was threatened by the Zealot freedom-
fighters and also by the alternative community life of the Essenes.
At first sight, it seems that Jesus also threatened to overthrow
structure. In fact, He did not want to abandon the structure, but
only to reinterpret it in terms of the new 'temple of His body' (John
2.21; see Acts 15.16) or the new people of God (1 Pet. 2.4–10) or
sacrifice (Mark 14.24) or the new Law (Matt. 5.1, 17–20).

At first, the Gentile mission appeared to be in conflict with what
God had revealed to His people in the Law (Acts 15.1, 2). Paul's
mission to the Gentiles challenged the Church at Antioch and
Jerusalem (Acts 14.27; Rom. 15.25–31); and the gifts of the Spirit
experienced by ordinary Christians in Corinth challenged Paul
himself (1 Cor. 12–14). In all these ways communitas disturbed and
challenged structure. This has continued to happen throughout the
history of the Church, as the following examples show.

Movements of communitas often appear as renewal or revival in
the power of the Spirit. But they are often not welcomed in their
early stages. They come from *below*, challenging those above who
have authority and leadership; they are structurally powerless, but
spiritually powerful—and they attract many followers. Movements
of communitas usually come from *within* a particular culture. They
both reflect that culture (they are relevant) and they challenge it
(they want it to change) because they meet the deeply felt needs of
the people. Many examples of it are mentioned in this Guide (e.g.
Special Note F; chapters 12, 13, 15).

The charismatic movement emerged as communitas confronting
structure (see p. 151). When this movement first reached England,
those who welcomed it were expelled from Churches, institutions
and even missionary agencies. The charismatic movement was
attacked as heretical. At that time it was not clear whether its
followers would leave the mainline denominations (as John Wesley
had been forced to leave the Church of England in the eighteenth
century) or stay within them. For the most part, charismatic
Christians have stayed within the structures and in the end changed
them. After a few years, charismatics were accepted because of the

STRUCTURE ⟵⟶ SPIRIT

Figure 14 The charismatic movement as communitas confronting structure.

new spiritual life they brought to the old structures—but only after a lot of argument and suffering!

Every Church is 'structure'—but is it also alert to those spontaneous movements of the Spirit which at first seem to criticize and threaten the Church but which actually offer renewal and hope? Will the Church welcome them? Will it even recognize them? Will the Church surrender some of its power to the Spirit? (see Figure 14).

But there is also a challenge to 'communitas' people. Do they realize that (because they are human) they will soon create new structures within their own movements, and may even use—and transform—the old structures which they are challenging? Are they going to separate themselves from the old structure and become (as they imagine) 'First-Class Christians', or will they patiently invite the whole Church to come along with them on the path to new life? The examples in this Guide mention some who were forced out (e.g. Simon Kimbangu, p. 132) and some who stayed in (Edmund John, p. 147; the East African Revival, p. 143). Jesus stayed in, and even submitted to the structures—and by doing this he transformed them completely! Paul went first to the structure (synagogues) and he was accountable to the Church in Antioch (Acts 13) and to other Churches (Rom. 15.24), as the evangelists were accountable to the Church at Jerusalem in Acts 8 and 10.

Almost always 'communitas' comes to us as something strange. It will probably not be the same as renewal movements we have known in the past, and our first instinct will be to reject it. But if we do so, we may be in danger of rejecting the Holy Spirit who wants to lead His Church into new places of wonder and power.

STUDY SUGGESTIONS

WORD STUDY
1. Give the meaning of the following words:
   (a) homogeneous
   (b) cheap grace
   (c) structure
   (d) communitas.

CONTEXTUAL APPLICATION
2. What sorts of growth might *not* be God's will for your Church?
3. (a) How do the four dimensions of growth correspond to the four ways in which Jesus grew (p. 112)?
   (b) How do the four dimensions relate to the three circles on p. 63?
   (c) In which of these four dimensions is your Church strongest? In which dimensions is it weakest? Give specific examples.
4. In the diagram on p. 113, which Church seems to be (a) growing more, (b) more healthy? Give reasons for your answer.
5. What barriers in mission is your Church crossing?
6. In what ways might each of the 'problems' mentioned on p. 114 actually turn out to be for the good of a local Church?
7. (a) A 'P' which is not mentioned on p. 116 is Prayer: what do you think is the importance of prayer in evangelism?
   (b) At what point do you think 'Power' fits into the logical sequence Presence-Proclamation-Persuasion?
   (c) What signs would you expect to see accompanying evangelism? What signs have you seen?
8. How missionary is your Church when tested against the five signs on p. 117?
9. What sort of people are specially open to the Gospel where you live?
10. Do you think local Churches should be homogeneous or culturally mixed? Give reasons for your answer.
11. Compare the usefulness of the goals of the five-year plan on pp. 72–74 with the guidelines given on p. 121. Do the goals of the five-year plan fulfil these guidelines?

12. What specific goals does your Church have?
13. Compare Barth's teaching (p. 123) with the theology of Mark (p. 32). What sort of weakness can be an asset in mission?
14. How do you think the Church can avoid offering either 'cheap' or 'expensive' grace when, for example, it gives baptism to (a) a polygamist (b) a homosexual, and (c) a rich businessman?
15. Which elements within your Church are structure and which are communitas? Are they in conflict? How can this conflict result in genuine Church growth in its different dimensions?
16. How do the questions on p. 128 challenge your Church?
17. Imagine that you live in a district where there are many Muslims who have made friends with many of your Church members. What features of your Church might be difficult for Muslims to accept? Which are most likely to be effective in reaching these Muslims: elements of structure or elements of communitas?

10. Africa: Indigenous Churches

All over Africa large numbers of independent or 'indigenous' Churches have grown up. Many of these Churches were born and developed *independently* of those Churches founded by missions from outside the country (though they have often been influenced by them). The independent Churches are also indigenous because their life and faith is *indigenous* to local African culture and philosophy. In this chapter we look at one of these Churches, and see what missiological lessons we can learn from it.

SIMON KIMBANGU

One night in 1918, at the village of N'kamba in Lower Congo (now Zaire), in the middle of a flu epidemic in which thousands of people were dying, the word of God came to Simon Kimbangu, saying, 'I am Christ; my servants are unfaithful. I have chosen you to bear witness before your brothers and to convert them. Tend my flock.' Simon tried to make excuses, saying that he had no training, but the voice spoke to him night after night. He ran away to the capital, Kinshasa, but he had no success in the jobs he tried, he could not escape the voice, and he finally returned home to continue cultivating his fields.

On the morning of 6th April 1921, on the way to market, Simon Kimbangu felt compelled to enter the house of a sick woman and lay hands upon her in the name of Jesus. She was instantly healed. At first Simon was accused of being a magician, but after several more healings, thousands of people left their work—and their Churches—and flocked to him in a great revival movement. His preaching was as powerful as his healings, and his followers repented and gave up fetishism and polygamy, they turned to Christ and pledged themselves to obey His word. Dead children were restored to life, the deaf heard, cripples walked and the blind regained their sight when they washed in the sacred spring at N'kamba. The people thought that Pentecost had come again.

Simon had no desire for this ministry, but he had no choice. He had been brought up as a Baptist and had worked as a teacher-evangelist in the Baptist Mission, where he had married. To the end of his life, he taught morality, love for your enemies and obedience to authorities. His whole ministry was the fruit of missionary labours and the translation of the Bible, but he had been anointed by the Holy Spirit to be the black Apostle for the Congolese. 'We have found the God of the blacks', the Congolese said, 'the religion which suits Africans.'

The white settlers (who were losing their servants) and the Catholics and Baptists (who were losing their congregations) opposed Kimbangu, on the false grounds that he was a political threat to whites. The authorities tried twice to arrest him, but Simon's followers, the Kimbanguists, responded by speaking in tongues and singing hymns all night. Finally, on June 6th, only two months after the first healing, Kimbangu went into hiding. But in September God said to him, 'Go to N'kamba and give yourself up'. He was arrested there, but he warned his followers not to use violence and to face suffering courageously. The only people who used guns were the soldiers. Kimbangu was treated cruelly and sentenced by a military court to 120 lashes and death. The sentence of death was later reduced to life imprisonment by King Albert of the Belgians at the request of Baptist missionaries. After giving his wife and sons a final blessing, Kimbangu was taken to Lubumbashi, thousands of kilometres away. He never saw his family again, and the Belgian authorities completely destroyed N'kamba. He received few visitors, and was usually kept in solitary confinement. He was a model prisoner, and the governor recommended his release, but this was opposed by the settlers and the Catholic archbishop. He died on 12th October 1951. Nobody bothered to inform the family of his death, but Simon appeared in a vision to his son, Joseph Diangienda, saying, 'I now live with God in heaven'. When Joseph asked the Belgians, they confirmed that Simon had in fact died a few days before.

SONGS OF SUFFERING

Music and singing are especially important both in the history and in the present life of the Kimbanguist Church. Their hymns are prayers which relate to their situation. Here are the words of two hymns used in the early days of the Church (1922–1925):

> Come, Jesus, our Redeemer, come with thy power!
> We have run into difficulty.
> With thy Name 'Jesus' help us, help us.
> The enemy is persecuting us.
> We are resisting him with our prayers
> In which we ask for thine aid.
> The devil is persecuting us all the time,
> But when he sees thee he will flee.
> When Satan surrounds us do snatch us from his hands!

In times past we did not know thee, Jesus,
We did not know thee in our hearts.
Today we know thee; let no evil befall us.
All our evangelists have been deported
For the sake of Jesus' Name.
We shall do our utmost so that they will let us alone.
Jesus, come help us
If we must go into the Upper Congo [i.e. into exile].
Jesus, thou wert the first to go,
We are following thee.

*   *   *

God has created the heavens and the earth,
None is mightier than he.
God will end the conflict of these days.
Come quickly, let us pray; we are following thee.
Someone wants to inflict evil on us.
Our God, Jesus, our Brother, Jesus, snatch us from misery.
Come, Jesus, help us here on earth;
We are listening to thee.
For our enemies we are performing all the labour
They demand of us,
But they do not see the truth about our cause.
Our Father and Mother, we are obedient.
If conflict arises, then we shall resist with our prayers.
Jesus was a prisoner, Jesus was smitten;
They are smiting us, too.
We, the blacks, are prisoners, the whites are free.
The enemy has snatched from us the Staff [Simon Kimbangu].
All kinds of suffering befall us.
We are afflicted, our tears flow.
Come, help us, Holy Spirit, come, come, help us!
We are all following thee.
Blacks and whites are praying,
And we do not know the day of thy return.

THE KIMBANGUIST CHURCH

The full name of the Kimbanguist Church is 'The Church of Jesus
Christ on earth through the Prophet Simon Kimbangu'. Kimbangu
does not take the place of either Jesus or the Holy Spirit, though
some of the sects which have developed out of the Kimbanguist
Church claim that he does. The Kimbanguists feel, however, that
Christ relived His earthly life through Simon, and that Simon
received the Holy Spirit and was the Spirit's tool (and even possibly

the Spirit's manifestation). After his death his followers felt that he could present people's prayers to Jesus in heaven. N'Kamba is still seen as the New Jerusalem where people come for healing.

After Kimbangu's arrest, the Belgians tried to suppress the Kimbanguist movement by deporting his followers to camps scattered all over the country. This ensured only that the movement spread to the whole nation, at Belgian expense! Evangelism, healings and prayer took place everywhere, and new hymns to traditional music were composed and sung. But in 1925 the movement had to go underground, and its members joined other denominations. In the 1930s, people who were known to be Kimbanguists were forced to move from their homes every two years. From 1947, Joseph Diangienda (though outwardly a Catholic and holding high government office) tried to encourage the small, secret groups of Kimbanguists. From 1951, they began to claim their 'human rights' under the United Nations charter. In 1957 they were still persecuted by the government and denounced by other Christians, but a huge number of them gathered in the Kinshasa football stadium. Joseph stayed in his car to pray while a delegation presented a petition to the Governor-General saying, 'We are always suffering . . . so in order not to burden the police too much, we are all in the stadium, unarmed, where you can arrest us or shoot us all.' That day they were granted religious freedom after 36 years of persecution. Two years later the Kimbanguist Church was officially recognized and joined the World Council of Churches. Today it is the largest indigenous African Church, with more than five million adherents in Congo, Angola and Zambia as well as Zaire.

In all Kimbanguist congregations, water from N'kamba is kept to consecrate people and things, and especially to heal. But baptism is not practised. The first celebration of the Lord's Supper took place in Kinshasa on 6th April 1971, the fiftieth anniversary of Simon's first healing. Bread was baked from a mixture of maize, potatoes and bananas, and honey was used for wine. The Lord's Supper is celebrated three times a year, 'so that it does not become a mere habit'. Prayer for healing is common, but only a few ministers are officially allowed to lay hands on the sick. The Bible and the singing of songs have a central place in all worship. The Church owns large farms and it has extensive programmes of social service. It encourages self-reliance through generous giving and in its modern seminary produces some of the best-educated clergy in Africa.

Although the Kimbanguist Church's culture is African, the key to its life is the biblical tradition of Christ. This is not the case with the sects, the 'Ngunzist' (or prophetist) movements which arose in

Like Simon Kimbangu, William Wade Harris of Liberia was a prophet who inspired new Churches. He is shown here carrying the bamboo cross and other symbolic objects with which he performed healings and exorcisms. Why were prophets like Kimbangu and Harris so successful in bringing Africans to Christ?

imitation of the Kimbanguist Church. Many of these said little about Christ, but replaced Him by Kimbangu. They gave special honours to their leaders, and publicized sensational miracles. The leaders of the Kimbanguist Church reject and dissociate themselves from the Ngunzist movements. For them Kimbangu does not replace Christ, he reflects Him.

THE INDIGENOUS MOVEMENT

Kimbangu was not an unusual phenomenon in Africa, and prophets like him were not only found within the Christian Church. For many years all over Africa people have believed that prophets sent by God have delivered them from major threats to the life and stability of the tribe. The threat to the tribe may be natural disasters like drought, local tribes or other invaders, or spirit-powers; whatever the threat, at such times people turn to the Creator God and He sends His messenger. Such a messenger emerged in Southern Tanzania in 1904 when the people were oppressed by the German colonialists. Kinjikitile came with magic water (*maji* in Swahili) which, he claimed, would turn German bullets to water. The people turned to him and swept the Germans out of the area in a planned movement of local unity called the Maji-Maji Rebellion, until they were finally defeated by superior fire-power.

God seems to have used the generally accepted African phenomenon of traditional prophets to interpret the Gospel to Africans in an authentic African way. When these prophets founded new Churches it was usually by accident. William Wade Harris of Liberia, for example, was a Methodist who at the age of 45, while in prison in 1910, had a vision of God calling him to be His prophet to West Africa. Dressed in a white turban and robe, and carrying a bamboo cross and a Bible, he travelled all over the Ivory Coast, urging people to abandon their fetishes and follow Christ. He scorned the power of demons, and healed many people through the symbolism of his cross and Bible. After two years Harris was expelled from the Ivory Coast, but new Churches were springing up. These new Churches were often led by former leaders of traditional religion, so the pattern of life in the villages did not change. When Methodist missionaries arrived ten years later, they were immediately able to enrol twenty-five thousand catechumens! Harris defended polygamy and preferred to reform African tradition rather than abolish it. Some of his followers began the Harrist Church, but many became Methodists.

In 1970 African Indigenous Churches (or AICs) had fifteen million members in six thousand denominations, but that figure grows by a million every year. The estimated figure for 1994 was fifty million members, or sixteen per cent of the population of Africa. Zaire alone had five hundred independent Churches in 1970, when the law required all of them to register as one denomination. Many of the Churches in Zaire were not accepted for registration and they remain independent and unregistered. The largest number of indigenous Churches is in South Africa (where whites are most dominant). In 1970 South Africa had three thousand denominations, with four million members. By 1992 there were an estimated five thousand different AICs in South Africa, representing about thirty-five per cent of the black population. The largest is the Zion Christian Church, with two million members.

The indigenous Churches within South Africa fall into two main groups: the 'Ethiopians' who broke away from the mission Churches but retained their doctrine and organization, and the 'Zionists' who sprang up spontaneously with charismatic black leadership. The Zionists have joyful, informal worship in which everyone can take part. They emphasize the healing ministry and are generally not involved in politics. The mission Churches often criticize them for this, and for allowing polygamy and wanting to worship ancestral spirits; but much of this criticism is not well founded (see e.g. p. 131).

The Aladura Churches of Nigeria emphasize prayer; the African Independent Pentecostal Church (Kenya) emphasizes the restoration of African customs like circumcision and polygamy. Other indigenous Churches emphasize healing and the return of Jesus. Almost all of them emphasize the Holy Spirit, oppose witchcraft, and pray on all occasions, because of their awareness of the presence of God.

Other local prophets and indigenous Churches seem to have received a genuine revelation from God but do not focus their faith and life on Jesus Christ (see p. 211, for example). Some of these Churches focus on law, sacrifice, or the requirements of external ceremonial. They find the Old Testament more relevant to their culture than the New Testament. We can share their joy in the grace that God has given them—but we also need to help them to recognize Jesus as the centre of their new life.

REASONS FOR THE GROWTH OF INDIGENOUS CHURCHES

The Belgian officer who arrested Kimbangu wrote,

Everyone can readily see that the religions of Europe are completely shot through with abstractions and in no way corres-

This African Indigenous Church baptism is taking place in the Indian Ocean on the coast of Mozambique. What can the Churches founded by missionaries learn from the AIC?

pond to the mentality of the African, who longs for tangible facts
and protection. The teaching of Kimbangu suits him because it is
supported by palpable facts . . . It is therefore necessary to
oppose Kimbangu since he has a tendency towards pan-
Africanism.

We do not need to revise this opinion, even though the officer
meant to criticize Kimbangu. We today would understand these
words as praise. Missions were often guilty of a 'failure to love'.
This does not mean that they supported colonialism; often they did
not. It does not mean that they lacked compassion; they wanted to
improve the condition of Africans, and many missionaries gave
their lives for this cause. It does not mean that they despised
Africans; on the contrary, they translated the Bible into African
languages, so that Africans could discover not only the Good News
about Christ but also the Good News that human beings are made
in the image of God and possess dignity and worth in His sight. The
missionaries failed, however, in four ways:

1. They did not listen to Africans. Therefore they often failed to
relate the Good News to African issues such as witchcraft, spirits,
ancestors, land and community. They also failed to bring the
holistic deliverance from evil which Africans longed for. Most
missionaries were not sure how to deal with African spirit-powers,
and they were nervous of calling on the Holy Spirit to conquer evil
powers. Some possible reasons for their fear are given on p. 163.

2. The missionaries did not realize that the Bible they had
brought would judge their culture just as it judged African culture.
It offered Africans a new independent standard by which they
could evaluate all cultures, especially when the Bible was translated
into their own languages.

3. The missionaries could not see that, just as Jesus did not
abolish the Law and the Prophets but fulfilled them, He could in the
same way also fulfil African tradition, and could be worshipped in
terms of African culture.

4. The missionaries competed with one another, and thus
threatened African tribal life with conflict and instability. For
example, Moshoeshoe, King of the Sotho people, asked the
Roman Catholics, the Anglicans and the Paris Evangelical Missionary Society to baptize him. When they told him he must choose
between them, he refused, and warned his son against the conflicts
of the 'peace-bringing' missions. About twenty years later, in 1885,
a child called Matita was born and, after a series of miraculous
events, became a prophet. At first Matita urged his converts to join
the mission Churches, but he was finally persuaded to found the

Moshoeshoe Church of Lesotho, which has now become an Associate Member of the Lesotho Council of Churches.

The indigenous Churches now have so much life and spiritual power that much of the continuing evangelism of the African continent is in their hands. Archbishop Milingo, of the Zambian Catholic Church, believes that the Churches founded by missionaries need to learn from them. He criticizes people who go to Church to pray for the 'decent' problems, while the Church has no time for the real problems. Many Christians still go to the traditional witchdoctor to get help with these problems, and they will continue to do this until the priests learn to deal with questions which are outside the teaching they received in their merely academic studies. Professor Ali Mazrui says that in Africa 'Christianity has to adapt— or perish'. If wholeness comes from God, why does the Church not offer it? Milingo himself has learned to exorcise evil spirits and to minister healing in response to prayer; but the Catholic Church transferred him to Rome because he encouraged these practices.

The indigenous Churches also face the challenge of adapting. They need to adapt to city life and to modern culture in order to survive (see pp. 149 and 153). The newer African Pentecostal Churches have been able to do this, but they still continue to pray for power over spirits, sickness, unemployment, failures, family breakdown, etc.

STUDY SUGGESTIONS

WORD STUDY

1. What do we mean when we call African Churches
   (a) independent
   (b) indigenous?

CONTEXTUAL APPLICATION

2. Do you know any Churches which are 'independent' of the main denominations? What are their chief characteristics? Why are they independent?
3. Why did Kimbanguism spread so rapidly?
4. If the indigenous Churches arose because the missions partly failed, should we thank God for that failure? What failures in the Bible brought great blessing to people?
5. Music and song are important in much spiritual renewal in Africa. How important is Christian music in your area and how indigenous is it? (For example, does it use traditional tunes?)
6. God used local prophets to do His work in Africa. What other

examples do you know of God using a common feature of human life to bring blessing to people?

7. What evidence of (a) power, and (b) weakness do you see in the indigenous Churches?

8. Do people get help in the Church with the 'real' problems of life? If they do, give examples; if they do not, where do they seek and get such help?

9. 'Churches founded by missionaries need to learn from the indigenous Churches' (p. 140).
   (a) What can they learn?
   (b) What can the indigenous Churches learn from the Churches founded by missionaries?

10. 'Adapt or perish' (p. 140). How does this challenge the Church you belong to?

11. Africa: Movements of Renewal

Chapter 10 showed that the normal experience of African Indigenous Churches has been either to leave the mainline mission Churches or to be expelled from them. Other movements of the Holy Spirit, however, have succeeded in remaining within the mission Churches, often after a long period of debate and conflict. See Special Note D, 'Structure and Communitas'. We now consider some examples of this.

REVIVAL IN EAST AFRICA

In 1934 the Anglican Church in Uganda and Rwanda had lost its vitality. The spontaneous worship of the early days had died away. It was difficult to realize that this Church had a noble tradition of martyrdom and joy in the face of persecution. Now it was chiefly school children who attended Church. Missionaries had lost their enthusiasm, relationships were bad and materialism, racism and immorality were appearing. At Gahini, in April 1935, the students at the Evangelists' Training School went on strike and some of them packed up and left. One of the teachers, Blasio Kigozi, was so worried by his powerlessness to remedy the situation that he disappeared into his house, excused himself from activities and spent two weeks alone reading the Bible and asking God for power.

When Blasio emerged from his house, he was a changed man. He first asked his wife to forgive him for things he had done wrong at home, and he began to urge other people to repent. He wrote:

> In the past people felt remorse for sin—like Judas, who went and hanged himself. But there is another word, 'repentance'—like the prodigal son who repented of sin openly and turned his back on it . . . My old teachers never emphasized strongly enough the need to be 'born again'.

The first effect of this teaching was widespread spiritual opposition. Bitter accusations were brought against Blasio and his teaching about 'being saved', but he did not seem worried or angry or even defensive. He just smiled and seemed able to love his worst enemies. At a Church Council meeting, two elders stood up to accuse him—but they found themselves confessing their sins instead. Praise meetings went on all night and there were dreams and tremblings of a pentecostal kind. Missionaries were astonished; some of them thought that paganism was invading the Church; others testified later that they were converted at that time.

Revival teams travelled all over East Africa. One team visited a school at Katoke, in Tanzania. The staff and pupils were not very interested until two senior boys confessed that they had stolen money. Many other confessions followed and pentecostal meetings took place day and night with speaking in tongues and deep emotion. The Principal, an Australian missionary, tried to organize a formal service of evening prayer, but he was denounced as 'Satan'. The Bishop ordered the boys to say the Litany every day in order to quieten things down. The Principal later said that he was converted to Christ through the visit of this team.

The Revival has been going on for nearly sixty years, although there have been some setbacks from time to time. In all that time it has been the main source of spiritual life in the Protestant Churches of East Africa. The following were the main features of the Revival.

1. It reflected the priorities of local culture, especially in the area of community and relationships.

2. It challenged other aspects of that culture, e.g. people did not want to lose face and so they would not admit their failures.

3. It translated words of good news into concrete action. One of the most startling features of the Revival was the way in which people began to confess dishonest actions committed many years ago, which could never have been discovered. Those who confessed insisted on making restitution to their employers, even when these were big, profit-making companies or the colonial government! It shook society; thousands of people were challenged and 'saved' through such witness. Everybody knew that if you needed an honest person to look after large sums of money, you should appoint one of the 'Balokole' ('the saved ones').

4. The leaders of the Revival were not the clergy but the laity. Often the leaders had no education, and often they were women. Decisions were not taken by vote but by consensus; and any problem (e.g. seeking a marriage partner, a car or a cow) was brought to the leaders of the fellowship for their advice.

5. The worship had a clear pattern but, unlike in church, everyone contributed and it was all relevant to life and full of praise.

6. Judged by the standards of the missionaries, administration seemed chaotic. However, the Revival organized conventions which were attended by three times as many people as attended meetings organized by the missions, and money problems were rare, even though the followers of the Revival thought it was 'unspiritual' to keep accounts!

7. The most important thing of all was to 'walk in the light' with

This cross marks the site of the first Anglican mission in Malawi, which was a complete failure. Why was the Revival in East Africa so successful? In the light of the recent history of Rwanda, did the Revival also fail in what it tried to achieve?

one another. The late Bishop Festo Kivengere tells how this worked out early in his life:

> The Holy Spirit reminded me that I hated a white man, but since he lived fifty miles away, that did not seem to matter. But the Spirit said to me, 'Go on your bicycle to see this man: now he is your brother.'
>
> 'My brother? An Englishman?' I nearly fell over.
>
> 'Yes, your brother. You have hated your brother.'
>
> 'What shall I do when I see him? You know him, Lord.'
>
> 'Yes, I know him. Tell him that you love him.'
>
> That fifty miles had never seemed so hard. The rivers seemed much wider and the hills much steeper than they had ever been before. Approaching the house, I was tired and frightened, and hoped he was not at home. But he was, and suddenly I was standing in his proper English living room telling him what Christ had done for me, and that now I was his brother, having been saying bad things about him for years.
>
> 'Please forgive me'. I said.
>
> English though he was, there were tears in his eyes, and we hugged each other. On the way home, my bicycle flew as though it had a motor on it. My world was different, and in that house there was no longer a lonely 'European' but a brother—a true brother to this day.

The Revival changed Festo Kivengere and countless others. It changed the Church. It changed East Africa. (But see Appendix on p. 234.)

RENEWAL IN ZULULAND

The great missiologist Roland Allen said that you could tell when a local Church was truly indigenous, i.e. rooted in its local culture, because the Holy Spirit was at work within it bringing about 'a new discovery of new aspects of the Gospel and a new unfolding of new forms of Christian life' (see p. 87). One area where this happened about fifty years ago is the Anglican diocese of Zululand in South Africa. In 1944 two young Zulu priests, Alphaeus Zulu and Philip James Mbatha, realized that their Churches were lifeless and that they were powerless to revive them. Together they gave themselves to prayer—for three years, until the Church began to change. This is how Bishop Lawrence Zulu recalled what happened.

> Today we have a movement called Iviyo Lofakazi Baka Kristu, 'The Legion of Christ's Witnesses', which began when some of

145

our parish clergy were tearing their hair out trying to see what to do with people who took seriously the challenge to repent, and the clergy found they had nothing to direct them to, once they had given up the life that was outside of Christ and had turned to Christ. Then they stumbled upon a rule of life of the Fraternity of the Resurrection, which is related to the Mirfield Fathers. They found that they could adapt the rule of life which the Fraternity members were using, and out of that emerged certain disciplines which people would pledge themselves to uphold, such as being in Church to worship on Sundays and on major festivals of the Church, saying their prayers regularly, preferably daily—and well beyond just family prayers—each one praying by themselves, observing the standards of Christian sexual purity, giving generously for the work of the Church, trying to win at least one person a year for Christ, and a few other things of that kind.

Now when these people began to meet regularly to receive teaching, they found themselves having gifts of the Spirit, speaking in tongues, teaching, healing, evangelism, caring for others and things like that all taking place—it has taken a much longer period to order the gifts and help members to understand the need for discipline in their exercise of them. There was a tendency to go for the dramatic gifts, but slowly we are winning the battle on that one and people are coming to see that every gift comes from God and has its place and its value.

So this movement has empowered the Church, but it went through a phase when it had to be debated in Synod whether it should continue or should be closed down, and the proposal was that it should be banned from the Diocese because it was turning the good, stolid Anglicans into raving Zionists and revivalists—and that had never happened in the Anglican Church. After the debate for and against had ended, the then Bishop of Zululand, Thomas Savage, said, 'If that is all that can be said about this movement, then I wish to God every Anglican was a member!' That was the last time they had any difficulties, but then under Bishop Alphaeus Zulu the clergy received enormous help in both accepting members of this Legion and also gaining the wisdom to guide and direct them, because it often happens to people in the Spirit that they are fairly powerful, and if the clergyman is a spiritual weakling he can find it very difficult to cope with them. They demand a lot of teaching, they have ideas about how things should be done, they have limitless energy, and that is not how Anglicans normally operate. One then has to decide whether to join them or to silence them, and trying to silence them had not worked, so many began to join them.

The movement began to open its doors, with open Conferences, to all sorts of people who were not members, and people
began to discover that it was not as dangerous as they had
thought. So by now it had got to the stage when even ordinary
Anglicans who were not members of the Legion had themselves
been renewed in the Spirit. By the time renewal started to sweep
through the white membership of the Church in South Africa
[and then on into the mainline churches of the USA and Britain],
we had been going through this very slowly and undramatically
for years. The whole Diocese had had this experience of being
sensitive to the things of the Spirit right through.

HEALING IN THE CITY

The elderly evangelist stood by the bed. There were beads of
perspiration on the sick child's face. Her heart was beating more
slowly now; her eyes were closed. The mother stood anxious and
wide-eyed, gazing from child to evangelist in silent despair. The
evangelist found himself, he did not know how or why, stretching
out his hands to the child's head. A sense of Jesus' presence and
power was overwhelming him. Now he was praying for the child's
recovery, with a confidence which surprised him. As he finished, he
felt strangely peaceful, and that peace seemed to transmit itself to
the child's fevered face. Calmness took the place of fear, and he
was hardly surprised to hear the next day that the fever had gone
and the dying child was making a rapid recovery.

That was how Edmund John discovered the remarkable gift
which God had given him. He had retired early from working for
Radio Tanzania, in order to lead a little Church in a poor suburb of
Dar es Salaam. Soon, in response to a voice which he heard clearly,
he organized little groups which met to pray for the sick and for
other needs. Many people were healed, and in May 1973 he was
asked to pray for the sick in a city Church. He did so, on condition
that only people who were sick came for prayer, not people who
were disabled. But one of the first to be led forward was a cripple.
Edmund was alarmed, but felt God leading him to tell the cripple to
stand and walk in the name of Jesus. The cripple walked out of the
Church. Blind people had their sight restored, and even a dead
child was restored to life. Huge crowds gathered and even broke
the windows to get in. For two years Edmund John held healing
missions arranged by Church leaders all over the country. This had
never happened before in the mission Churches in Tanzania, but
now it is a common feature everywhere, and prayer groups meet
regularly in Dar es Salaam. Edmund was an Anglican in the

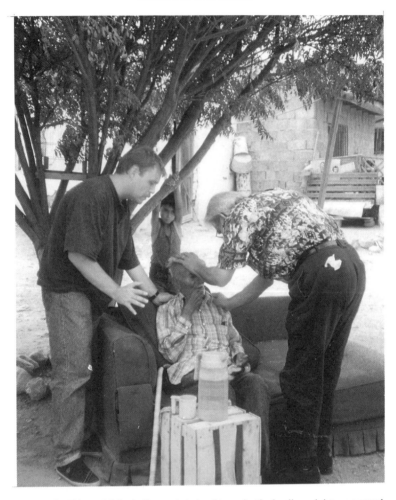

People like Edmund John in Tanzania helped to make the healing ministry a normal part of church life. Here Christians in Juarez City, Mexico, lay hands on a sick man and pray for his healing. Does your local Church have a healing ministry? How does this ministry help Christian mission?

catholic tradition, but his ministry became pentecostal. As a result, catholics and evangelicals came together and received blessings from one another which they would not otherwise have done. Here are some of the main features of Edmund John's ministry.

1. There were hundreds of traditional and Muslim healers in Dar es Salaam who had a profitable trade among people who feared witchcraft and the other unfamiliar problems of the city. People knew they needed help, and it was these felt needs which Edmund was able to address in the powerful name of Jesus.

2. Edmund John fasted for long periods before he prayed for the sick, and often he became very weak himself. He died in 1975, only two years after his ministry became known. His ministry of power was never easy for him and it was exercised in weakness.

3. He insisted that people should repent of all sin and turn to Jesus who is the only Healer. If they did not do this, their sickness was likely to return in a more severe form.

4. Edmund experienced persecution. The *Daily News* wrote about him, 'An individual passing himself for a spiritual healer has been haunting the city of Dar es Salaam. Poor people have travelled from as far away as Mwanza to come and see this "spiritual healer". Have they been cured? *None of them.*'

5. On one occasion in Dodoma, Edmund claimed that everyone who came to the meeting would be healed. But afterwards it was pathetic to see the crippled and the blind staggering or groping their way out of Church without their sticks after being assured that they had been healed; or to receive letters from believers who had been promised healing but had never been healed. This simply showed that Edmund was an imperfect human being who could make mistakes. The power was not his own.

CHRISTIANIZING AFRICAN CUSTOMS

Like Edmund John, W. V. Lucas in Southern Tanzania could see in 1913 that, unlike the traditional ceremonies, the mission Churches did not meet the needs which people felt most severely. He felt that (1) the Church should supply Christian ritual for any need felt by society; (2) the Church should preserve African traditions as far as possible, e.g. the blessing of fields, exorcism, initiation ceremonies and bride price; (3) local Christians should decide what traditional elements could be 'baptized' and what had to be cut out; (4) the Church should take the people's beliefs seriously, not dismiss them.

Lucas had noticed how immensely important symbols were in African life. He also saw that because the missions belonged to European post-Enlightenment culture (see Special Note E) they were replacing symbolism with head knowledge which could never have the same impact on people's lives. He saw, too, that Jesus had been more like an African than a European in His use of symbols and sacraments. So his idea was to combine Christian and African symbols in a new *jando* (initiation ceremony) which would preserve the community life which was so precious to Africans, instead of treating each person as an isolated individual. The Eucharist especially became the focal point of the new ceremonies. Africans welcomed the change, but many missionaries accused Lucas of paganizing Christianity.

MORATORIUM

This chapter began by looking at three spiritual movements: the East African Revival, Iviyo in Zululand, and the healing ministry of Edmund John. What Lucas offered was not a movement but a *strategy* to affirm and embrace African culture through the people. In 1971 another strategy was proposed, with a similar purpose. At a meeting in New York, John Gatu, of the Presbyterian Church in East Africa, called for a *moratorium* on Western missionary involvement in Africa. A moratorium is a temporary suspension or stopping of activity. Gatu asked the Western mission agencies to stop sending missionaries and funds to Africa for a set period of time. This would enable the Church in Africa to find its own identity, to value its own culture, to set its own priorities, and to discover the resources to carry out its mission from within its own fellowship . This missiological principle is similar to the principles of Roland Allen sixty years before, or of the African Indigenous Churches.

The West must stop interfering and guiding African believers as if they are children. If the Western missionaries cannot do that, and Africans cannot stop encouraging them to behave in this way, then a moratorium is the only solution, 'the only potent means of becoming truly and authentically ourselves'. 'In the midst of all our difficulties,' wrote Archbishop Desmond Tutu, 'we are trying to know Jesus Christ; please leave us alone for a while.' A moratorium must be the result of obedience to the missionary call, not a desire to escape from this call. It must be a moratorium *for* mission (leaving the African Churches free to find their own mission tasks), not a moratorium *of* mission (which would mean that no mission work was done at all).

There were several different responses to John Gatu's proposal. One 'response' was a statement actually made *before* Gatu spoke and it was one of the reasons why he made his speech. The statement came from Bishop Stephen Neill, who in 1971 was

Professor of Religious Studies at Nairobi University. Bishop Neill, who had written many books on Christian missions, felt that Christianity had never gone deep into the African people and that it could only survive through a constant supply of missionaries. This view caused a storm of protest in Nairobi at the time. The evidence of history and the Indigenous Churches does not seem to support Bishop Neill's idea.

A second response to Gatu's suggestion of a moratorium supported the removal of mission personnel, but wanted to continue to receive funding— indeed, to receive more because of all the money which would be saved if missionaries did not have to be paid. This, however, would merely change dependence on people into dependence on money.

A third response, which was the most common, applauded the speech, and then carried on exactly as before. All Church leaders faced the immediate problem of how to continue to run their institutions tomorrow. They could not afford the luxury of a long-term strategy.

John Gatu's hopes were not realized. The African Churches were not set free to discover themselves and their resources, and to rethink Church order, administration and finance in ways which were authentically African. The Western Churches were not set free from involvement in foreign countries so that they could discover new missionary opportunities in their own lands. The most disturbing result, however, was that those African Churches never received the space they needed to develop an authentic African form of Christianity which could in its turn enrich all the Churches of the world. The Indigenous Churches had developed this kind of authentic African Christianity but, even today, few of them have close contacts with mainline denominations. However, all the Churches need to *exchange* personnel constantly, and to recognize that all parts of the Church need one another, as members of one family. In the past all the traffic seemed to move in one direction (see p. 8), but the call for a moratorium showed clearly how unhealthy that was for the Church.

Movements of genuine renewal frequently resemble other such movements in other places or at other times. For example, the charismatic movement came to England as a response to needs which English people felt. The movement directly challenged evangelicals and others who for many years had concentrated on understanding and analysing their faith rather than experiencing it. Many theologians and Church leaders resisted the charismatic movement so much that as a result some Christians lost their jobs, some lost their homes, and others were even expelled from training for missionary service. But after a very few years, the Church learnt to be more flexible so that it could accept the people who were involved in the charismatic movement. These people also became mature enough to receive criticism and to continue to think through their theology and correct their mistakes.

The charismatic movement has certainly spread across cultures but only because it has been free to adapt and change to fit any new context. What happened among the Zulus had a rather different form when it moved to white South Africa, then to the USA, and then to Europe. It is always difficult to export such a movement out of one culture into another without changing it. The East African Revival was brought to England but it never had the vitality or joy which it had in Africa. Some people suggested that it could only work well in places where people were more conscious of relationships than of individuality, where they valued experience more than analysis, and even (perhaps) where they spoke the more musical and symbolic languages of Africa. Other people have tried to export the charismatic movement back to Africa in the same form as it has taken in England. However, this has not really been a success when it is compared with the impact of the indigenous renewals in East Africa, Zululand or the Indigenous Churches.

Special Note E

MODERN WESTERN CULTURE

Very frequently in this Guide we have needed to recognize the influence of modern Western culture. This culture has dazzled the world with its developing technology, and much of this technology seems to have formed part of the Good News of Christ which was brought by Western missionaries. 'The Gospel' was seen as education, rapid transport, technology, health care—which all proved to be passports to progress in one way or another (see p. 81). With this culture, which has become known as *modernity*, came complete confidence in the power of human reason (see p. 99) to control the environment and to expose much traditional culture as superstitious or childlike (see p. 139). Reason could ignore or explain away the world of the supernatural. This has happened with narratives in the Bible (p. 69), traditional beliefs (p. 89) and symbolism (p. 150), and the modern signs and wonders movement (p. 163). We may criticize this Western culture for its arrogance, narrowness and blindness to other realities—but no one today can ignore it.

Gutmann discovered that this was true (p. 97) when he saw the Chagga people more attracted to Western technology than they were to their own traditional culture which Gutmann valued so highly. Modern culture and technology are irresistible and inescapable. They have invaded the traditional world so fast that pastoral peoples (like the Masai) find that they have moved from a pastoral to an agricultural to an industrial to a technological culture in only one generation—a process which took Westerners many hundreds of years. Those who want to succeed today (wherever they live) must come to terms with modernity. At the same time, modernity has proved that it can resist the Christian Gospel just as well as any other culture can—and perhaps more than most of them. Therefore Christians need to understand modernity and communicate with it.

Modernity began with the period known in European history as 'the Enlightenment', which began in the sixteenth century and was fully established by 1700. The Enlightenment was the natural outcome of the Renaissance (the rediscovery of classical learning) and the Protestant Reformation. It had four central features:

1. The period of the Enlightenment was the *Age of Reason*. The motto of this period in history was the saying of the French philosopher Descartes, *Cogito ergo sum* ('I think, therefore I am'). The ability to reason gave human beings their identity and sense of worth.

2. Together with this went the *scientific method*. This method enabled human beings to stand back from the natural world in order to observe, analyse, understand and, eventually, control it. The effect of this was revolutionary. People no longer saw themselves as victims of nature or unseen forces; supersitition was banished; people no longer accepted what the Church or tradition told them about nature, and they learnt new truths of science such as the law of gravity (Newton) and that the sun was the centre of the universe (Copernicus and Galileo). A new body of 'public truth' emerged which all reasonable people were expected to accept.

3. The Enlightenment was an age of *individualism*. People were free to think and behave as they wished in order to succeed and be happy in life. This freedom is enshrined in the American Constitution, which aims to give the people of the USA 'Life, liberty and the pursuit of happiness'. Individualism is also the reason why modernity can tolerate a great variety of 'private options' outside the area of public truth. Religious beliefs come into this 'private' category (see p. 163). Relationships and the sense of community

lost the central importance which they had in Europe in the Middle Ages (and which they still have in almost all traditional cultures).

4. The concept of *purpose was eliminated* from scientific study. Reason claimed that it could explain why things happened or existed, in the sense of what *caused* them, but not in the sense of what their *purpose* was. To know the cause of everything but the purpose of nothing is a recipe for human hopelessness—which is exactly what has happened to people in the Western world.

The development of this modern way of thinking has profoundly affected not only the Western world and its missionaries but people everywhere. Although modernity began in the Western world, many Westerners (especially people who have not had tertiary or higher education) do not think in modern ways. Many non-Westerners, on the other hand, are very 'modern'. Note the conflict between modern and traditional ways of thinking in the examples which follow.

1. Modernity divides life and experience into different compartments. Religion concerns the human soul, knowledge concerns the mind, and health concerns the body. Each of these different aspects can be studied separately from the others. As a result, people's lives are broken up into several parts. But the person remains one person and traditional culture continues to see life as a whole, with all its aspects interconnected.

2. Modernity not only analyses, it also measures everything against accepted standards and norms. As a result, people become dissatisfied with how things are and are always striving for improvement: this is called progress. This attitude can be commended—within limits. This is how a group of Pacific islanders responded to people who wanted to measure their children's development:

> The psychologist sends his research team to the village and asks mothers: 'Did your child do this or that at the same time as other children?' The village mother answers 'Yes'. They know that when White Coats come . . . it's best to say 'Yes' to whatever funny things they ask. Where the White Coats come from they catch children and measure them from the day they are born . . . any child who is not fast enough gets found out . . . torn from their family their souls fly away. We do not measure children so in our village. When a child is ready to walk, he will walk; when he has reached the point of telling what he saw in the field, he will tell it.

3. Under the influence of modernity, evangelism has become the transmission or passing on of concepts or ideas. People are asked to respond to these ideas by making a decision to invite Christ into

A doctor in the Philippines uses modern Western technology (a microscope) to help his patients in a jungle village.

their lives, and then to believe that He has come in, and not to expect to feel or to see anything different. Becoming a Christian is all about the individual and the mind. This is quite different from New Testament evangelism, which pointed to what was *happening* through God's activity among human beings—whether this was the coming of Jesus (Acts 10.38) or the gift of the Holy Spirit (Acts 2.1–13) or signs and wonders (Luke 11.20). If nothing was happening, there was no Good News! In the same way, becoming a Christian made a visible difference to people (Acts 8.18), just as it does today in most parts of the world (see p. 143, and the whole of chapters 10 and 11). Westerners have learnt to be content with analysing and understanding. The reason why the Gospel has spread rapidly in China and Africa is that it has had a visible and dramatic effect on people's lives.

4. Modernity's emphasis on individual reason conflicts with the central issue of most traditional cultures, which is relationships. In answer to Descartes' *Cogito ergo sum* ('I think, therefore I am'), Africans would say, *Sumus ergo sum* ('We are, therefore I am'). Their identity and sense of worth come from the community where they belong and have a valued role. This fits in much better with the Gospel of the Kingdom of God. In the Kingdom, relating to God and to one's fellow human beings is absolutely central (Mark 12.28–34), rather than simply holding correct ideas.

This is illustrated by the story of the Masai schoolboy who broke a window one day as he was kicking a football. A new teacher asked him if he was the one who had done this. He replied 'No', and the more the teacher scolded him, the more lies the boy told. A more experienced teacher came up later and began to chat to the boy about his school work and to praise him for being so good at football. Before long the boy began to boast about how far he had kicked the football—'and even through that window over there!' In the Western world-view, the purpose of words is to *establish the truth*. In the Masai view the purpose of words is to *establish relationships*. In terms of his culture, the boy was quite right to tell lies to a teacher whose angry words were in danger of breaking a good human relationship. The boy used words to try to maintain that relationship. In conversation with the other teacher he felt free both to tell the truth and to keep a good relationship. The danger in transmitting a Western view of the Gospel to a non-Western culture is that those who receive this new message will probably hold it only superficially, and continue to think and live according to their own culture. They may be right to do this, because their culture may relate better to Jesus' message of the Kingdom of God, and be more compatible with it, than modernity.

5. Westerners themselves have found that modernity cannot satisfy them. They need something which touches not only the mind but also the emotions and experience. In the West today people are no longer asking 'What is true?', but 'What is relevant to me and my experience?' This is an important aspect of a new Western culture which some people call 'post-modernism' (the world-view which comes after modernity and rejects some of modernity's ideas; see below). As a result, many people are ready to accept a message which affects their emotions and links them in close fellowship with other people, rather than the Gospel presented to them in the form of 'truth' to be understood. The charismatic movement (see p. 151) and the signs and wonders movement (see chapter 12) were welcomed precisely because they brought new physical and spiritual experiences of healing, tongues, prophecy, tremblings, jumping, faintings, laughter, etc., which went beyond the mind. If people are to live with hope, they also need to be aware of the purpose of things, not merely their cause. The story of the bus accident (p. 91) shows that to discern only the cause of an event is deeply dissatisfying when what people really want to know is the purpose of the event for them in their lives.

Post-modernism seems to have three aspects: (a) it acknowledges and enjoys the benefits which modernity has brought to the world; (b) it recognizes that human beings have many basic needs which modernity cannot satisfy; and (c) it seems to go back to some of the values of 'pre-modernity', i.e. the sort of culture which existed before the Enlightenment and which was holistic and concerned with community, relationships and creation. Pre-modernity, modernity and post-modernism can sometimes be seen together in a healthy form of co-existence in African and Asian Christianity. The cultural values of the past are remembered and rediscovered, especially in the Indigenous Churches (pre-modernity); the benefits of modernity have been imported, mainly through Western missions (modernity); and there is a new vitality in the Pentecostal Churches, which are now growing so fast all over the world (post-modernism). These Pentecostal Churches criticize both traditional culture and the rigid forms of worship in the mission Churches, and they appeal to the hearts of ordinary people everywhere, especially the young people who join these Churches in large numbers.

6. The world as a whole is tired of this dominance of Western culture and technology—especially now that people can see clearly that it is quite unable to supply a satisfying pattern for human life (see p. 4 and chapter 8). As a result, various forms of 'fundamentalism' have emerged in connection with all the major faiths. Jewish

Zionism focuses on the land; Hinduism focuses on the nation; Christian fundamentalism focuses on the Bible; Muslim fundamentalism focuses on the practical effect of Islam in order to make the world sit up and take notice of it (rather like a Muslim form of liberation theology). This does not mean that people do not welcome the very real achievements of the Enlightenment. On the contrary, many fundamentalists are modern, highly educated people. Nevertheless, they see clearly that modernity, secularism and materialism on their own have no power to satisfy the needs of the human soul. All over the world, people have a longing to worship. In Russia, after seventy years of atheist domination, a young Church leader said 'Faith lies deep in the souls of the Russian people.'

Christians do not have an automatic answer to all the cultural conflicts of the world, especially since Christians themselves were some of the chief builders of modernity. They can be proud of this, provided that they also recognize its limitations. The Gospel of the Kingdom of God which Jesus brought into the world provides all the ingredients needed to set people's feet on 'The Way' which will encourage human progress and at the same time respect and enhance our human relationships—both with God and with one another. This is the essence of the Good News, and it is holistic enough to embrace every dimension of human life. The Gospel events were acted out on the stage of real human history, and they cannot be treated as a private religious point of view. They are worthy to be proclaimed without shame as the initiative which God has taken to put the human race back on the right path to enjoy and care for all that He has made.

STUDY SUGGESTIONS

WORD STUDY

1. Give the meaning of the following words:
   (a) Iviyo
   (b) moratorium
   (c) post-modernism.

CONTEXTUAL APPLICATION

2. What features of the ministry of Jesus described by Mark (p. 31) were reflected in the East African Revival (p. 143)?
3. What (a) similarities and (b) differences do you notice between Edmund John and Simon Kimbangu?

4. What importance do the Churches of your country give to the ministry of healing?

5. What were the effects of Edmund John's ministry?

6. Many of the events described in this chapter show that God gave His power to people who were in themselves weak and even mistaken and sinful (see pp. 142 and 149). In what way is this 'power in weakness' similar to the mission teaching of Mark and Luke (see chapters 3 and 4)? What examples of God's power at work in human weakness have you seen?

7. (a) In what ways was Lucas similar to Ricci and de Nobili (p. 103), and in what ways was he different to them?
   (b) How did Lucas put into practice the insights of Roland Allen (see pp. 85–87)?

8. What meaningful symbols, pictures, stories etc. are used by your Church in its mission? Which ones could be used more? What symbols convey meaning to people in your locality?

9. If every Christian possesses the Spirit, then every Church must possess the resources it needs for its mission (see Allen, p. 87). What forms might a 'moratorium' take today so that your Church could fully explore and develop its God-given resources?

10. It is impossible simply to import a spiritual movement from somewhere else, but such a movement might have a good influence on other parts of the world Church. How do you think this might happen? If possible, give examples to illustrate your answer.

11. Looking back over chapters 10 and 11, what examples can you find of (a) communitas, (b) structure and (c) how structure and communitas help one another?

12. What can we do to ensure that we baptize local culture without paganizing or secularizing the Gospel?

13. In what ways has modernity influenced your country? What has been good about this influence, and what has been bad?

14. In what ways could pre-modernity, modernity and post-modernism exist together in the Church in your country? How could this 'healthy form of co-existence' be encouraged?

PART 3
MOVEMENTS IN MISSION TODAY

12. Signs and Wonders

A few years ago a book was written about Christian pastoral care of the sick. It contained explanations of the idea of health, the relationship between sickness and sin, how to see God at work in the midst of sickness, how to pray for the sick person's spiritual well-being, how to pray with the carers and support them, and how to help people prepare for dying. But there was nothing in the book about the possibility of the sick person getting better! Yet one-fifth of the stories in St Luke's Gospel are about people being healed in some way. Many Christians read these stories in Church and at home, yet seem to ignore them in practice. One cannot help wondering which Bible they are reading. They seem to be praising Jesus for how great He was long ago! But there has been a rediscovery of this ministry of healing in the twentieth century.

TYPES OF HEALING MINISTRY

There are three chief ways in which people have tried to heal the sick.

1. They have used natural remedies made from leaves, roots, fruit and animals. Herbalists and medicine-women all over the world are experts at using these kind of remedies. Many of them claim that their knowledge is given by God. Some of them combine this skill with a belief that sickness comes to people because they have been bewitched by an enemy or even by the spirit of an ancestor. In this case the healers are often called witchdoctors or shamans and use magic remedies as well as natural ones. Their trade thrives not only in rural areas but also in cities, where the new immigrants are not familiar with the spirits who are at work in cities and therefore need help from witchdoctors. Some of these 'healers' may do more harm than good because of their ignorance of hygiene and science; and some people may become enslaved by their power just as much as they were enslaved by fear of the spirits and witchcraft.

2. The second form of healing ministry is based on scientific diagnosis and medical research developed in the Western world,

especially over the last 150 years. The killer diseases, like malaria, syphilis, TB and smallpox can be almost eradicated by these methods. Other parts of the world have developed other, equally scientific, methods, e.g. Chinese acupuncture. Most Christian missions have followed this second form of healing ministry, although some of them, like Adrian Attiman, a Liberian who worked in Tanzania, have practised as Christian herbalists.

3. The third form of healing ministry follows the example of the Gospels. It makes the sick and disabled whole, and casts out evil spirits in the powerful name of Jesus. This ministry has been called 'Signs and Wonders' (Acts 2.22). John Wimber has developed this ministry in the USA over the last twenty years, but it was present in many Churches all over the world for many years before that. There are examples in this Guide on pp. 131 and 147.

JOHN WIMBER'S TEACHING

After trying various programmes for many years in the Church where he served, John Wimber, like Ray Bakke (see p. 192), felt that he and his congregation should rely more on the Holy Spirit. As a result, he began to discover the gifts of the Spirit, especially in healing. Wimber makes the following important points:

1. Christians should 'give God back His Church' i.e. allow Him to show the way rather than ask Him to bless what has already been planned by the leaders.

2. Signs and wonders help the Church to do evangelism more quickly because people can see the results of faith before they can fully understand faith.

3. Signs and wonders are not against reason, but they are not limited to what can be rationally, or scientifically, explained and understood.

4. Christians should expect God to work in people's lives. When this happens, we can see what He is doing but we are not responsible for it ourselves. This means that we can never command signs and wonders, or blame anyone for not being healed.

5. It is more important to receive signs and wonders than to ask questions about them. So all the conferences which John Wimber leads include actual ministry and prayer.

DIFFERENT WORLD-VIEWS

Many people in the West feel uncomfortable with the idea of God working directly in wonderful ways. Because of the way in which Western thought has developed, Western people have become

161

A traditional healer (right) and a modern clinic (below) in Mexico illustrate two ways of trying to heal the sick. What is the third way, which John Wimber teaches?

used to the world of *public truth* where people act on the basis of scientifically observed facts. Westerners are also ready to allow people the *private freedom* to believe, pray and worship as they wish, even if their beliefs are foolish—provided that they do not try to impose these beliefs on other people (see Special Note E and Figure 15). But they are troubled when the two worlds of science and religion interact. This happens, for example, when sickness is removed through prayer to God, not through medical means. Western people often regard this as unscientific and even superstitious, and they may seek some scientific explanation for what has happened, e.g. the person was not really sick at all, or the healing is all in the mind (psychological).

Western missionaries who enter Third World cultures are conditioned by the world-view described above. Therefore they sometimes deny the existence of spirits and demons and bring a 'Gospel' which does not relate to that world (see p. 89). They often try to heal sicknesses through the public science of medicine, but to bring 'salvation' through private and personal faith. But people from less 'scientific' societies are already convinced that God and spirits interact with our world, i.e. they have a 'holistic' view of life. When they are troubled by sickness, they ask who caused it, and are ready to turn to God (or to a witchdoctor) for help. Therefore it is not surprising to learn that signs and wonders have for a long time played an important part in spiritual movements in the Churches of the South. People like Wimber acknowledge that they have learnt a lot from them.

WORLD OF RELIGION	PRIVATE BELIEFS	Faith Prayer Visions
/ / / / / / / / / / / /	/ /	/ / / / / / / / / / / / / / /
EXCLUDED MIDDLE	INTERACTION between World of Religion and World of science	Demonstration Miracles Answered Prayer
/ / / / / / / / / / / /	/ /	/ / / / / / / / / / / / / / /
WORLD OF SCIENCE	PUBLIC TRUTH	Observation Knowledge

Figure 15 The relationship between the world of religion and the world of science.

There are therefore two world-views in conflict: the Western view usually *excludes* the middle category in the diagram above; the second view accepts it as a normal part of life. The second view was shared by the writers of the New Testament—but many scholars would say that this was because they belonged to their time and that we ought to follow their faith (private beliefs), but we should be glad that we have grown out of their ignorance and superstition (public truth).

The signs and wonders movement claims to be turning away from the 'closed' Western world-view and rediscovering the supernatural world of prayer and power. This is partly true, but in another way this theology cannot claim to be free from the Western world-view. On the contrary, it is captive to it. In the North, for example, we see many comparatively rich Christians, who already have good medical care, education, nourishing food, warm, comfortable homes and rapid world-wide travel, claiming yet more power from God to deliver them from what seem to be minor pains and problems compared with the difficulties faced by many other Christians in the world, especially in the South. What about the millions of people in the South, who are also made in God's image, who are starving and diseased partly because of conditions created by those rich Northern nations? Why does it so often seem as if the real signs and wonders of this loving God are not available to the people in the South?

Those charismatic Christians who enjoy constant signs and wonders have not turned away from the Western world-view at all. They are claiming yet another layer of comfort for their already over-luxurious lives and (perhaps) failing to reflect the compassion of Jesus for the wretched people of the earth who need His signs and wonders the most. 'Which God do we worship?' is a question we must also ask—as well as 'Which Bible do we read?' The New Testament says that evil people can also perform wonders (Matt. 24.24; 2 Thess. 2.9) and that wonders can be desired for wrong reasons (Matt. 7.21–23; John 4.48). Perhaps signs and wonders done by those who neglect needy people are really evil powers, not good powers.

To discover the right place for signs and wonders, we should look at the power ministry of Jesus which was always exercised out of weakness, sorrow, conflict, suffering and even defeat (see p. 32). Like Jesus, many people have been anointed with God's power in the midst of persecution and pain. Many of them are described in this Guide. God's power is at work not only *for* the poor and weak but also *in* the poor and weak, and there is no escape from the way of the cross. Even God's own supreme demonstration of power was when He lived and died as a human being. Jesus healed our sorrows because He bore them Himself.

POWER EVANGELISM

The evangelism aspect of signs and wonders is often forgotten—yet Jesus did his miracles chiefly among people who were not yet disciples. Sometimes they responded in faith, but not always. The healings of Simon Kimbangu, Edmund John and the Zulu renewal movement led the way for the spread of the faith. But in some parts of the Church, signs and wonders are a luxury for the enjoyment of believers. Christians need courage to respond to the leading of the Holy Spirit and to trust God to work in power out in the streets and on the frontiers of the Church.

This may involve a healing ministry; but it may involve feeding the hungry; or giving money; or bringing a prophecy; or living a life of love for brothers and sisters in Christ; or receiving words of knowledge for our pastoral ministry. There is no limit to the gifts which the Holy Spirit gives in His Church—but we need to remember that the graces (the fruits of the Spirit, see Gal. 5.22) are always more important than the gifts. All the gifts and graces are given to spread the knowledge of Jesus everywhere. Here are three practical examples from recent times:

1. A respected Muslim railway worker in Tanzania was admitted to hospital. About the same time, a Christian pastor was admitted to the same ward. The Muslim was surprised to see how many visitors the pastor received, all of whom encouraged and comforted him with prayer. He said that he could see them living out the life that Jesus lived, and he himself decided to follow Jesus. He devoted the rest of his life to witnessing to the love of Jesus as he travelled the railway network.

2. Sister Briege McKenna of Ireland is invited to conduct many retreats for Catholics all over the world. Priests come to her for help with their personal problems—in fact, so many come that she does not have time to listen to all their stories. Instead, God has given her the gift of being able to perceive their situation, problem or sin, so that she can bring His message to a large number of needy people. Some people call this perception 'words of knowledge'. Priests say that they can easily ask her for help because a sister who is not ordained has no power to be a threat to them.

3. In the Mexican town of Juarez there are many poor people who live by selling or even eating rubbish which they collect from the garbage dumps. A group of charismatic Catholics tried to take the Good News of Jesus to these people; but they heard God saying

to them, 'Go and feed them'. So they announced that they would do this and took enough food portions for 1,500 people. To their dismay, 3,000 people turned up. They felt they had to feed them all as best they could, and in the end everyone was fed, no one went hungry, and there was even some left over. They believe that God increased the food as they obeyed His word.

'ALREADY' BUT 'NOT YET'

In chapter 3 we saw that the first part of Mark's Gospel tells of the signs of the King, but the second part tells of the suffering of the Servant. It is not only the life of Jesus which is like that, but also the lives of all His followers. For example, He has *already* saved us from the guilt of sin, but *not yet* saved us from the presence of sin. He has *already* taught us His truth, but *not yet* given us perfect understanding. He has *already* given us eternal life, but *not yet* set us free from bodily death. In just the same way, Jesus has *already* carried our sicknesses (Matt. 8.17) but has *not yet* removed all pain and crying (Rev. 21.4). Meanwhile Christians live between the 'already' and the 'not yet'. In practice this means that Christians see Jesus transforming their sicknesses, sometimes by healing them immediately, sometimes by making the sickness into a new opportunity to praise Him. Only He knows what is best for us at any one time.

A Christian student once discovered this in her own experience. She fell down a mountain and received brain injuries which made her fall asleep in the daytime, caused headaches and reduced her intellectual ability. Repeatedly she asked for prayer in healing services. Then she stopped asking. The pastor asked her why she no longer came for healing. She replied, 'I think the Lord has answered my prayer; all my symptoms are still there, but I believe He has made me whole.' The pastor agreed, for he could see that she had been transformed into a new gentle and loving person. She is now a pastor herself with a loving ministry and a beloved family. *Already* God has done His work in her; He has *not yet* healed her completely. Are we ready to accept God's wisdom rather than our own? Holiness (i.e. being like God) is more important than signs and wonders (Matt. 7.22, 23).

Dom Helder Camara of Brazil says that Christians must stop 'pressing the absurd claim of being the best, and present ourselves as brothers and sisters for others'. In one Latin American city, the Church ran a fine programme for slum children. Then the money ran out. There seemed to be only two alternatives before them: either to close the programme or to ask for help from a rich

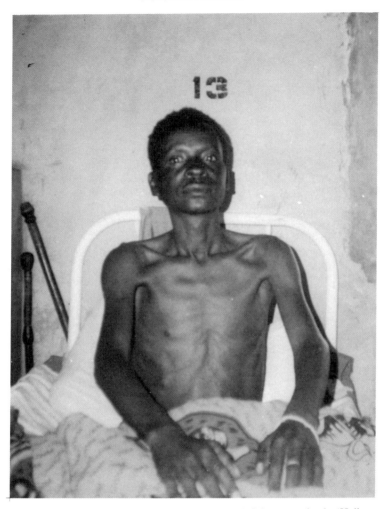

God can work in people even when he has *not yet* healed them completely. 'Holiness . . . is more important than signs and wonders' (p. 166). How would you explain this to someone like this man, sick in a mission hospital in Africa?

Western country. In fact they did neither. Instead, they told the children and their parents about the problem. The Church had never done such a thing before—it was there to solve other people's problems, not to share its own difficulties. What was the point? Those slum people could not even feed their own families, let alone help the Church! But this time a group of the poor parents sat down with the account books and suggested savings here or cuts there; others started a project to raise money—and even the children did a project. A large number joined the Church's prayer meeting—this had never happened before. For the first time adults came to Sunday worship. Only a weak and needy Church can show weak and needy people the way to the love of God. 'My power is made perfect in weakness' (2 Cor. 12.9).

Christians, therefore, should expect—and pray—to see God's power at work in the world. Like the people of Jesus' home town, if we expect little, we shall see little (Mark 6.4–6). We should also expect the good health which comes from being at peace with God and within ourselves, both because God wants the best for us, and also for the psychological reason that a calm mind keeps stress away from the body. Like Jesus, however, we are engaged in warfare against the Evil One. Because He has won the final victory, we cannot be afraid but we can look forward to sharing what He has promised us.

STUDY SUGGESTIONS

BIBLE STUDY

1. What was wrong about the signs in each of these verses: Matt. 7.22; 24.24; John 4.48; Acts 8.19; 2 Thess. 2.9?
2. Make a list of the Gospel blessings which Christians have *already* received, and another list of those blessings which they have *not yet* received. How does the contrast between the two types of blessings affect how we live day by day?

CONTEXTUAL APPLICATION

3. What do you think are (a) good and (b) bad features of traditional healing as described on p. 160? Should Christians use or support healers of this type?
4. What movements, or individual examples, of healing through faith and prayer do you know about in your area? What evangelistic effect have these had? What evidence is there that they are connected with special gifts of faith or with the power of the Holy Spirit?

5. What examples have you already found in this Guide of people exercising spiritual power in wonderful ways? What elements of (a) power and (b) weakness did you find in them, and what blessings came from this power and weakness?
6. What connection have you noticed between prayer and signs and wonders?
7. What methods can we use to raise the expectations of Christian people so that they will look for great things from God?
8. What sort of happenings (in this and other chapters) would you call 'signs and wonders'? Make a list of actions and events which might come into this category.

13. Liberation Theology

During the twentieth century, three new movements which began in Latin America have affected the mission of the Church all over the world.

1. The first is the Pentecostal Movement, which has become the fastest-growing part of the Church in the world since 1960 (see p. 157). This growth was first seen clearly in Latin America (beginning in Chile, 1909, and moving on to Brazil), where masses of working-class people were drawn to the lively worship of the Pentecostals. One huge Church in Sao Paulo, with a congregation of 25,000 and a hundred satellite Churches, had to put up a notice warning people going up into the gallery, 'No dancing on the stairs'. All new Christians were expected to tell their story of faith in open-air services. No one could become a pastor until he or she had actually planted a new Church.

2. The second movement is Theological Education by Extension, which began in Guatemala in 1963. The residential theological seminary in Guatemala City was educating pastors to such a high level that they lost touch with ordinary people, and most of the graduates were unwilling or unable to minister in the growing Churches of the poor. So it was decided to take the seminary to where the people were, by means of 'distance learning' at home and in extension centres. Fifteen years later the number of trained pastors had increased by 500 per cent, and there were 240 similar TEE programmes in sixty countries in the world.

3. This chapter, however, is about Liberation Theology, which began in 1957 near Rio de Janeiro in Brazil. A woman complained to Bishop Agnelo Rossi that all the Catholic Churches were closed and dark on Christmas Eve 'because we cannot get a priest', while three Protestant chapels (which did not depend on priests) were full of people singing. Two years earlier the Bishops of Brazil had recognized a three-fold problem facing the Church: a shortage of priests, the growth of Protestant Churches, and the growth of Marxist groups offering liberation to the poor. In 1962 Rossi and others drew up an 'Emergency Plan' to (a) identify the natural community in every place; (b) start from the life-situation of people, not from theology; and (c) give leadership to lay people.

BASE CHRISTIAN COMMUNITIES

As a result of this 'Emergency Plan', local groups began to meet, led by 'people's catechists' who were trained to lead prayer and

Bible study and to visit people at home. Lay women and sisters in religious orders played a major part in these local groups, which were called Base Christian Communities (BCCs). (The word 'base' means the lowest level of society.) Four further factors must be noted in the rise of these Base Christian Communities:

1. *The social situation* Large numbers of people were being exploited by others and were never asked for their opinion. Some of them were driven off their land or bought out cheaply by landowners who wanted to plant cash crops for a quick profit. Others were forced to pay very high rents for small strips of land or tumbledown shacks. These people were asking 'Where is God in our suffering?' They wanted to share with others, say what they thought and take responsibility for their own lives (see p. 125). Base communities gave them a chance to discuss and act in e.g. sewing groups, education and health groups, etc.

2. *The Basic Education Movement* Paulo Freire was a Brazilian educationist who changed the way in which adults were taught to read and write. He recognized that they had good ideas and would learn quickly if they could see the purpose of learning. Freire would begin his teaching with a poster portraying people's life and work experience. They would then spend some time discussing the aim and meaning of the activity portrayed—then he would write up words used in the discussion and the people would begin to learn. This method was called 'conscientization'. Instead of those who know everything teaching those who know nothing (the 'banking' method, which puts information into people's minds in the same way that you deposit money in a bank), Freire's method assumes that the learners know a lot already, know what they need to learn, and can take charge of their own education. They even teach the 'teachers' and they gain responsibility and power.

3. *Church leaders*, like Dom Helder Camara of Brazil, not only challenged corrupt politicians but also left their homes and cars and went to live in shanty towns and ride bicycles. They did not become poor but they showed solidarity with the poor. Julius Nyerere, formerly President of Tanzania, has written,

> Almost all the successful revolutions have been by people who were themselves beneficiaries under the system they sought to replace. Time and again members of the privileged classes have joined, or led, the poor or oppressed in their revolts against injustice. The same thing must happen again.

So the privileged are not helpless—provided that they respect the poor and learn from them (see p. 68). In fact, BCCs only worked well when the bishop of the diocese supported them.

4. *Catholic Bishops' Conferences* formulated policies which reflected the Base Community movement. First, at Medellin (1968) they declared that instead of working *for* the people (giving them charity), they would find a new way of being *with* them and supporting their self-liberation through base communities. At their meeting at Puebla (1978) they spoke of God's 'preferential option for the poor', i.e. the poor are the first, but not the only, people on whom God focuses His attention. Unlike Pope Paul VI, who thought that the Church should evangelize the Base Communities, the meeting at Puebla said the BCCs were not the objects of mission, but the agents of mission (see p. 38). The Church needs the poor more than the poor need the Church.

LIBERATION THEOLOGIANS

As this movement progressed, theologians began to observe and analyse it. Karl Marx wrote books which are difficult to read, and liberation theologians tend to write the same sort of books. We must remember, however, that they are not writing for ordinary people. They are writing to theologians and other leaders about the dreams of the people. For example, many people think that only theologians can do 'theological reflection'. Gustavo Gutierrez of Peru disagrees. He says that, on the contrary, (1) theological reflection is just ordinary believers working out their Christian life and commitment every day— often only half-consciously. This he calls 'wisdom', which people acquire through living in the world. (2) On top of this 'wisdom' it is possible to build 'theology', i.e. a rational knowledge which systematically explains this Christian faith and life. (3) We need to criticize the practice and faith of the Church in the light of the word of God. This is what leads to change, but it starts with grass-roots wisdom. The views of Gutierrez can help us to understand some of the definitions of Liberation Theology which have been made by theologians, e.g.:

A critical reflection on Christian *praxis* in the light of the Word (Gutierrez).

A concrete theology related to daily life and based on an analysis of various situations in the light of the gospel message (J. Sobrino).

Not the application of the divine word to present reality but the other way round . . . in an attempt to interpret God's word directed to us here today (J. L. Segundo).

Liberation Theology grew out of South American slums like these. Liberation theologians tried to put into words the hopes and dreams of the oppressed.

A theology cast in political terms . . . rejecting a theological debate which proceeds as if abstracted from the total situation in which reflection takes place (J. M. Bonino).

A theology of salvation rather than of revelation; not directed primarily at the understanding but at the transformation of reality, seeking fulfilment not in the realm of the mind but in history' (J. M. Bonino).

Liberation theologians would agree with St Francis of Assisi: 'Humankind has only as much knowledge as it puts into practice'. They remind us that we do not learn only by observing and thinking, but also by doing (*praxis*, a Greek word meaning practical action arising out of experience).

THE GROWTH OF LIBERATION THEOLOGY

1. The Base Christian Communities movement began because Latin American Christians were taught Western Christian theology and were then expected to apply it to their situation in South America, and this did not satisfy them. They wanted (a) to understand their situation and then (b) to ask what the Bible had to say about it. This has become known as 'walking on two legs' (see Special Note F).

2. The movement belongs to the local people; it cannot be copied by other people or imposed on anyone. It has usually flourished among certain sorts of people, i.e. those who are poor and politically aware, and who have a religious foundation for their lives. It cannot be exported easily to a different sort of society. For this reason it has spread to the black people of South Africa and the USA, and to many poor Christian groups in Sri Lanka, South Korea (where it is called Minjung theology), the Philippines and some Mediterranean countries. Bishop Ting of China tells us that the Church would never have survived through the Cultural Revolution if Christians had not begun to meet in small communities all over the country. Not all Christians everywhere are called to imitate Latin America. They *are* all called to discover forms of obedience together in terms of their own story and who they are. They can learn (a) how to respect and empower the poor in their communities, and (b) why the poor read the Bible differently—and even imitate them. But even in Latin America only about 20 per cent of the Catholic population support the BCC movement.

3. Study of the Bible is central to the movement, even though

the BCCs may choose different topics for study—or may read them differently—from those chosen in Western theology. For example, God's deliverance of the oppressed at the Exodus is as central for Liberation Theology as it was for Israel. Genesis 1–4 is interesting, not because it throws light on theories of creation or evolution, but because it says (a) the world we live in is good; (b) human beings, even the 'nobodies', are made like God; (c) God has given us responsibility for caring for our world; (d) the land is God's gift to everyone; (e) marriage is shared loving; (f) sin breaks relationships, like the relationship between Cain and Abel. All these six points affect how people see life in the fields or the shanty towns of Latin America. They challenge what they see around them, e.g. people exploiting natural resources for private profit; some people having no right to land or justice; men having the right to 'possess' a woman; sin as a private matter between an individual and God.

4. Even non-Christians who want to change things for the better can be invited to share in the fellowship and action of Base Communities. Often they may even worship with local Christians. This helps them to understand the Gospel better, and it helps the Christians to understand the world better. The division between sacred and secular is broken down.

5. The movement's principles have influenced thinking about world poverty and development. In past centuries, the rich were encouraged to give 'charity' to the poor. The missionary movement had a more comprehensive approach, and missionaries brought education, health and agricultural ministries. Since the 1950s, this approach has given way to development projects, i.e. bringing modern Western technology to the Third World. However, development projects kept power in the rich North, which had no need to change, and kept the Third World as humble receivers who had nothing to offer anyone. Now the Third World is littered with the remains of the useless and rusting machinery left behind by these rich donors. In any case, if all the six billion people in the world succeeded in achieving the same 'development' as the North, no one would be able to live in this world any longer. The Liberation Theology movement, however, shows that the poor know best what their own needs are and how to put things right. Africa has the best farmers in the world, and 75 per cent of them are women who need help to take charge of their own future and to challenge oppressive political situations. The result of this liberation will not be independence for some and dependence for others but a new interdependence for everyone. It will mean change for the North as much as for the South (see p. 82).

An essential part of Liberation Theology are the Base Christian Communities like this one, seen celebrating the Eucharist together. What could your church learn from such communities?

A NEW THEOLOGY FOR LIBERATION

This sort of thinking about liberation for the poor does not fit easily into the traditional structures of the Roman Catholic Church. Roman Catholic authorities have therefore had to rediscover New Testament teaching about the Church, ministry and sacraments. The pattern based on the Pope who, as the apostolic successor of St Peter, leads the priests to lead the faithful, has been turned upside-down. This is the pattern shown in Figure 16 below. Many people are now beginning to see a new pattern of ministry, i.e. that God sent Christ, who sent His Spirit, to send His people to live and minister as His Church in His world with His Word and Sacraments. The Spirit assists them in this task by setting apart within the Church men and women who devote themselves to the pastoral ministry (see Figure 17 on p. 178).

This has been called 'the re-invention of the Church', and it has taken place through *praxis*, i.e. the experience of Base Communities, not through academic theological study. From now on the Church sees that it does not get its life from the Pope via the priests, but from Christ and His Spirit present in the Church. The Church thinks about itself from the foundation upwards (this is what the word 'base' means), not from the roof downwards. The Church is not *transplanted* from Rome to anywhere else, but *implanted* within every different culture (inculturation). This new theology of the Church affects everything the Church does. For example:

1. In the Eucharist, Jesus told us to 'Do this in remembrance of me', and both Roman Catholics and Protestants define the Church as a gathering of people where the Sacraments are properly administered. But there are many congregations who perhaps receive the Eucharist only once a year because of the shortage of priests. In the traditional Western Church a priest can have the Eucharist without a Christian community, but the community

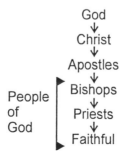

Figure 16 The traditional structure of the Roman Catholic Church.

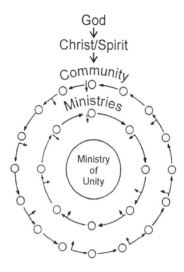

God
↓
Christ/Spirit
↓
Community

Figure 17 The 're-invention of the Church'.

cannot have it without a priest. This situation robs believers of what Christ has promised them, and makes the priesthood more important than the Church where God's Spirit lives. For this reason liberation theologians want lay people in every community (perhaps even women) to be authorized to preside at the Lord's Supper—and in some places they have begun to do this. One Brazilian priest, Leonardo Boff, was banned by the Pope for expressing views like these. But it is a problem for other denominations (e.g. Anglicans) as much as for Roman Catholics.

2. In the ministry of the Word, pastors need to consult with congregations. One Saturday night in Rome Abbot Franzoni, the head of a community of monks, spent two hours with 150 disabled people, with their Bibles open, preparing the sermon (on the disabled and their place in the community) for the next day. In a literal sense, it was a *popular* sermon, a sermon by the people!

3. In Church government, Franzoni's congregation also began to decide questions about divorce involving some of its members. One day during Mass a young couple stepped forward and asked the people to witness and bless their marriage vows. Eventually, Franzoni was banned from presiding at Mass. Then the question arose, 'Shall we get another priest? If no priest will come, shall we appoint one of us to preside? Did Jesus not tell us to do it?' These

questions remind us of what Gutierrez wrote about theological reflection (p. 172 above).

CRITICISMS OF LIBERATION THEOLOGY

This form of theology has a number of dangers, most of which are recognized by liberation theologians. Here are some of them:

1. Even though God may be on the side of the oppressed, it does not follow that the oppressed are always on His side. It is dangerous to assume that whatever such people say is God's message to us. We must listen to the Church as well as to 'the people'.

2. The situation ('the context') must not take over from the Bible ('the text') as the chief authority for Christians. God's revelation in the Bible of who He is and what He has done judges all human thoughts and actions. In its enthusiasm to focus on the world's agenda, the Church must not forget that it, too, has an agenda, entrusted to it by God. The Church is equally one-sided when it sees itself purely as 'servant' as it is when it sees itself purely as 'saviour'. A better model is that of 'partner', for God expects us to work on both agendas.

3. Base communities can provide opportunities for people to become leaders for the wrong reasons. For example, they may want to 'express their personality' without any orderly control from outside. They may enjoy having other people dependent upon them. Or they may be politicians who oppose the government but cannot find a place where they are allowed to speak except the Church—so they pretend to be Christians; this happened under Communism in Eastern Europe and under apartheid in South Africa.

4. Base communities can offer some hope for changing people's circumstances a little, and people are content with that even though the unjust structures of society remain unchanged. Then what happens is that those who used to be poor gain the power to start oppressing other people.

5. The Bible is central for Liberation Theology, but it is easy to 'domesticate' the Bible, i.e. make sure that we only study what it says about the questions which we want to consider. However, we need to set the Bible free to ask us its own questions—especially those questions which we might prefer to avoid.

6. Jesus taught that the Kingdom of God is God's gift to us which we can receive, wait for, enter, seek, etc., but never control or build or extend. Liberation theologians often sound as though they want to be in charge of the Kingdom. J.M.Bonino answers, however, that God does in fact build His Kingdom not only in the

future but also here in human history. Human beings are called to share with Him in His action by doing those works which belong to the new age, and so have an eternal future. Western theology asks 'Where is the Kingdom today?' Liberation Theology asks 'How can we work for and with the Kingdom now?' (see p. 62).

7. Some people have accused liberation theologians of being Marxist. Marxism is a useful tool to analyse society and economics. Liberation theologians use this tool and are ready to work with Communists, but they usually question the Marxist approval of violence, and they reject Marxist atheism and materialism.

This brief survey of Liberation Theology has shown that this movement has helped Christians to understand better that their God is a God of justice who acts in historical events, as He did throughout the history of Israel. Liberation Theology has also helped Christians to see that Jesus often had to oppose religious leaders in order to serve God faithfully, and that they may sometimes have to do the same. Finally, Liberation Theology has helped Christians to renew their confidence in the Holy Spirit who gives power to weak and poor people and who can change people and situations in unexpected ways. The Church itself must always be ready to change in order to have a message for the many different cultures in this 'post-modern' world. Liberation Theology, and the Base Communities which started it, can help the Church in this process of change.

Special Note F

READING THE BIBLE IN BASE COMMUNITIES

The people who meet together in Base Christian Communities often do not find reading easy. They may not know the Bible well and sometimes they do not have the confidence to discuss what they have read with other people. They are, however, confident about discussing the experiences and problems of their daily lives. Therefore most Bible Study models for BCCs give a simple step-by-step plan, and also give plenty of opportunity for people to discuss the relationship between their own lives and the Bible. They often do this with the help of large coloured posters, which are particularly useful for people who do not enjoy reading. The four models given below come from *Gospel Sharing*, published by The Lumko Institute, Johannesburg. You can see an example of each of them on pp. 182–185.

1. The most basic model is called *The Seven Steps*. For each of the four models, the leader trains the group to use the different

methods of Bible Study. He or she suggests to the group how each step could be done, and gives them an opportunity to discuss what is done and practise it for themselves. Look at Figure 18, *The Seven Steps* on p. 182. Step 1 invites the Lord to be present at the meeting. In Step 2 a passage from the Bible is read. In Step 3 anyone in the group can pick out a word or phrase from the Bible passage which has struck them as important. They speak it aloud so that everyone can meditate on it, but at this stage there is no discussion. Then there is a time of silence (Step 4) so that the group can think about what the Bible passage says to them. Step 5 provides an opportunity to share reactions and feelings about the text. In Step 6 the group looks back at the task which they undertook as a result of previous Bible Study, and then decides what action they must take as a result of the passage they have just studied. The meeting ends with a brief time of prayer (Step 7).

2. *Group Response* (see Figure 19, p. 183) also begins with reading the Bible in a similar way, but it quickly uses the text to trigger memories or thoughts which group members may have about their own problems. After a time for reflection, the members of the group share what they think God is telling them to do about these problems.

The last two models do not begin with the Bible, but with people's stories.

3. *Look-Listen-Love* (see Figure 20, p. 184) selects an experience related by one of the group for discussion and analysis. Those who are poor or marginalized will probably have many stories to tell of things which have deeply affected them. Group work shows them that together they can understand the reasons for what happened, they can evaluate it, they can come to know the mind of God about the event, and finally they can take responsibility for some action. By this method, the members of the group start to realize that they do not always need to be victims. They can exercise power as a group.

4. *Life-Bible-Notes* (see Figure 21, p. 185) follows the same sort of method. The group studies both the text (of the Bible) and the context (of their lives), and all the studies finish with people taking action.

Finally, here is the story of one Bible Study held in a home in a very poor district of England. A visitor who attended wrote of it in this way:

The host was not a Christian, though he took a full part in the proceedings. Of the ten people present, some were Christians, others were enquirers. The meeting began with cans of beer and

1. **We invite the Lord**

   Will someone, please invite Jesus
   in a prayer.

2. **We read the text**

   Let us open .... chapter ....
   Will someone, please, read verses ....

3. **We pick out words and meditate on them**

   We pick out words or short phrases,
   read them aloud prayerfully,
   and keep silence in between.

4. **We let God speak to us in silence**

   We keep silence for .... minutes
   and allow God to speak to us.

5. **We share what we have heard in our hearts**

   Which word has touched us personally?
   *We may share also on any "spiritual experience," e.g. how some have
   lived the "Word of life."*
   *We do not "discuss" any contribution, even if some do not "share"
   but "comment" on the text)*

6. **We discuss any task which our group
   is called to do**

   a) Report on previous task
   b) Which new task has to be done?
      WHO is doing WHAT and WHEN?

7. **We pray together spontaneously**

   (We end with a prayer/hymn which all know
   by heart).

Figure 18 The Seven Steps.

Today we follow a Bible-method called "Group-Response". We shall NOT share with each other how the Word of God has touched us personally. Today we rather think of our community, the problems which we have together in our parish, village, town or country. After we have read the text of the Bible we shall ask the question:

*"Which problem in our community is mentioned in the text?
What is God's will for us in a group?"*

1. We read the text

* We read the text twice.
* We pick out words or phrases — read them aloud and keep silence in between these phrases

2. Which problems of our community are mentioned in the text?

* Let us now discuss in little groups. Each one should talk to his immediate neighbour.
We discuss the following question:

"Which problems of our parish, village, town or country are similar to the problems mentioned in the text?"

The same question in other words:

"The text reminds us of which problems in our own community?"

* We discuss this question for five minutes.
* After five minutes each group reports back.
* Let us choose one problem which we are going to discuss further.

3. What does God tell us about our problem?

* We keep silence for about three minutes.
During this time of silence we ask ourselves:

"What did God tell us in our text? What does he tell us about our problem?"

* After three minutes: We tell each other what we think God is advising us about our problem.

4. What does God want us to do?

WHO will do WHAT and WHEN?

Figure 19 Group Response.

Introduction:	Today we do not begin our meeting by reading God's Word, but we begin by looking at the reality of our daily life. We follow the steps of the "Look-Listen-Love" method.
LOOK **at Life**	**"We ask several of us to relate a recent experience."** "Please tell us of an experience which you found important, an event which you were involved yourself. Please tell us briefly in a few words. It can be an event of your daily place in work, or an event in public life, or in your neighbourhood or in your home."
	"Let us now select one of these experiences for discussion." When the experience has been selected the helper leads the discussion asking the following questions: **"What exactly happened?** Do we know all the facts? Can we be told more about it? **Why did it happen?** Let us look for the reasons why it happened. **How do you feel about it?"**
LISTEN **to GOD**	**"What does God think and feel about this event?** Let us listen in silence for about 5 (or 3) minutes to Him. In these few minutes let us put aside our own feelings about this event, and listen carefully to the way God feels and thinks about it. We do not open our Bibles but remember silently words or events which we know already from the Bible. We just imagine: if God would speak about this event now, what would he say?" **"Please share with us now what you think God feels about this event."** Relevant words from the Bible may be read or told from memory at this time. If no suitable passage comes to mind, continue with the next step.
LOVE **in Action**	**"What does God want us to do?"** **"Who will do what and when?"**

Figure 20 Look—Listen—Love.

1. **Situation of Life**

   The problem of our life today ....
   ....

   Guiding questions:
   * Who knows more details and facts about our problem?
   * How do people feel about this problem?
   * Why do we have such a problem? But why .....? But why ....?
   * Who suffers and who gains in this situation?
   * Other questions which look at our particular problem from different angles:

   ....
   ....
   ....
   ....

2. **God's Word**

   A Bible text in which our problem is reflected: ....
   Guiding questions:
   * At which word or sentence did you think: "That is right. I am happy to hear that."?
   * At which sentence did you think: "I did not expect that."? Tell us why you thought differently.
   * What is public opinion saying about our problem? What do we hear on the radio or see on TV about our problem?
   * What do you think is God's opinion about our problem?
   * Other questions which can help to connect our problem with the message of the Bible:

   ....
   ....
   ....
   ....
   ....

3. **Our Response**

   What does God want us to do?
   "**Who** will do **WHAT** and **WHEN?**"

   ....
   ....

DATE: .... COMMUNITY: ....

Figure 21 Life—Bible—Notes.

conversation. The room filled up with people and smoke. One woman was particularly distressed. She was overweight and not well, and was waiting for a hospital appointment. On top of all these problems, one of her neighbours was being aggressive and had reported her to the authorities, accusing her of neglecting her child. The group gathered round the woman and began to discuss her problem and advise her what to do.

All sorts of homely advice was offered. At first most of the advice was of the 'eye-for-an-eye' sort, encouraging the woman to attack her neighbour in return. Then people began to share their own experiences and think about what was happening to the neighbour. They began to discuss what a Christian ought to do, and to search for relevant and helpful stories from the Bible. This was theological reflection! Towards the end of the meeting, the leader produced a Bible and talked briefly about the passage set for the day, James 5.7–20, on patience and prayer. It was now relevant, alive and full of meaning! The atmosphere was electric. Finally the group prayed for the woman.

I had never been to a Bible Study that worked in that way before. The leader told me she was afraid she had done it in the wrong way. It was not a 'proper' Bible Study. But I realized that we had discovered the Good News by 'critical reflection on the economic and social realities of society in the light of the given Word'.

STUDY SUGGESTIONS

WORD STUDY

1. What does the word 'base' mean in the name 'Base Christian Communities'?
2. What is Christian *praxis*?

BIBLE STUDY

3. What principles of Rossi's 'Emergency Plan' (p. 170) can be found in 1 Thessalonians 1?
4. What practical message do you find for your own situation when you read (a) Exod. 3.7–12; and (b) Gen. 2.15–25?

CONTEXTUAL APPLICATION

5. What do you know about (a) Pentecostal Churches and (b) Theological Education by Extension in your own country? What good features have you noticed about them?
6. What opportunities do ordinary lay Christians get in your

Church to (a) freely express their opinions; (b) discuss their problems in supportive groups; (c) get the help they need from fellow-Christians?

7. What are the three levels of theological reflection described by Gustavo Gutierrez on p. 172? Who reflects in these ways in Churches which you know? If the second and third levels of reflection are usually done by Church leaders or theologians, how can we help all Christians to think on all three levels?

8. In (a) your country and (b) your Church, which method of education is most favoured: the 'banking' method or the 'conscientization' method? What are the benefits and weaknesses in each method? Which one do you think Jesus favoured in His teaching?

9. What benefits could the poor bring to the Church?

10. (a) What do you understand by 'theology'?
    (b) How are the definitions of Liberation Theology given on pp. 172–174 different from your understanding of theology?

11. How could a Christian group in any locality set about starting a Liberation Theology movement?

12. When would you (a) encourage non-Christians to work and share with Christians and (b) discourage them—and why?

13. What sort of local development projects in your locality would be in harmony with the principles of Liberation Theology?

14. According to the 're-invention of the Church', where does the Church get its spiritual power? If this new theology of the Church was a reality in our lives, what difference would this make to our attitude to (a) signs and wonders, and (b) Christian mission in general?

15. How would you solve the problem of p. 177(1)? What other problems would be created by your solution?

16. Do you think it is a good idea to prepare sermons collectively? What is good about this method? What is less good about it?

17. What do you think are wrong reasons for seeking leadership in the Church (see p. 179)? What can Church leaders do to avoid falling into temptations like these?

18. Evaluate Liberation Theology by making two lists: (a) one list of ways in which it can help the Church and (b) another list of ways in which it might hinder the Church.

19. Try using the four methods of Bible study outlined on pp. 181–185 in a small group you belong to. Evaluate each method when every member of the group has given their opinion.

14. Urban Mission

The world missionary movement has been specially concerned to reach new peoples with the Gospel. Many missionaries have gone to live in remote areas in order to learn new languages and identify with the people. But the cities of the world have been comparatively neglected. This neglect may have happened because cities seemed to belong to the Western world rather than the Third World. Or perhaps the missionaries thought that cities were godless places which would be harder to redeem than the countryside.

THE URBAN SITUATION

Christians have become much more concerned for cities over the last twenty years. There are four main reasons for this:

1. The Bible shows God's concern for cities. Abraham prayed for God to spare the city of Sodom; Jeremiah told the exiles to pray and work for the welfare of Babylon; Jonah discovered God's love for Nineveh; Jesus wept over Jerusalem; Paul concentrated his mission work in big cities; John sent letters to seven major cities; and the centre-point of God's new heaven and new earth is the city of New Jerusalem (Rev. 21.2)—so we know that all Christians have an urban future!

2. The cities of the world are growing in two ways: (a) by birthrate (8 million babies are born in cities every month; Cairo has one new baby every 20 seconds) and (b) by migration (75,000 people move into cities every day). More than 50 per cent of the world's people will live in cities by the year 2000. People who used to be far away from one another are now close together in cities: Turks in Frankfurt, Bengalis in London, Indians in Durban, Central Americans in Miami, Thais in Singapore. Yet many Christians are moving out, leaving the city to people who are exploiting the poor for personal gain. But there is no doubt that the city is the place for today's missionary—and perhaps even more for international teams of missionaries who can use their gifts to provide resources for one another, be a model of the unity which the Gospel brings (see p. 118), and relate well to the variety of ethnic groups to be found in modern cities. Such teams need to be ready, however, to accept leadership from local Christians so that any Church which emerges will be indigenous rather than foreign.

3. Cities can change the world. They are centres of new ideas and communication. The powers of evil are indeed at work in them; yet the Good News of Jesus can touch a community of immigrants

(in strange surroundings, they are often open to new ideas) and spread not only to them but also to the areas they come from, perhaps on the other side of the world. By teaching the faith in the great city of Ephesus, Paul reached people all over the Province of Asia without going there!

4. Cities are places for compassion and love. The Salvation Army began with William Booth's concern for London's poor; the whole city of Dar es Salaam was affected by Edmund John's call to heal the sick in 1973. Today's smart city centres are surrounded by huge shanty towns of slum dwellers who live off toxic garbage dumps which poison the water and the air. Child prostitutes are bought and sold in Bangkok to satisfy rich tourists. Presidents build new hotels and airports for international visitors but spend nothing on water or sanitation for the poor. Eighty per cent of city dwellers, and nine out of the world's ten biggest cities are in the Third World. In such places Christians are called not only to preach but to work for change (see Isa. 58.6–12).

Cities have changed a great deal over the centuries. In the year 1600 the world's five largest cities (Peking, Istanbul, Agra, Cairo and Osaka) were hostile to Christianity. By 1900 the five largest cities (London, New York, Paris, Berlin and Chicago) were centres for Christian mission. But now the picture has changed again and urban growth is in the Third World (Mexico City, Sao Paulo, Tokyo, Shanghai and Beijing) and although most people now live in cities, most of them are not Christians (see Figure 22 below).

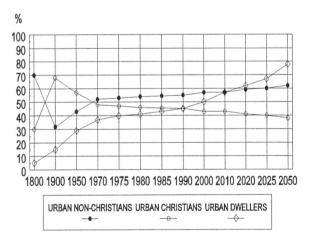

Figure 22 The rise and fall of urban Christianity, 1800–2050.

189

N.B. The bottom line in Figure 22 ('urban dwellers') shows how the number of people living in cities has grown from five per cent of the world's population in 1800 to fifty per cent in the year 2000. The two top lines show that in 1800 only thirty per cent of all city dwellers were Christians (at least in name). The number went up to nearly seventy per cent in 1900, and down again to forty-five per cent in 2000.

This change in the population of cities challenges the Church to change its mission strategy. City dwellers are encountering more new people and more new ideas than ever before. Among these new ideas is Christianity. This means that even though Christians are a smaller proportion of city dwellers than before, with modern technology they have greater opportunities than ever before to be witnesses to Christ—so they may be able to do more evangelizing (see Figure 23 opposite). But the Church must do this job without the support from city leaders which it used to get in the old cities of Europe. At the same time the Church is called to challenge the city when it fails to sustain and nurture its inhabitants. The first graph opposite gives the same information as the two top lines of the graph on p. 189. The second graph shows how it is possible in the modern world for a small percentage of Christians to evangelize more people than a larger percentage of Christians could do in earlier times.

MODELS OF URBAN MISSION

There are hundreds of different models of urban mission. The modern city has room for them all, and different people with different models can work in partnership. Here are a few of them:

1. Give power to the powerless poor by encouraging them to work together to demand justice and to resist those who exploit them. The World Council of Churches favours this model.

2. Organize a bold mission thrust which uses TV and radio to get the Gospel message out to as many unbelievers as possible—whether they respond or not. This is called 'mega-evangelism' and is the policy of the Southern Baptists of the USA.

3. Use telephones or newspapers to say something to the whole city about the Gospel or about human need. The aim of this model is not to convert people but to alert them to the possibility of change.

4. Plant new congregations which will reach out to their immediate neighbours, concentrating on 'homogeneous' units (see p. 118). This is the model of 'Church Growth'.

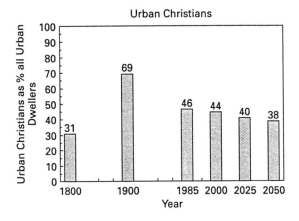

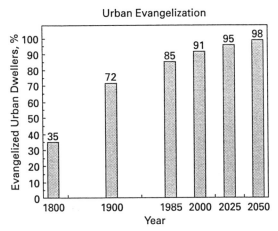

Figure 23 Models of urban mission.

5. Equip Christians to serve the needs of the poor by basic educational programmes to help them to develop and to cope with the problems of living. This is long-term community development.

6. Provide intensive youth worship which uses cultural forms that appeal to the youth culture of cities. This has been done in Prague, Sheffield and by Youth with a Mission in Amsterdam.

This chapter does not recommend any particular one of these models, because there is no one best method for mission. Fixed programmes for mission or evangelism can make people feel guilty, either because they find they have not got the energy to do all the work which the programme demands, or because they do not really like the programme anyway and therefore do nothing. Some of the people who do join in with enthusiasm can become seriously exhausted. Some of these programmes seem to trust management skills more than the Holy Spirit. Therefore John Wimber has said 'Give God back His Church' and Ray Bakke has said 'Give ministry away' (this chapter relies greatly on Bakke's work). Both are good slogans for a city Church, because (a) God ought to be the leader of all mission, and (b) human leaders should not try to control everything themselves but should set ordinary Christians free for mission. Urban mission should value all models, because different Christians have different gifts, different theologies and different objectives. The Lord has given His Church vast resources, and the city gives scope to them all—if Christians co-operate.

This need for many different models is reflected in a recent survey of Nairobi which suggested a three-fold mission strategy: (1) develop small, community-based congregations and house-churches in the poor areas of the city, sharing resources; (2) trust lay people to be led by the Holy Spirit without the clergy controlling everything; (3) develop new links between evangelism and social action, e.g. relief services, family counselling, medical help, income generation and work training.

A development of this kind took place recently in an urban district in England. After the City Council had redeveloped the area and rehoused the people, it became obvious (a) that the Council had made no provision to support the community or provide community services, and (b) that the four big local Anglican church buildings were unsuitable to meet the needs of the community. The Anglicans therefore decided to create a 'local indigenous Church' which would take the community as its starting point rather than tradition. The aim was not to impress the area but to reflect it, and to relate to the whole of its life, its homes, its people, and its problems. The new building was criticized for being 'not like a proper church'; 'like a music-hall'; 'a barn'. It was not

A weekday play group at Easton Family Centre in England (see p. 194).

even dedicated to Saint Somebody! The building is called 'Easton Family Centre' and it is open six days a week. It provides a drop-in centre for the unemployed, a crèche for babies, lunches for the homeless, a family guidance centre, facilities for hobbies, a conference centre, and specialist groups for the blind, mothers-and-toddlers, young people, alcoholics, the elderly and the disabled. It is easy for non-Christians to come in during the week—and since Church on Sunday is in the same place, they can attend without feeling strange. A poster in the entrance hall proclaims 'Jesus is Lord', and Christian staff (two pastors, a Youth Worker, a Community Worker and an Asian Community Worker, two part-time administrators and lay volunteers at the welcome desk) are always available to help anyone. Leadership is more in the hands of the people than of the pastor. The aim of the Centre is not to evangelize the community but rather to meet people at their points of need, i.e. unemployment, crime, child-abuse and loneliness, and in this context to bear witness to Jesus who meets people at the same point.

NETWORKING FOR SUPPORT

No one can work alone in a modern city. That is the route to loneliness and fear. The result of fear is usually that pastors become authoritarian dictators who want to control everything. As a result, they lose their best lay leaders, and finally may lose the Holy Spirit. City pastors need to admit that they need the support of others. True vision must be shared vision (see Eph. 3.18).

1. *Training* is the first need, i.e. time spent in supervised study of the city and different patterns and theologies of mission. Those who work in big, multi-cultural cities need specialized missionary training.

2. The second need is for continuing *group support*. For example, in one city about six ministers (preferably both men and women with different styles of ministry) might meet together one full day every month (away from spouses, families and Church members). The group might look something like this: all members are totally committed to one another; no one is allowed to be absent; they share joys, problems, successes, failures and pain; if the group criticizes or corrects one of the members, he or she can hear it because they know that the other members do it out of support and love. Shared support of this sort is one of the best features of urban life. Those who get it feel secure and encouraged. A pastor who fears and hates the city cannot minister there. He or she must first unpack their bags and settle there, as Jeremiah told the

Jewish exiles to do when they were deported to Babylon. Then a pastor may begin to know the city and love it—and be able to minister in it.

It is impossible to arrange such support if we see other pastors and other Churches as our rivals with whom we are in competition. If we feel like this, we shall envy the success of the other pastors, rejoice in their failure, and even try to imitate their ministries, instead of exercising the special ministries God has given to us—and perhaps to us alone. Two pastors in an English city with a big Hindu population once spent much time criticizing one another's theology and strategy—until they went to a meeting where both of them admitted that their attempts to do evangelism amongst Hindus had been a complete failure. Then, out of mutual weakness, they began to help one another. The first step in getting support is mentioned on p. 199 below.

In addition to this, city pastors often need a special sort of support because of the environment in which they work. The drug and sex culture of modern cities makes traditional Christian patterns of family life very difficult. The Church in these areas lives on the cultural frontiers, just as it does when it engages with polygamy in rural areas (see p. 79). If the Church wants to reach people with Jesus' love, it must, like Jesus, show them this love without condemning them. Unmarried couples live together, people change or swap their sexual partners, children are given away to surrogate parents, prostitution is common. And it will often be these very people who are attracted by the true love which is offered in the Church. But they are often confused about the meaning of the word 'love', and look for it in the wrong places and in wrong ways. At this point all pastors, both women and men, are in danger. Women with bad relationships may desire a loving pastor as a substitute sex-object; children may desire a man or woman pastor to be a substitute parent. This may have three results: (a) the pastor (who is himself or herself a sexual human being) experiences sexual temptation; (b) the Church is deeply resented by the other partner or parent; (c) the Church, which should be a refuge for needy people, actually ends up not affirming but destroying the last vestiges of family which they had.

In these circumstances, the following support strategy is suggested:

1. Church ministers should respect the non-Christians in any family as much as they respect the Christians. Listen to them, value their ideas, be responsible to them.

2. Let the Church share in the instruction and upbringing of the

children, perhaps by supplying responsible godparents or sponsors when a baby is baptized or dedicated.

3. Try to ensure that every local Church has both female and male ministers available.

4. Have all letters, telephone calls and interviews monitored by another person.

5. Appoint one or two reliable, mature women (and one or two men) to check and guide the ordained or lay pastors in their relationships with people of the opposite sex.

In the list of Jesus' ancestors in Matthew 1, the most interesting feature is that five women are mentioned. The first four (Tamar, Rahab, Ruth, Bathsheba) each had something surprising or shameful in her sexual history. No 'honourable' women are mentioned. So there was no attempt to conceal the fact that Jesus' family was quite disreputable. This is how life is and how people are, and Christians must not pretend to be different (yet how often we do!). Jesus' mother Mary also had a problem with public opinion, for she had become pregnant before her marriage to Joseph. It almost seems as if the four women were mentioned so that they could serve as an encouragement and a support group for Mary. The Gospel of Jesus really does specialize in people like this. They are the 'all nations' which Matthew mentions at the end of his Gospel (28.19), the people for whom Jesus came.

NETWORKING FOR EVANGELISM

There are no short cuts to evangelism. Most people become Christians through observing the lives of Christians over a long period. This means that the Church must become visible through its members. Quick-fix programmes through knocking at the doors of strangers, distributing leaflets to houses, or urging people to make a response to Christ are not effective in the city. City people are tired of being given advice; they are overloaded with advice. What they want is good news which will make them feel good about themselves— and that is just what Jesus has always offered. Unfortunately the Church has often failed to offer the same.

Instead of urging believers to make new contacts for evangelism, networking helps them to use the contacts they already have. For example:

1. *Biological* Get people to make a chart of, say, twenty relatives with whom they are in touch, choose four or five of them, and then find out what their basic needs are and how the Church member can support them. Meanwhile the believers have learnt and practised how to give a two-minute testimony about what Jesus has done in

This photograph shows the delegates from all over Africa who took part in a conference organized by the World Council of Churches to set up a worldwide network of Bible teachers, so that they could share needs, experience and ideas. Networking is also an essential part of urban mission.

their lives. Given the contacts, the practical help and the testimony—and prayer, evangelism will take care of itself! Figure 24
shows the kind of chart you could make for yourself to list your own
opportunities for evangelism.

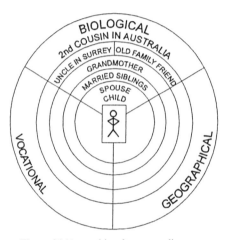

Figure 24 Networking for evangelism.

2. *Geographical* Again, fill in a chart to see the contacts in your
district. There are often significant people in poor urban districts,
and nothing happens without them—they are the gate-keepers.
Often these significant people are women, often they are uneducated, but are listened to. They are never appointed; it is a
process of natural selection by consensus. The Church has to
recognize these people. Rich districts operate differently: in one
rich district a Christian couple asked their neighbours to their home
for 'cheese and wine' one evening. It was a new experience for the
neighbourhood. They all knew what sort of cars their neighbours
drove, but they did not know their neighbours' names or what sort
of people they were. That evening they were overjoyed to make
new friends in a place where they had felt alone. Among such
contacts, again, evangelism can take care of itself.

3. *Vocational* Often the Church drags people away from their
colleagues at work by putting them on Church committees and
telling them to attend Christian meetings. Instead, Christians
should be given time to play a full part in Trade Union and other
activities connected with their daily work —and to do so as

believers. Small support groups can pray for such people on the 'front line'. Pastors should encourage this by visiting their people in their work places as well as at home, and also by meeting their colleagues. Such visits will help the pastor to relate his or her own public ministry to the real world of the people; and before long the Christians will probably be sought out by colleagues for help with problems and will have plenty of natural opportunities for witness.

Networks such as these provide more than enough natural contacts for Christian witness, and there is no need for the Church to devise ways of artificially creating new contacts. These are seldom fruitful amid the pressures of urban life.

NETWORKING FOR UNDERSTANDING

Coca-Cola and McDonalds are the same all over the world—the same in Beijing as they are in Boston, totally unaffected by the environment. Churches often operate in the same way—Roman Catholics, Anglicans, Southern Baptists may simply export a packaged product, without taking time to understand the nature and culture of the people who receive the package. This often results not in evangelism but in stealing Christians from other Churches, e.g. Presbyterians 'winning' Coptic Christians in Cairo. The Church, however, is called to do genuine market research in two stages: (1) the first stage is to discover what are the perceived needs of the people and to begin to relate to those needs. One Brazilian couple in Recife made no real contact with the shanty-dwellers until one Christmas they took a food parcel to the poorest home of all—the food they gave was only symbolic, but it was a breakthrough. (2) The second stage is to move on to share with those people the inside information we have about their deep, spiritual needs which can be met by Jesus. But we often try to take the second step before we have taken the first! One way to take the first step is by Mission Audit (see p. 120 and Special Note G). For an example, see pp. 192–193.

NETWORKING CHURCHES

Just as Jesus invited others to talk with Him and serve Him (John 4.7), so a new pastor arriving in a city should try to meet as many other pastors as possible, because he or she is someone who needs to learn and get support. The new pastor might say to another pastor who has been there longer, 'I'm new here and I wonder if you could tell me the most important lesson you have learnt here since you began?' Often pastors make the mistake of seeing one another not as resources but as rivals or even threats.

Just as cities specialize in different activities (business, car manufacturing, education, tourism, etc.) so do Churches. Some (e.g. Ethiopian Orthodox) are proud of their ancient tradition and resist change, and yet they attract many people who want security. Other Churches (e.g. in Singapore) are efficient business enterprises with high achievement levels and managerial pastors; these Churches attract people who want to be busy. Another may be a city-centre charismatic Church offering celebration for big crowds and a Master of Ceremonies as pastor; it attracts people who want to be both excited and hidden in the crowd. Another Church is a happy family who need to be together and to be loved, and who want a Big Daddy for a pastor. Another Church is a servant with a conscience to help the weak and create a caring society; it has a pastor with political wisdom and attracts people with a call to stand alongside the poor and needy. Another Church is artistic and looks for beauty and music and a sense of God's transcendence; it attracts people who dream dreams and want to 'be' more than to 'do'. No Church specializes in only one of these approaches, and no Church has them all. *Local* Churches must offer a general ministry for everyone, made up of worship, evangelism, discipleship, stewardship, fellowship and service. *Urban* Churches can afford to specialize, provided that they also affirm the ways in which other Churches specialize and refer needy people to them. The city has room for them all; the wise pastor recognizes this and is glad.

For too long the Church has had a rural bias, and has tried to create rural-type local Churches even in the cities where such a model is unsuitable. In cities the Church must forget the idea of territorial parishes and take into account the realities of urban social and cultural life (see p. 192 above).

NETWORKING AGENCIES

A young woman out walking early found a dead man in a car. He lived in a street nearby and had committed suicide. The local pastor asked the police for the man's address in order to visit and comfort the family. But the police did not know the pastor and refused to give him this confidential information. Another city pastor knows all about the life and problems of his district because he has made friends with the police, social workers, teachers and shopkeepers. This saves him hours of time when a crisis occurs because these people know him and trust him. We should never think 'I am too busy to do this'; rather we should realize 'I am far too busy *not* to network like this.' No one feels successful in the city—all of us need support from one another.

NETWORKING LOCALITIES

Christian workers need to 'put one arm round the Church and one arm round society' and draw them together. Many Christians (especially rich Christians) are afraid of society. One pastor in South Africa could see that the rich white people in his parish were afraid of the poor black people in the nearby township—because they did not know any of them. So the pastor took the white people with him, one by one, on his visits to the black area until they found they could be friends with the black people and could share problems and learn from one another.

The city Church can see the whole pattern of life in a way that few other people can, and it can embrace and gather together those who are trying to serve the city. One way of doing this is to have a 'celebration' party every six weeks, and invite urban workers to come and to express their appreciation of one another through information and short speeches. Or one particular ethnic group could invite those of another group to a cultural evening.

The presence of different cultural groups makes the city one of the most interesting and exciting places to be: the whole world is in the city, and we can see what God is doing in His global kingdom. The biggest city in the world before 1800 was Rome in the time of Paul. It had over a million inhabitants, 60 per cent of whom were slaves. Refugees flocked to Rome as they do to big cities today—among them was a runaway slave called Onesimus. He came across Paul's urban mission team (Acts 28.30), became a Christian, went back home to Laodicea and joined a house-church which contained rich and poor, slave and free alike. He might have been the same Onesimus who was later Bishop of Ephesus. Paul wrote to Onesimus' master, Philemon, that God had a purpose in allowing this urban refugee to come to Rome (Philemon 15)—a purpose which involved not only Rome but two big cities of Asia (Laodicea and Ephesus) as well. Soon after the affair of Onesimus, Pliny, the Governor of Bithynia, wrote to the Roman Emperor that there were huge numbers of Christians in Asia, of every age and class, men and women, rural and urban. Today there are 12 million reluctant urban refugees—what plans might God have for them, and for the world through them?

Creating and maintaining networks of support and information should form part of every urban pastor's regular programme. At the outset of a new ministry, this activity could take up 50 per cent of his or her time. A later pattern might be: 20 per cent of the time spent on study, teaching, preparation; 20 per cent on caring, pastoring; 20 per cent on administration, equipping; 20 per cent on networking; 20 per cent on self and family. This seems to reflect the shape of Jesus' ministry.

A NOTE ON HISTORY

Many city dwellers are nostalgic about the past. They remember it, they dream about it, but they do not learn from it. The past is gone and the best they can hope for in life is to survive. What needs to be done is to unlock the nostalgic memory so that it becomes a functional memory. Spend time with older lay people and ask them three questions:

1. What is your story, and your experience of God?
2. What did you value most at Church over the years?
3. If you could create a new future, what would it be?

Then those who preach and teach could tell the stories and dream the dreams in public, perhaps mentioning the name of the person who told them. By this means memory and dreams become (a) valuable and (b) functional, i.e. they will give rise to action. The mood of the Church changes, the members look for new things to happen, they expect prayers to be answered. If we have no good memories of the past, we can have no hope for the future; and without either past memories or future hope, present life is just a desert of despair.

A NOTE ON ART

Art can be found in all the world's cities, even in shanty towns. People paint a wall; or make a toy; or plant a shrub; or create music; or act a little drama; or dance. These things are not planned, they just happen. In Exod. 31.1–11 it happened to a disorganized rabble of slaves wandering about the desert and always complaining. God gave them gifts of creativity as signs of hope to lift up the spirits of people who thought they were of no value and could do nothing. How can we encourage these gifts? Here are some suggestions:

* Don't pay a professional to produce the Church bulletin, but ask a few Church members who are learning to type to produce it—then everyone will proudly own it as their work, even if the lines are crooked and the spelling wrong.
* Use a crumbling Church building to discover and develop the skills of Church members (some perhaps unemployed) in painting, plumbing, plastering, electricals.
* Instead of the pastor's sermon, use the youth group's skills in drama or music, and have the pastor preach around their presentation.

202

In a city Church, *what* is done is far less important than *the way* it is done (i.e., by whom). 'Give ministry away.'

One day three rural lay people brought a proposal to Diocesan Synod. Their proposal had already been passed by the parish council and Deanery Synod. If it was accepted by the Diocese they would take it to National Synod —imagine how nervous they felt! After they had made their speeches, a clever Archdeacon stood up and demolished their arguments in five minutes. He sat down. He had won; they had lost. But one thing was certain—those three people would never again dare to share any good ideas. *Their* lay ministry had been destroyed for ever, and the people who had *really* lost were the whole Diocese, including the Archdeacon.

NETWORKING FOR ACTION

In 1984 people who lived in council flats in Liverpool had a problem with cockroaches. Week after week they asked the City Council to deal with the insects, but they were ignored. Finally they decided to take action. They organized a competition to see who had the biggest cockroaches. They all collected them in coffee jars and brought them to the Council Chamber to be judged. In the middle of a debate, the people let out their huge cockroaches and asked the Mayor to judge whose was the biggest. The councillors were very angry, and the people were expelled from the Chamber. But next day, men came round to clean up the flats!

This method of direct action often solves the immediate problem, but it does not change much in the long term. A better way is for a group to work together in positive action to remove injustices in the community. By this means they first discover power, and then they increase their power, just as you strengthen muscles by exercise. But there are some important guidelines to follow:

1. Begin with a group of Christians who support one another to protest against bad conditions, and choose a memorable name for the group (e.g. People in Faith United = PIFU).

2. Have a vision for what changes might take place. Isa. 65.18–25 might offer some ideas.

3. By means of networking, find out what the local people see as their needs.

4. Select one small need, e.g. the loneliness of old people, and see what can be done when a group works together. Realizing that change is possible is a turning point in the process.

5. Do a small project, e.g. a lunch club for the elderly. It is important to start small because poor city dwellers are used to

being losers and will give up if they try a big project which fails, so that they lose yet again 'because we are bad people'. They need to get used to winning.

6. Later, begin to look at a bigger problem, e.g. the youth culture, unemployment, housing.

7. If the problem is too big for the group, find other people and groups who want to help—they will be glad to join a small group which has already started, and the network will be enlarged and have more resources.

This process is a form of 'community development' in which local people take the initiative. Most of the obstacles to mission in the city come from inside the Churches, not from outside. Perhaps Christians are more interested in enjoying fellowship within the Church than in networking and changing the city. Perhaps they are not co-operating. Above all, perhaps they have forgotten to pray. A group in Amsterdam goes on prayer walks round the city. Any group can take responsibility for the neighbourhood and its people by organizing prayer for them, perhaps street by street. Jesus did not only weep over Jerusalem; He prayed for it.

Special Note G

A MODEL FOR MISSION AUDIT

One of the mistakes which missionaries make most often is to speak before they have taken time to listen. Any local Church which fails to listen seems to be saying to outsiders:

'We don't think you have anything of value for us to hear.'

'We know it all, and you should listen to us.'

'We don't love you as you are, but we might if you become like us.'

This is not like the ministry of Jesus, and it turns people away from the Christian message. *Mission Audit* can help us not to make this mistake, for an audit is a way of 'reading' the context and culture in which we live. It makes us ask questions about (a) the people and the society around us; (b) the Church we belong to, and (c) how Church and society should relate to one another. The purpose of Mission Audit is to enable the Church to change, so that all people can hear its message clearly in terms of their own language and culture, and ultimately be changed by it themselves. Effective audit can therefore only be done by people who belong and it will probably show Christians whether or not they truly belong to the locality where they live. (Many Churches do not belong, but are like islands unrelated to the people.)

Audit must be preceded by *Prayer* and followed by *Planning* and *Prioritizing*. Prayer shows that we are open to God and want to follow Him first of all. We *expect* to discover more about Him and His will, both for the Church and for society, through the Audit. Planning and Prioritizing show that Audit is not just gathering information. It will have visible results in the Church: *we* must change before we can expect other people to change. The members of the Church as a whole must *want* to do this, rather than be persuaded by a few enthusiasts.

There are two kinds of Audit.

1. The first is a *Limited Audit*. A Limited Audit considers one specific area of concern, e.g. Leadership (Who are the leaders? How do they make, communicate and implement policy?). Or Local Youth (What are the needs of young people in our area? How are these needs being met? How can the Church help?). Or Politics (How does it affect the lives of local people? How far can the Church support or influence local policies or help the people to come to terms with them?).

2. The second kind is a *General Audit*, which will take much longer, perhaps one or two years. In fact, because human society is changing so fast nowadays, Audit should ideally never end, but become a continuous feature of the Church's life and self-understanding. This is represented by a diagram of the *Action Cycle* in which we:

LOOK - THINK - PLAN - ACT

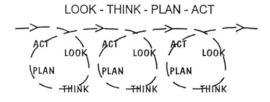

Figure 25 The Action Cycle.

LOOK   at *the local community*, its history, geography, people and resources; how its people relate to and regard the Church; and what values, beliefs and activities are important to them;

at *the Church*, its history, membership, internal leadership, relationships, worship, customs and resources;

at *God*—His written word, His activity among both Christians and non-Christians in the area, and His will for the people.

THINK   about how far the Church matches and communicates with the local community, whether it both reflects it (speaking its language) and challenges it (having a relevant message and vision).

PLAN   any changes the Church needs to make (a) within itself (e.g. relationship with God, leadership, structures, membership, worship, etc.); (b) in its ministry to the area; and (c) in its vision for the area.

ACT   to put the plans into action by having objectives which can be achieved and measured and which will involve everyone, be closely monitored and use whatever resources and training are available.

Many resources may be available, but they will differ as much as Churches differ. Here are three different kinds of resources which are often useful:

1. Local government resources, e.g. census details which tell us about age groups, housing, education, etc.

2. Outside advisers, e.g. two experienced helpers who are not members of the Church—one of these could even be a non-Christian.

3. An appropriate questionnaire to discover more about local people (e.g. their age, sex, race, language, work, interests, religion, values, experiences, beliefs, problems, including social issues). Get Church members to go round asking the questions, because there is no better way for them to learn to relate to people as they are.

Some local Churches may be afraid of starting such a challenging and changing exercise. In that case, it is a good idea to start with a short exercise, auditing just one part of the Church, or to do a practice audit on a nearby Church which has already done a Mission Audit. Or Church members could be encouraged to audit one of the New Testament Churches, discovering all they can about, e.g., the Church at Philippi and its locality (Macedonia) through using Bible passages like Paul's letter to the Philippians; Acts 16.12–40; 20:1–6; 2 Cor. 8.1–9; 9.1–5. Or people could survey a nearby small urban district and try to 'read' the context in order to answer questions like 'What would a Church need to be like in order to relate effectively to these people living here?' or 'What forms of worship would be most relevant in this place and for these people?'

Audit will help us to discover the people who are unevangelized and those who are likely to be receptive to the Gospel, e.g. certain ethnic minorities, age groups seeking a spiritual meaning to life, people concerned for the environment or for justice and peace. Audit will show what contacts Christians have with such people—or even with the people they meet at work day by day. Audit discovers local needs—in the shanty towns, among the unemployed or under-employed, the homeless or AIDS sufferers—and may enable the Church to be the first to discover and challenge these social evils, instead of being the last to see and to act (as so often happens).

Audit defines the areas in which the Church needs to change in order to be true to its mission—and the shape of mission is changing fast. We can no longer assume that a missionary is a white European; she is more likely to be an Asian or African witnessing to a living and joyful faith on a French University campus or in a poor urban district of Chicago, Beijing or Rio. Audit includes learning more about our neighbouring Churches and about fellow-Christians from far-away lands who are here to help us in our mission. Audit is an organized and structured way of involving the whole Church in 'networking' (see p. 199).

A new version of the Three Circles diagram can summarize for us the proper areas for Mission Audit (see Figure 26, p. 208).

If the whole Church is to be involved in the Mission Audit, then the results of the Audit must be communicated to the whole Church. Christians need to know what the relationship between society and the Church *was* like (its history), what it *is* like (its sociology) and what the hope is for its future, what it *will* be like as a result of planning and praying. Pictures, posters, graphs and charts can help everyone to know, and to want to be part of the future.

Finally, Audit must begin, continue and end with *worship*, including prayer and listening to God. Otherwise Audit will be just another example of our activism, and we shall be in danger of failing to hear the will of God and see His action among us.

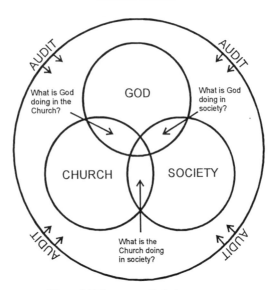

Figure 26 The scope of Mission Audit.

STUDY SUGGESTIONS

BIBLE STUDY

1. What indications of success or failure do you find in Paul's mission in (a) Thessalonica, (b) Ephesus, and (c) Rome? What effect did his urban mission have upon non-urban districts?

CONTEXTUAL APPLICATION

2. (a) Find out the rate of population growth or decline in the city you know best.
   (b) How receptive or hostile to Christian mission do you think this city is?
   (c) What specific examples of Christian compassion and care for the needy do you know of in that city? Isa. 58.6–12 and 65.19–23 might give you some ideas.
   (d) Evaluate how effective these efforts are.
3. Do you feel that the Church in your country has put more effort into rural mission or into urban mission? What evidence is there for your opinion? Why might the Church favour one mission or the other?
   4. Note the strategy proposed for Nairobi (p. 192). If your Church adopted a similar strategy, what difference would it make?

5. What support or training do leaders in your Church get, along the lines described on pp. 194–195? How could such support help them?
6. What special trials or temptations face urban ministers?
7. Make a chart of *Networking for Evangelism*, like the chart on p. 198, and fill it in to show your own contacts in family, locality and work. Compare your completed chart with the charts of one or two friends.
8. What 'gate-keepers' helped Paul in Corinth and Philippi?
9. Does your Church offer a general ministry for everyone in its locality, or does it exercise a specialist ministry? What, if any, are its specialized activities, and who are they for?
10. How many of the people who serve your local community do you know by name? How many of them know you, your Church or your minister?
11. As far as you know, what different nationalities and cultures are present in reasonable numbers in the capital city of your country?
12. Give any examples you know of memories of yesterday being put to effective use in mission today.
13. What creative arts are present in your Church? (a) How are they being used, and (b) could they be used better in the Church's mission?
14. How, in your experience, have Christians been able to improve the quality of life in their neighbourhood? Give any example you can of a small improvement which led on to a bigger one.
15. What are the arguments for and against the Church inviting non-Christians to join with it in its mission to society?
16. Do the exercise on p. 207 which relates to Philippi, or the one which relates to an urban district you know.
17. What is the importance of prayer in Mission Audit, and how would you make it part of the structure of the Audit?
18. How could you effectively involve and encourage all Church members in Mission Audit and in finding a vision for the future?

15. Inter-Faith Encounter

The hardest theological question which faces the whole Church in the twentieth century concerns its attitude to people of other faiths. (Many Christians see the modern secular world-view, which seems to encourage people to live self-sufficient lives and to do without God, as an even bigger challenge.) The question of people of other faiths is a missionary question, which has been familiar for a long time to the people of Asia but is now becoming the daily concern of Christians in Africa, Europe and the Americas. For example, any pastor who proposes to engage in serious dialogue with Muslims will have to struggle with one group of Christians who insist that since 'Christ is the only way' (whatever that means) the only thing you can do with people of other faiths is preach the Gospel to them (this is called the *exclusivist* position). The pastor will also have to contend with another group who think that all religions are equally valid and true ways of relating to the one God (called the *pluralist* position). Many people say that the pluralist position is like the blind men in the Indian story who met an elephant for the first time: one of them leaned against its side and thought the elephant was like a wall; another touched the trunk and thought it was like a snake; the next touched the tusk and thought it was like a spear; the last blind man found the tail and thought the elephant was like a rope—each man was partly correct, but you must put all their opinions together to get the truth. The pastor may see himself, however, as an *inclusivist* who believes that religion is indeed a sign of people's instinct for God but He can only be known for sure in Christ. (Note, however, that each of these three 'positions' can be expressed in a great variety of different ways.)

Many long and complex books have been written on this topic, but this chapter begins with some questions in the form of stories; it suggests some guidelines for tackling these questions, and finally it uses the Bible to build a framework within which to understand the place of religion in human life.

But first, let us realize that this is a deeply painful problem. In 'Christian' England 200 years ago, or in Uganda or Poland today where the Church is strong, it may not be a big issue. But if you are one of the 400 Christians in Morocco, how do you even think about your 24,000,000 fellow-Moroccans who cannot be anything but Muslim? And how do British Christians face the fact that their message is irrelevant and incomprehensible to millions of their fellow-citizens today? Has God really forgotten His love for all these people, just because His Church has proved inadequate or disobedient in mission?

QUESTIONS

The stories which follow raise questions which are difficult for Christians to answer. These stories all raise doubts about our neat theological ideas, and send us back to God to ask for His help, because He is somewhere in the theology, and somewhere out there in the world of the questions.

1. A Muslim scholar who was invited to speak to a group of Christian students, began by saying 'Do you believe that Jesus is the Way and that no one comes to God but by him? Well, so do I, for that is the witness of the Qur'an. Muhammad acknowledged Jesus as God's Messiah and followed his teaching.'

2. Malam Ibrahim, a teacher of the Holy Qur'an in Nigeria, taught that prayer should be made to God in the name of *Isa Masih* (Jesus the Messiah) because the Qur'an gives him a unique dignity. For this heretical teaching, Malam Ibrahim was crucified in Kano market-place thirty years before the Christian Gospel was proclaimed in Kano. His followers are still there, they are still Muslims, and they are still praying through *Isa Masih*.

3. A chief, also in West Africa, dreamed that white people would bring a message to his village from the Creator God. He shared the dream and told his people to obey the message when it came, and the dream and the message became part of the folklore of the village. Many years later missionaries proclaimed Jesus. With one accord the villagers believed and were baptized. But the chief and his elders had long since died, not having heard of Jesus or been baptized into His name.

4. In East Africa witch-doctors, the guardians of community welfare, deal with many cases of demon-possession. Muslims, too, have their remedies. But some spirits seem particularly resistant to 'treatment'. 'Ah, then special power is needed to deal with your case; you can't be healed by anyone but Jesus—you'll have to go to the Christians,' say the Muslim elders, preaching Christ.

5. One day in 1969 a strange, prophet-like figure walked into the villages of Central Tanzania. Clothed in skins, with the smell of the bush still upon him, he could not speak Swahili (the national language) nor read or write. He had never met any Christians. But God had spoken to him in a series of dreams and told him to proclaim the message to everyone. So he stood up in the village and did so. He was taken into village churches where his local dialect was translated, and they were amazed to hear him reciting (though

not word for word) the visions of the Revelation of St John, and telling people to repent and mend their ways. It was not quite the Gospel, but it seemed authentic, and he had obeyed . . .

'If God is God', wrote one bishop, 'He is likely to be the most common of human experiences.' Many of these 'common experiences' occur throughout the world, both within organized religion and outside it. Recent research in Britain has found that over 60 per cent of the people have had such experiences. However, they are quite reluctant to talk about them because they are afraid that their friends might laugh at them and they often find that the pastors don't understand what they are talking about.

There are similar stories in the Bible of people who also had a partial understanding of Christ. Abraham is perhaps the chief example (see p. 222, below). The Wise Men (Matthew 2) learnt from a very unscientific study of the stars that God was doing something special in 'the house of Judah' and they responded. They are well-known to us because they were rich enough to travel long distances and offer costly gifts. But did they become believers only when they bowed before Jesus (a very different Jesus from the one who is in our minds when we bow and worship)? For them the crucial turning point was surely their response in faith to what they understood as God's message. The book of Jonah tells of pagan sailors and pagan Ninevites who made similar responses (see p. 19), and there are probably many other examples which are not recorded by history. Through Cornelius, Peter realized that God was at work more widely than his theology had ever admitted (although it was God-given); see p. 92.

Although God is at work outside the area of the Church's witness, there have also been times when the Church's witness to Christ has been so false that God cannot have been in it. The obvious example is the Crusades, which were so cruel that Christians should be ashamed to use the word at all. What response should Saladin and his Muslim armies have made to the Christ whom they saw then?

Surely conversion to *that* Christ would have been an act of disobedience to God? One contemporary, the Franciscan Ramon Lull, certainly had his doubts:

Many knights do I see who go to the Holy Land thinking to conquer it by force of arms. But . . . it appears to me, Lord, that the conquest of that sacred land will not be achieved save by love and prayer and the shedding of tears as well as blood . . . Let the knights become religious . . . let them be filled with the grace of the Holy Spirit, and let them go among the infidels to preach the truth concerning thy passion.

In 1505 the Portuguese explorer d'Almeida arrived at Kilwa, a Muslim trading city famed for its culture and civilizing influence on the East African coast.

> As soon as the town had been taken without opposition, the Vicar-General and some of the Franciscan fathers came ashore carrying two crosses in procession and singing the *Te Deum*. They went to the palace and the Grand Captain prayed. Then everyone started to plunder the town of all its merchandise and provisions. Two days later d'Almeida fired it, destroying the greater part of this city of abomination.

The city never recovered its former prosperity.

The Good News had become bad news for Kilwa. Even today we must ask what sort of 'Good News' the 'Christian' Serbs have brought to the Muslims of Sarajevo. Perhaps Muslims have not really rejected Christ; perhaps they have never really seen Him, because we have hidden Him from them. An English woman recently turned to Islam because, she said, 'the Church always made me feel so guilty'; in Islam she was accepted as she was.

We need to hear true stories like these to stop us from being self-confident and to compel us to listen—before we speak.

PRINCIPLES

ENCOUNTER IS A BETTER WORD THAN DIALOGUE

Dialogue usually means a discussion about religion. But it is normally more valuable to meet with our fellow human-beings and talk with them about our real human needs—and then to move more naturally into understanding one another's faith. A group of Christians living in one inner-city area of England could make no contact with the multi-faith community of local residents. One day they went out to clear away rubbish, put lids back on the dustbins and smarten up the area. Then the barriers on both sides came down, and they could openly share their witness for Christ. In a time of famine in the deserts of Northern Kenya Christians distributed food to poor Muslims and so changed their attitude to the Christian message, even though some Muslims quite under-standably object to rich Christians influencing poor Muslims by means of humanitarian aid. For a similar example from Brazil, see p. 199. A group of Muslims, Christians and Hindus in an English town held occasional meetings which suddenly became significant on the night after Mrs Indira Gandhi was assassinated. Then, out of the despair felt by the Hindus— and then by all of them—they were able to pray together with a new urgency.

What brings people together is the support we give one another in the struggle to make sense of human life in a troubled world (see p. 225). It is not surprising, therefore, that the Church is growing in those parts of the world where, as in the Bible, God's gift to us all of our common humanity is understood to be part of the Good News. Christians in the North have often failed to make this a significant feature of their evangelism. We are not only one when we are in Christ; we also enjoy a oneness as human beings made in God's image.

WHY RELIGION OF ALL THINGS?

Some of the worst crimes in history have been done in the name of religion, because the world of religion is the world not only of God but also of demons. Much inter-faith dialogue assumes that religion moves people towards God— but that is not always true either in the Bible or in human experience. People are almost always religious, and that is part of the human problem, not the answer to the problem. Jesus was crucified by the world's most religious people. The Gospel of Jesus saves people from religion (which Barth called 'unbelief' and 'the affair of the godless man') and brings them to God.

But Jesus saving people from religion includes the Christian religion.

In the light of Christ's example and the example of the prophets, Christians must be prepared to be as critical of their own religion as they are of the religions of other people. It is just too easy to criticize the faults of other faiths as if these faults were the norm, and to have an idealized view of our own faith even though we never live up to the ideal. For example, Christians criticize Muslims for their aggressive teaching about 'Holy War', yet they forget the story of the Crusades, and often do not know that in Islam Holy War is more about internal discipline than about external aggression.

THE ELEMENT OF SURPRISE

God reveals Himself much more often in the ordinary experiences of life than He does in the places, such as our religion, where we plan to meet with Him. He takes us by surprise, because He is generous to those who are irreligious and severe to people who are religious. Both the irreligious and the religious are astonished

214

Relations between Christians and Muslims have varied greatly over the centuries.
Do you think Christians should try to convert Muslims like these, or simply share
their faith with them in dialogue?

(Matt. 25.31–46)—but religious people were always deeply disturbed by the teaching of Jesus (Luke 7.47; 15.11–35; Matt. 22.1–14). We cannot possibly know in advance which people have got their seats in heaven securely booked and which people have not. But religious experts often think they know—and as a result, they talk instead of listening and they may even shut themselves off from the God who repeatedly reveals Himself to us as the stranger, and surprises us by His appearances.

THE NEED FOR PERMISSION

It is not easy to go beyond the walls of the Church to meet people of other faiths. When we do this, we risk our theology, our fellowship with other Christians, even our faith itself. There are no guarantees that it is 'safe', but it was not 'safe' for Jesus to be born, to live and to die. His disciples have no choice except to follow Him into the world, trusting only in God. We discover God when we lose ourselves in mission but we lose God when we try to stay secure in sheltered territory. We need three kinds of permission to allow us to go out to meet people of other faiths:

(a) We need permission *from God*, that to go out like this cannot take us outside His will or beyond His love;

(b) We need permission *from our fellow-Christians*, that however disturbing our discoveries may be, they will never turn away from us;

(c) We need permission *from ourselves*, that we really can be faithful to Christ as the only Saviour and Lord, at the same time as we are open to receive revelations of God in places where Christ is confessed in different ways, or not confessed at all.

Real mission among people of other faiths is always costly. It was costly for Jesus and He warned that it would be costly for us (Luke 12.49–54). A Hebrew Christian who came from a Jewish family was invited to read Deut. 6.4–9 at a conference about Christian missionary work, but she had read only two verses when she cried out 'I can't read this after what we've been discussing', and ran out in tears.

Mission also proved very costly for a young European missionary in India. She had made friends with a Hindu girl and was warmly accepted into her friend's home. She joined in their family festivals and shared their big family bed. One day she arrived to find that one of the family had died, and they were all mourning and filled with grief. She made her excuses to leave them on such a private occasion, but they said, 'No, you can't; you are one of us, in the family'—and she stayed there for the days of mourning. She had never experienced so much love and welcome in her life as she did from this Hindu family. How could she ever repay it? Then one day when she was in Delhi, her friend called to tell her that she had accepted Jesus and was going to be baptized. The missionary should have been glad—this was why she had accepted God's call to India. But all she could feel was utter misery. What a betrayal of that wonderful friendship given so unconditionally! How could she ever face that family again? It seemed that the 'Good News' of Jesus had taken their daughter from them and broken up that loving Hindu family. 'Is it good news?' she asked herself. 'What will they think of Jesus now?'

THE DANGER OF DOGMA

Naturally and rightly, new Christians want to learn more about the teachings of Christianity. But these teachings then become a problem if they are made into a high fence which is placed across the entrance of the Church to give believers a sense of security and to keep 'unbelievers' out. Many of our doctrines, as they have developed over the centuries, do not make much sense, or seem relevant, to people of other cultures and faiths—especially, perhaps, to those people who belong to modern Western culture. Why should we expect them to accept, or even to understand, what we say about the divinity of Christ or the Trinity, when the first Christians took many years to work it out? For some examples, see p. 229.

This is *not* how God originally intended Jesus to be presented to the world. If we can present Him more simply, we shall not rob new disciples of the wonderful adventure of discovering for themselves who this Jesus is, in terms of their own cultures and world-view—as the Masai people did (see Special Note C). In any case, how foolish we are if we think we know Him so well that we can tell other people about Him clearly and adequately! Paul realized that *no one* could fulfil such a calling; the love of Christ is beyond human ability to know or to express (2 Cor. 2.16; Eph. 3.19).

LIBERATION THROUGH INTER-FAITH ENCOUNTER

The peoples of Africa and Asia find it easy and natural to talk about God. When they have gone from those continents to the North, they have helped Northern Christians (1) to see the value of our shared humanity (as reflected in Acts 14.15–17; 17.24–30; Amos 9.7), and (2) to talk more freely about the meaning of their faith in Christ. But talking freely about our faith is not really possible unless we value our shared humanity, and we need help from one another to be set free.

Many Christians all over the world find it easier to keep their distance from people of other faiths. We are afraid to admit that we do not know everything about salvation or that other people may be as good as we are—or even better. It is absurd, but that is how Jonah felt about the people of Nineveh and Peter felt about Cornelius. Some English Christians find it hard to accept that God's chief agents for mission in the cities may be black-led Churches. Some African Church leaders feel the same way about the growing African Independent Churches (see pp. 131–140). To see and admit that God is at work in non-Christians is even more difficult— it seems to threaten the most sacred ground on which we stand, and even God seems to be overturning the faith we hold. But God surprises us by meeting us in unlikely places, and we have to take risks if we are to go and meet Him in those places. When we do, we discover a new joy and freedom. The Gospel is not lost at all, it is rediscovered—yet we nearly ran away from it! Christians are often too anxious about defending the Gospel against attack. The Gospel is like a lion; you do not defend it; you turn it loose, and it defends itself!

One other area where we can experience liberation is when we join together with people of other faiths to remind our secular world that the Creator has called us all to be responsible stewards of creation. We all have to account for our stewardship to Him and His just requirements; and Jews, Muslims and Christians ought to say together those things on which they agree as part of the faith they have received.

THEOLOGICAL EDUCATION

The more people learn theology, the more they think that they know it. But God will never allow us to 'know' with such self-confidence. We need to have disturbing experiences which question this 'knowledge' (see p. 211, above). Then we can see the difference between knowing about God and knowing Him, as the Muslim scholar, Muhammad Al-Ghazali of Egypt (died AD 1111) did. He had been thrown into despair by years of theological scholarship and had been rescued by a personal experience of God through the Sufi mystics. He described the relationship between knowing about God and knowing God as similar to the relationship between infancy and adulthood. If we do not remember this, theology will lead us away from God, as it led many of the opponents of Jesus.

Christians need to combine unlimited confidence in the Gospel of Christ with many doubts about how clearly we can either understand it or communicate it (see p. 217). We never know *exactly* what the Gospel is in any new situation—so we always have to discover it afresh. Those people who teach theology should create space for such discoveries to take place. The Church is never the possessor of salvation but only the witness to it. When the missionary, Vincent Donovan, came to the Masai, they asked him, 'Has your tribe found God?' To his surprise, he found himself replying in a small voice,

> No, we have not . . . For us too He is the unknown God. But we are searching for Him. I have come a long distance to invite you to search for Him with us . . . Maybe, together, we will find Him.

This journey to find God is risky. It seems to give up truth and certainty, and even to betray what has been entrusted to the Church. Therefore Christians need to have a faith and a theology which will allow them to set out on this journey.

A THEOLOGICAL FRAMEWORK

GENERAL REVELATION AND RELIGION

In Romans 1 Paul described how the Gentiles had responded to God's revelation of Himself in creation and in their consciences. He seems to have decided from what he saw in Greece that all people know about God, and all people abuse that knowledge (Rom. 1.20, 21, 28). This results in idolatry and immorality (Rom. 1.23–32). Therefore human religion involves:

1. General revelation which shows truth to people (Rom. 1.19, 20);

2. Human sin which has falsified this revelation (Rom. 1.21–25);

3. God's common grace which restrains people from being as sinful or ignorant as they might be (read Rom. 2.14, 15);

4. Human diversity which is reflected in the different cultures.

Because of their sin and ignorance, therefore, people cannot turn away from their religion and go back to a pure 'Natural Theology' which once existed (see Figure 27 of 'God's Revelation' on p. 221). In spite of this situation, Paul could appeal to truths which people still knew in their consciences and through creation as proof of human sin against God and the need for human beings to begin to see God in a new way (Acts 14.15–17; 17.23–28). But religion itself represents a falling away from the truth and from a 'Natural Theology'. Because religion cannot witness clearly to the truth, it does not lead towards God but away from Him. Religion does not offer any bridge which people can cross in order to come to the knowledge of God, although perhaps it can show that people *want* to know Him better but do not know how. Religion itself offers no hope for the relationship of human beings to God.

REVELATION AND THE JEWS

In the case of Israel, the starting-point for knowing God was different, but the response was the same. God had truly revealed His will in the Law, but the Jews had made the Law into a charter of national privilege which gave them a claim upon God and a right to demand His favour because they were His own people, not because they obeyed Him (Rom. 2.13, 17–24). They also did not respond to Him with humble repentance and faith. They were more concerned with their Law and their worship than with the Giver of that Law and the Object of that worship (see also p. 103). They became active people rather than people who received from God, people who talked rather than people who listened. Just like the pagan Greeks, the Jews put their religion in the place of God's revelation. Their religion, too, is under His judgement. Much of what the Jews did has often been equally true of the Christian Church (see Rom. 3.2; 9.4).

THE GOSPEL AND THE CHURCH

The light of the Gospel has broken upon this dark scene, the Good News of a personal relationship with God through Christ for everyone equally (Rom. 3.27–30). But those who receive this Gospel become the Church, and the Church always needs to remember God's judgement upon it and to return to the Gospel which brought it into being in the first place (1 Pet. 4.17; Rev. 2.4, 5; 3.3, 20). Like pagans and Jews, the Church drifts away from what God has revealed and always needs to reform itself by becoming more like its Lord.

This can be seen in Figure 27. Notice that dialogue usually takes place between those who want to discuss religion, because that is what they know and where they feel secure. But Paul, the Church's evangelist to the Gentiles, did not appeal to the religion of the Gentiles, but to its roots in God's general revelation through creation and through their consciences (Acts 14.17; 17.28). Jonah and Peter also, in their different ways, were brought back to the roots of their faith in God's revelation of Himself (Jonah 4.2; Acts 11.17). The aim of dialogue, therefore, should not be to trade bargaining points between the religions, but to admit that we all have a journey of faith to go on, either to the roots of religion in 'Natural Theology' or to the root of the Church in the Gospel. Perhaps people of different faiths can sometimes go on part of this journey together as they talk with one another. Paul the believer

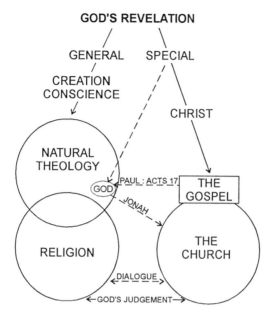

Figure 27 The Gospel and the Church.

urged Gentiles to do this; but Jonah the believer was himself urged to do it by his experience with the praying sailors and the repenting Ninevites (see p. 19).

God came to call sinners, not the righteous. So Figure 28 on p. 222, which shows stairs leading down and up, expresses more simply the fact that God generally meets us at the bottom of our religious stairways when we are empty and helpless, not at the top, as we climb up and increase in knowledge and holiness. In Jesus' day the religious professionals were not very good at talking with people on the streets, and the same may be true today. The most effective witnesses are people who have been changed by the wonder of God's universal love and who stand at the foot of His cross (see Acts 11.20,21). Jesus, who emptied Himself, is a good model.

THE GOSPEL BEYOND THE CHURCH

As we have seen (p. 211, above), God can speak directly to people in unexpected ways. That is how He spoke to Abraham. But the Jews claimed that their forefather Abraham was perfect in all he

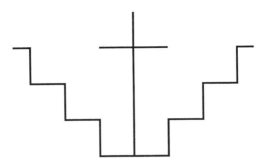

Figure 28 God meets us at the bottom of our religious stairways.

did. He had no need to repent and he could boast of the merit of his faith (see Rom. 4.2). They had 'domesticated' Abraham to conform to their religion. Christians have done the same—Abraham is now 'one of us', a Christian. But of course he is not. We should notice both the differences and the similarities: Abraham was given a special promise (Rom. 4.18–25) and although the promise seemed unbelievable, he responded to it by weighing up his circumstances on one side of the scale and putting the power and faithfulness of God on the other side. He lived BC, and believed the special revelation that God had given him without the help of Jesus. Abraham's faith was not very different from the faith of anyone who has responded to a special message from God. Some of the people who respond may never have heard of Christ at all, some may only have heard of Isa of the Qur'an, and some may have heard of Jesus from the Church in forms which either make no sense or which misrepresent Him. Such people are 'BC', like Abraham, and their faith may be as authentic as his. This sort of 'special revelation' is shown in the diagram of God's Revelation on p. 221 by a dotted line running from SPECIAL REVELATION to NATURAL THEOLOGY. But it is still true that God can only be truly known in His Son Jesus Christ—if only we could truly proclaim Him! However, five definite points need to be made in order to clarify the situation in the light of the Bible:

1. No one can be right with God by means of his or her own goodness, sincerity or religion, however impressive these may appear to be. Salvation is based only on what God does.

2. Christ is the only means of redemption. God did not pass over the sins of past believers like Abraham because He had forgotten to be just but because He would deal with them in justice in the death of His Son (Rom. 3.25, 26). The same must be true of other believers, although they are ignorant of Christ.

All human beings 'belong to a group to whom God is already reaching out in mercy . . . This is the basis on which we ought to meet people of other faiths' (p. 225). Do you agree?

3. Any true light which people receive comes from Christ (John 1.9), even though this light may not be brought explicitly in His name.

4. As far as we know, no one can recognize and respond to God's love except through hearing about Jesus. There may be exceptions to this rule, but these exceptions should only make Christians more ready to witness to Jesus, because (a) they know that God is already at work out there (see Acts 18.9,10) and so they need not be discouraged by their own weakness; and (b) they know that the only certain way of salvation is through turning to Jesus Christ.

5. In the end, we cannot know what is, and what is not, a genuine revelation from God, apart from the revelation given in Christ, or a genuine response of faith. Fortunately, therefore, we cannot expect to find answers to the questions raised by the stories on pp. 211–213. And if, as a result of this failure to find answers, we have to admit that our theology is not very neat or logical, we shall at least be more ready for any other surprises God may have in store for us.

A COMMON HUMANITY

Sometimes Christians speak of 'receiving Christ as *my own personal* Saviour'. While it is true that Christ deals with people as individuals, it seems that even more often He deals with them collectively, i.e. in terms of the group to which they belong (e.g. the West African villagers, p. 211 and the Masai, p. 108). This idea is prominent in all the writings of Paul.

In this connection Paul often used the word 'firstfruits'. For example, most of the baptisms recorded in the New Testament were not of individuals but of household groups—God's grace was shared by everyone. These in turn were the *first-fruits* of the harvest to be reaped throughout the region (Rom. 16.5; 1 Cor. 16.15). The conversion of households was a pledge of what God was going to do for the whole group.

God's special dealings with the remnant of Israel as the first fruits mean that we can be sure His purposes will extend to the whole lump, i.e. all Israel (Rom. 11.5, 16, 26). And if God has called one partner in a marriage to faith, we can be sure He wants to include the other partner also, for they belong together (1 Cor. 7.14). Paul used a similar argument to show his readers that the Holy Spirit within them was the first fruits, or pledge, that all the blessings of the new age would be theirs as well (Rom. 8.23).

If God deals with people in groups like this, no wonder Paul wrote in Rom. 5.18, 19 that just as the destiny of the sinner Adam is shared by all who belong to him, so all who belong to Christ share Christ's obedience and righteousness. Christ is the first fruits, those who belong to Him are the harvest (1 Cor. 15.20). We already enjoy the blessing of liberation from bondage (Rom. 8.19–23) and in due time we shall bring this blessing to the whole creation of which we are a part—the first fruits. If this is true of creation, could it be equally true of all human beings? Mercy is God's chief characteristic, and if He has shown mercy to some, both Jews and Gentiles, the visible first fruits, must He not intend eventually to show the same mercy to all (Rom. 11.28–32; James 1.18)?

But if God does show mercy, He does *not* do it because people are *religious* but because they are *human*, i.e. they belong to a group to whom God is already reaching out in mercy, even though His purpose for the whole group has not yet been realized. This is the basis on which we ought to meet people of other faiths. It is also the basis of our hope that they too are not outside the scope of God's mercy for ever.

When Teheran was bombarded by Iraqi air raids during the Iran-Iraq war, an Iranian bishop in the city wrote to his daughter as follows:

> All the routines of life are shattered . . . in this underground existence. People are thinking only of survival these days and share in everything—suffering, terror, uncertainty. They have never been so close, and this is something very precious. We discover we all have something in common, and that's our humanity, and we can thank God for the revelation of these mysteries and rejoice. Shared suffering removes many barriers, and thus people learn to accept each other as they are. Even religious and ideological prejudices become worthless . . .

Special Note H

MULTI-FAITH WORSHIP

Witness, yes; dialogue, yes; but all over the world there are pressures upon Christians to go further and engage in worship with people of other faiths. 'After all,' we are told, 'there is only one God, so all who believe in Him can worship together.' We are urged to do this sometimes by national or local leaders who do not want religious conflict, sometimes by people of other faiths, e.g. Hindus and Sikhs, and sometimes by our fellow-Christians. However, most Muslims and many Christians and Jews are deeply unhappy about this suggestion. For if all religions enable us to worship God together, what is the point of mission or of believing that any clearly revealed way to God, or truth, exists at all? That is the question, and Christians answer it in different ways.

Two weeks after I arrived in Tanzania in 1965, I stood casually in a crowd to watch a parade to celebrate Remembrance Day. Muslim, Hindu and Sikh leaders were there, but no Christian pastor had turned up. Suddenly someone recognized me as a new local clergyman and I was called up to say my Christian prayers alongside those of other faiths. I had no time to think—I simply had to act at once on the basis of the evangelical theology I had been taught: 'No compromise: preach the uniqueness of Christ and witness to him.' So I turned to the crowd and said, 'Thank you for your invitation, but I cannot join in prayer with people of other faiths. Jesus said "I am the Way . . . No one comes to the Father except by me." I can pray only with those who believe this.' That's what I *said*: what people *heard* (only a few days after Ian Smith had issued his unilateral declaration of independence in Rhodesia) was patronizing, imperialist sentiments spoken by a proud European. And now I know, after many years of inter-faith encounter, that I would never again speak quite like that.

That experience taught me three important lessons: (1) what people hear is more important than what we say; (2) for most people religion is not one part of life but a dimension which pervades all life; (3) Western Christians can probably learn a lot about relating to people of other faiths from people in the East and Africa who have been doing it for many generations.

JOINT SERVICES

There are many possible ways in which we can worship with people of other faiths. 'Multi-faith religious services' are only one of these possibilities and they are probably the least promising. These are normally organized events with little sense of urgency or need. Their aim is to demonstrate publicly a unity which is largely imaginary. At their worst, they can imply that salvation (whatever that may mean) can be obtained in all faiths equally, independently of the work of Christ. This casts doubt on the uniqueness of Christ and may lead to confusion. Above all, multi-faith religious services are often quite different from the occasions which really drive us to prayer and dependence upon God. Such occasions occur often in today's world, and it is then that we can find ourselves close to people of other faiths. These occasions I call *parallel* acts of worship rather than *joint* acts of worship.

WORSHIP IN PARALLEL

Such occasions might fall into three categories:

1. *National or community events* of grief, thanksgiving, prayer, repentance, etc. where leaders of the faiths participate in a public place, on equal terms, in parallel for the well-being of the whole community. All citizens should be encouraged to acknowledge their creaturely dependence on God—in fact we need to do this more often, to counteract the secular outlook which is so common today. Here at least our friends of other faiths will often take their stand together with us.

2. *Private and public crises* where people simply want to support one another in human solidarity. An example of Hindus in England being supported in prayer by Muslim and Christian friends was given on p. 214. And note again the story of the Iranian bishop on p. 225.

Recently an English Christian was invited by a group of Hindus to go on holiday with them to Portugal. While they were away, he heard that his wife had suffered a miscarriage. From her hospital bed she lamented about the pain he must be enduring, cut off from Christian friends and so isolated. But two Hindu friends had knocked on his door and sat with him, and prayed—and he knew he was not alone . . . As the bishop said about sharing an air raid shelter with Muslims in Teheran, these are mysteries indeed, which defy our neat, orthodox dogma. Situations like these are not planned; they just happen.

3. *Study or prayer groups*, where people of another faith are welcomed to join in and pray in the presence of and in parallel with others. An evangelical Christian attended a Qur'an study group and found Muslims sharing their experiences of faith and love—and listening to his experiences as well. They had doctrinal defects, he thought, but he could not deny the evidence of the Spirit of God in the gathering and he himself felt free to pray quietly to Jesus in his mind and in tongues. Above all, he came away with huge questions and the thought that it would have been more comfortable never to have gone—yet if he had not gone he would have been the poorer.

The above are clear examples of multi-faith worship—but as a *parallel* rather than a *joint* activity, where Christian witness is not difficult. What is difficult is to fit these experiences into our neat theological systems—but why should this be a surprise? In Acts, as in other parts of the Bible, the Holy Spirit frequently intervened to upset people's theological beliefs.

Roland Allen described the problem long ago, and the following is a shortened form of his argument. The apostles were profoundly conscious of the need of men for Christ, for without Him there is no justification, salvation or eternal life (Acts 4.12; 13.39, 46). So people talk of so many million souls passing into a Christless eternity. Yet on the other hand there are sayings in Acts, and in the Gospels, which seem to make less of that need of people for Christ. St Peter declares to Cornelius that 'in every nation he that fears God and does right is accepted with him' (10.35; see Matt. 25.31–46; Rom. 2.6–10). So some people argue

> that it is a libel on the Fatherhood of God to think of people perishing in their ignorance. The apostolic missionaries saw both sides of this story, they stated both sides, yet their zeal was not diminished at all. The solution of the difficulty does not lie in the intellectual but in the spiritual sphere.

The Holy Spirit assures us that Christ alone suffices, yet the same Spirit rejoices in signs of goodness, morality and awareness of God even when Christ is not apparently worshipped. There is no logical solution to the dilemma; the only possible way of understanding both the zeal and the tolerance of the apostles is to hold both sides of the dilemma in tension without resolving it. This procedure is not easy for people who are trained to think logically, yet it is there in Acts and in Christian experience all over the world.

We need to hold both sides of the dilemma in tension because of the doctrine of God as the Creator of everyone, and the doctrine of the Holy Spirit who is at work everywhere. 'God must be the most common experience of people—they must be bumping into him all the time', wrote Bishop John Taylor (see p. 212). We can even hope that God will reveal himself directly to many non-Christians who may respond to him in faith—often simply because we Christians have failed to communicate the Gospel to them (see p. 213). At the same time we believe that Christ alone can save. Therefore any forms of multi-faith worship must avoid two dangers: (1) casting doubt on this belief, and (2) suggesting that non-Christians are somehow beyond the reach of His love. So multi-faith worship should take place on neutral ground rather than within Christian church buildings.

A CULTURAL DIVIDE

During the last two centuries, European Christians have dominated other cultures aggressively and insensitively. Many of them never took time to uncover the riches which the Creator God had put within these cultures. In this respect Christians have been untrue to the Jesus of the Gospels who affirmed those people who were marginalized and unorthodox, and found God in them.

Christians who feel that they must refuse to take part in multi-faith worship should perhaps also feel the need to repent of their past (and present) cultural arrogance.

We must also re-examine the ways in which we express Christian doctrine. Over many centuries we have used images and symbols from our own culture to express doctrine. But if we use them unchanged in the midst of a multi-cultural society we shall falsify the truth we want to communicate. Christians need to work on new statements of faith which meet the heresies coming from today's world and answer its questions, just as the old ecumenical creeds met the needs of the Hellenistic world which was so different from ours. God, who has sent us out, will not allow us to continue to live in the past. For example, there are five common Christian beliefs which we may need to rethink if we want to communicate them to Muslims today:

1. Some Christians and Muslims say that Allah is quite different from the God of the Bible, but they do not offer any evidence for this statement. How can this be so? The Holy Qur'an claims to continue the revelation which God gave to Abraham and to Jesus; and Arabic-speaking Christians have no name to use for the God and Father of Jesus but 'Allah' (Christians in West Malaysia are in fact forbidden by law to do this). Even though there are differences in understanding, most of the 99 beautiful names of Allah in Islam could be accepted by Christians. Moreover, ever since John of Damascus in the eighth century, there has always been a long tradition of seeing Islam as a Christian heresy rather than as another faith. Much Muslim theology reflects biblical teaching, even though it may differ very much from today's popular Christianity of the North. Muslims and Christians must be prepared to explore honestly both the areas where they agree and those areas where they differ.

2. The doctrine of Jesus as the Son of God is a very difficult doctrine for people whose Muslim faith had to grow up in the midst of pagan beliefs in gods who had wives and sons and daughters. Therefore in Muhammad's time Ethiopian Christians who lived among Muslims portrayed the Trinity as 'The Merciful One, the Messiah and the Holy Spirit', in order to communicate the essential message without the hindrance of picture-language which was not helpful. We must make similar efforts today.

3. The doctrine of the Unity of God is at the heart of the Jewish Law (Deut. 6.4), the Gospel (Rom. 3.30) and Islam (where it is known as *tawhid*). So it is not surprising if Muslims feel that the Unity of God is threatened by the doctrine of the Trinity. We may need (a) to restate the doctrine of the Trinity in different words and

images and (b) be helped by Muslims to re-affirm the important doctrine of the Unity.

4. When we claim Christ is 'the only way', what exactly do we mean? The only way of revelation, which is clearly not true? Or the only way of redemption, which *is* true? Is it not possible that some people of other faiths or of no faith may, like Abraham (as I argued on p. 222), come to some knowledge of God—not *because of* their religion but simply because they are human and God can show himself to them?

5. Christians today usually confess Jesus as 'my own personal Saviour'. However, the primary confession in the group baptisms which were normal in the New Testament was 'Jesus is Lord'. Surely the New Testament confession, rather than the modern one, could build bridges to Muslims whose own Qur'an witnesses to the unique dignity of Jesus the Messiah, yet who find that 'being saved from sin' means little to them because they have confidence in the mercy and compassion of God towards them. And ultimately, whose fault is it if Muslims do not understand the Gospel which they claim to inherit? It is not so much their fault as ours, for it was Christians who failed to translate the New Testament into Arabic or into the Berber languages of North Africa, and in this way deprived Muhammad and his followers of the true light of Christ which had been entrusted to us for them. No wonder they went astray—let us now repent and try, in humility, to put things right.

A REFORMED CHURCH?

Rethinking our Christian beliefs in this way may also need to affect our ways of worship if we are to welcome the Christians of many different cultures among whom we live, or attract the non-Christians. Although we do need to proclaim Jesus Christ as revealed in the Scriptures, we must always be careful not to hide the true meaning of the Scriptures behind our own culture. Christians may not be able to find very much to boast about in the faith we have presented to the world, but we can find plenty to boast about in the Christ whom we have so often failed to discern, to reflect in our lives or to communicate to others. The believers of China, Africa, and Latin America are already leading the way in the expansion of the Church, now that they have been released from domination by missionaries. These Churches may look very different from the Churches which spread all over the world from Rome, Canterbury, Geneva and Wittenburg. But they will bring new life to those who will receive it with humility, and we should be glad that the new way of mission is international, interdependent and multi-cultural.

Do you think there is any value in multi-faith services like this one in a Buddhist temple in Britain? What are the dangers of such services?

Accepting new ideas is nothing new. The Church has known for a long time that it always has a duty to reform itself by the word of God. If we take this path without fear, it will reveal Jesus Christ as He truly is—not distorted by Islam, or reduced by Judaism, or misunderstood by a culture-bound Christianity. But, like Jesus, we shall become vulnerable. We shall not be tempted to imitate the tactics of Islam, which are never appropriate for Christians. After all, Muslims follow a great leader who chose the way of 'escape' from persecution and assumed military and political power. When Muslims do the same, they are only being true to their faith. If Christians use military and political power, however, they betray their Lord who chose the way of the Cross and told His followers to do the same. Endurance in suffering will be the way of life for us, not the way of defeat (see p. 43). That is how Jesus Christ will be revealed to the world—as a Person, not a set of doctrines; as a way of love, not of domination; in openness to our fellow human beings, not in fear of being tripped up by them; in giving away to them, not claiming from them. This attitude is our safest guide not only to the difficult problem of multi-faith worship but also to the total task of mission which Jesus Christ has committed to His Church. Far from fearing defeat by the world and by other faiths, we shall eagerly embrace every opportunity for meeting, for mutual respect and for witness.

STUDY SUGGESTIONS

BIBLE STUDY

1. (a) In what ways was the response to God of (i) Abraham, (ii) the wise men, and (iii) the people of Nineveh similar to that of someone who believes in Christ and is baptized?
   (b) In what ways were their responses to God different to that of a Christian?
2. How is the good news of people's shared humanity shown in Amos 9.7; Acts 14.15–17; 17.24–31? How could the Church communicate this good news today?
3. (a) In what ways were people's expectations turned upside-down in Matt. 25.34–46; Mark 2.12; Acts 10.45–47?
   (b) Give two examples from this Guide or from your own experience of people being surprised by what God does.
4. What features of human life does Paul commend in Rom. 1.18–32 and Acts 17.16–34? What does he find fault with?
5. (a) What criticisms of Jewish religion are made in the following passages:

Deut. 10.12–22; Isa. 1.10–17; Isa. 58.5–14; Amos 5.21–25; Rom. 2.1–24?

(b) What similar criticisms might be made of the Church? See Rev. 2.1–5; 3.1–4; 3.15–22.

(c) What steps can the Church take to reform itself according to the truth of God's Gospel?

6. People often feel sad when those whom they love refuse the salvation which God offers. What hope can they derive from Paul's teaching about the first fruits (Rom. 8.23; 11.5, 16, 26; 16.5; 1 Cor. 16.15)?

7. What do the following passages teach about people's relationship with God the Creator and God the Holy Spirit? John 1.3–9; Acts 16.14.

CONTEXTUAL APPLICATION

8. How might (a) an exclusivist, (b) a pluralist, and (c) an inclusivist respond to an invitation to take part in (i) an act of multi-faith worship in a big local church on New Year's Day, and (ii) a service of national mourning after many people have died in a big earthquake?

9. What examples do you know of people receiving a direct message from God without any human agency?

10. In what ways do Christians 'hide' Jesus from people of other faiths?

11. Why should Christians be confident when they meet people of other faiths?

12. In your experience, how far does the Church (a) criticize its own faults, and (b) appreciate genuine goodness among non-Christians?

13. (a) What was the cost of mission for (i) the Hebrew Christian and (ii) the missionary in India (p. 216)?

(b) In what ways have you, or people known to you, found that mission is costly?

14. What Church teachings seem to you to be (a) foreign to the people of your locality and their culture, and (b) relevant to them?

15. In what ways do Christians in your area join with non-Christian groups to improve the quality of life locally? In what other ways could they co-operate in this work?

16. What have you discovered about the relationship between experience and theological knowledge?

17. What do you think would be a proper response in your area to the invitation on p. 226 to pray alongside people of other faiths?

18. Do Christians and Muslims worship the same God? Give reasons for your answer.
19. A civic service, which will bring together Christian, Muslim, Sikh and Hindu leaders, is planned for a multi-ethnic district in which there have been some civil disturbances. You are asked to join in and give some guidelines to the planning committee. How will you respond?

Appendix: The Problem of Rwanda

In chapter 11 we read about the Revival which transformed the Anglican Church in Rwanda. The Roman Catholic Church has also been strong in Rwanda for many years. Ninety per cent of Rwandans claim to be Christians. But since chapter 11 was written, over half a million men, women and children have been killed in Rwanda by their fellow citizens; there are two million refugees and another million homeless. This was tribal conflict, i.e. genocide, or 'ethnic cleansing'. Many Christians were guilty of these murders. One bishop saw people whom he had recently confirmed, killing many others.

There are historical reasons for tribal conflict in Rwanda and Burundi, but the question for the Christian Church is 'What was the weakness within the Revival, and within the Roman Catholic Church, which allowed strong Christians, sometimes encouraged by Church leaders, to act with such hatred?' Some possible answers to this question may be as follows:

1. The chief message of the Revival was personal salvation through Jesus: the lordship of Christ over the whole of life was sometimes forgotten (see pp. 22, 230).

2. Missionaries preached about individual sin more than corporate sin, even though Africans need their faith to affect the community life which is so important to them (see p. 156).

3. Although the Revival healed much personal hatred (see p. 145), it did not face the deep ethnic divisions which ran through the whole country.

4. Most Revival leaders avoided politics completely because they thought it was 'unspiritual'. Many other Church leaders simply joined, and obeyed, the ruling party. In both cases, the Christians became unable to criticize, or even to see, the political wickedness around them (unlike Archbishop Janani Luwum of Uganda, who lost his life when he denounced the wickedness of Idi Amin).

5. The Revival preached personal salvation so much that it often ignored the ethical demands of the Gospel (see p. 123).

6. In times of ethnic conflict, Church leaders did not demand publicly that criminals be brought to justice (see p. 69).

7. Some Anglican and Catholic bishops lived in luxury instead of identifying with the poor and gave orders to the people instead of listening to them (see p. 171).

8. One Catholic priest said, 'We have sacramentalized the people, we have not evangelized them.' This meant that they regarded the Church as more important than the Kingdom of God (see p. 63).

9. Foreign governments and partner Churches were also at fault – even when they could see what was going wrong, they kept quiet or even supported the evil in various ways.

Some Books for Further Reading

Books marked with an asterisk (*) have been particularly useful in the preparation of this Guide.

Abraham, W., *The Art of Evangelism*. Cliff College, Sheffield.

Abraham, W., *The Logic of Evangelism*. Hodder & Stoughton, London.

*Allen, R., *Missionary Methods: St. Paul's or Ours?*. World Dominion Press, London.

Allen, R., *The Ministry of the Spirit*. Eerdmans, Grand Rapids.

*Anderson, W., *The Church in East Africa 1840–1976*. CTP, Dodoma, Tanzania.

Avila, R., *Worship and Politics*. Orbis, New York.

*Bailey, K. E., *Poet and Peasant & Through Peasant Eyes* (one volume). Eerdmans, Grand Rapids.

*Bakke, R., *The Urban Christian*. Inter-Varsity Press, Leicester.

Balasuriya, T., *The Eucharist and Human Liberation*. SCM Press, London.

Barrett, D., *Schism and Renewal in Africa*. Oxford University Press, Oxford.

Barrett, D., *World Christian Encyclopedia*. Oxford University Press, Oxford.

*Barrett, D., *World-class Cities and Evangelization*. New Hope, Birmingham, Alabama.

*Barrington-Ward, S., *Love Will Out*. Hodder & Stoughton, London, pp. 183–198.

Bediako, K., *Theology and Identity*. Regnum, Oxford.

Berryman, P., *Liberation Theology*. I. B. Tauris, London.

*Bosch, D. J., *Transforming Mission*. Orbis, New York.

Bosch, D. J., *Witness to the World*. Marshalls, London.

Brueggemann, W., *Biblical Perspectives on Evangelism*. Abingdon Press, Nashville.

Burnett, D., *Clash of Worlds*. Monarch, Crowborough.

Cotterell, P., *Mission and Meaninglessness*. SPCK, London.

*Cracknell, K. and C. Lamb, *Theology on Full Alert*. British Council of Churches, London.

*Donovan, V., *Christianity Rediscovered*. SCM Press, London.

Finney, J., *Church on the Move*. Daybreak (DLT), London.

*Finney, J., *The Well-Church Book*. Church Pastoral Aid Society, London.

Freire, P., *Pedagogy of the Oppressed*. Penguin, Harmondsworth.

*Fung, R., *The Isaiah Vision*. World Council of Churches, Geneva.

*Gibbs, E., *I Believe in Church Growth*. Hodder & Stoughton, London.

Gnanakan, K., *Kingdom Concerns*. Inter-Varsity Press, Leicester.

Haliburton, G., *The Prophet Harris*. Longmans, London.

Hebblethwaite, M., *Basic is Beautiful*. Collins Fount, London.

Hinton, K., *Growing Churches Singapore Style*. Overseas Missionary Fellowship, Singapore.

*Hirmer, O., *Gospel Sharing*. Lumko Institute, Johannesburg.

*Isichei, E., *A History of Christianity in Africa*. SPCK, London.

Kendall, E., *End of an Era*. SPCK, London.

*Kivengere, F., *Revolutionary Love*. Kingsway, Eastbourne.

Kraft, C., *Christianity in Culture*. Orbis, New York.

McCoy, M., *Good News People*. Church of the Province of Southern Africa, Cape Town.

*Martin, M.-L., *Kimbangu: An African Prophet and his Church*. Blackwell, Oxford.

Milingo, E., *The World in Between*. Orbis, New York.

Murray, S., *The Challenge of the City*. Sovereign World, Tonbridge.

235

Namata, J., *Edmond John, Man of God*. Acorn, Canberra.

Nazir Ali, M., *From Everywhere to Everywhere*. Collins, London.

Neill, S. C., G. Anderson, J. Goodwin, *Concise Dictionary of the Christian World Mission*. Lutterworth, Cambridge.

*Neill, S. C., *Christian Missions*. Penguin, Harmondsworth.

*Newbigin, L., *Foolishness to the Greeks*. World Council of Churches, Geneva.

Newbigin, L., *Mission in Christ's Way*. World Council of Churches, Geneva.

Newbigin, L., *The Gospel in a Pluralist Society*. SPCK, London.

*Newbigin, L., *The Open Secret*. Eerdmans, Grand Rapids.

Nicholls, B., *In Word and Deed*. Lausanne.

Niebuhr, R., *Christ and Culture*. Harper and Row, New York.

*Parratt, J. A., *A Reader in African Christian Theology* (TEF Study Guide 23). SPCK, London.

Rowland, C., *Radical Christianity*. Polity, Oxford.

*Sanneh, L., *Encountering the West*. Marshall Pickering, London.

*Senior, D. and C. Stuhlmueller, *Biblical Foundations for Mission*. SCM Press, London.

*Shorter, A., *Evangelization and Culture*. Geoffrey Chapman, London.

Stott, J. and R. Coote, *Down to Earth*. Hodder & Stoughton, London.

Stott, J., *Christian Mission in the Modern World*. Falcon, London.

*Wagner, C. P., *Church Growth and the Whole Gospel*. MARC, Crowborough.

Wimber, J., *Power Evangelism*. Hodder & Stoughton, London.

*Winter, D., *Putting Theology to Work*. CFWM, London.

*Wright, C., *Deuteronomy*. NIBC Series, Paternoster, Exeter.

Yates, T., *Christian Mission in the Twentieth Century*. Cambridge University Press, Cambridge.

Key to Study Suggestions

Chapter 1: Historical and Theological Foundations (Pages 6–15
1. (a) and (b) See p. 7, para. 1.
2. See p. 14, para. 1.

Chapter 2: The Mission of God in the Old Testament (Pages 16–25)
1. (a) and (b) See p. 16, para. 1.
2. (a) and (b) See p. 16, para. 2.
3. See p. 17, para. 1.

Chapter 3: The Mission of the Son in Mark's Gospel (Pages 26–35)
1. See p. 26, para. 3.
2. See p. 27, Section on The Story that Mark Told.
3. See p. 29, para. 2.

Chapter 4: The Mission of the Spirit in Luke's Gospel and Acts (Pages 36–47)
1. (a) and (b) See p. 40 (2).
    (c) See p. 42 (4).
    (d) See p. 44, para. 5.

Chapter 6: Mission and the Kingdom of God (Pages 60–75)
1. See p. 60, para. 3.
2. (a) See p. 65 (top).
    (b) See p. 64, para. 2.

Chapter 7: Bridging the Gap (Pages 76–94)
1. (a) See p. 77(3).
    (b) and (c) See p. 87, Section on Form and Function.
    (d) See p. 93 (middle).

Chapter 8: The Missionaries (Pages 95–110
1. (a) See p. 103 (bottom).
    (b), (c) and (d) See p. 105 (top).

Chapter 9: The Church Growth Movement (Pages 111–130)
1. (a) See p. 118(4).
    (b) See p. 123(7).
    (c) and (d) See p. 125, para. 1 of Special Note D.

Chapter 10: Africa: Indigenous Churches (Pages 131–141)
1. (a) and (b) See p. 131, para. 1.

Chapter 11: Africa: Movements of Renewal (Pages 142–159)
1. (a) See p. 145 (bottom).
(b) See p. 150, para 1 of Section on Moratorium.
(c) See p. 157(5).

Chapter 13: Liberation Theology (Pages 170–187)
1. See p. 171 (top).
2. See p. 174, para. 1.

Index of Bible Passages

INDEX OF BIBLE PASSAGES

Index